Richard F. Burton

Personal Narrative of a Pilgrimage to Mecca and Medina

Vol. 3

Richard F. Burton

Personal Narrative of a Pilgrimage to Mecca and Medina
Vol. 3

ISBN/EAN: 9783742807946

Manufactured in Europe, USA, Canada, Australia, Japa

Cover: Foto ©Lupo / pixelio.de

Manufactured and distributed by brebook publishing software (www.brebook.com)

Richard F. Burton

Personal Narrative of a Pilgrimage to Mecca and Medina

PERSONAL NARRATIVE
OF A
PILGRIMAGE
TO
MECCA AND MEDINA

BY

RICHARD F. BURTON.

COPYRIGHT EDITION.

IN THREE VOLUMES.—VOL. III.

LEIPZIG
BERNHARD TAUCHNITZ
1874.

The Right of Translation is reserved.

CONTENTS

OF THE THIRD VOLUME.

	Page
CHAPTER I.	
The Bayt Ullah	1
CHAPTER II.	
The first Visit to the House of Allah	38
CHAPTER III.	
The Ceremonies of the Yaum el Tarwiyah, or the First Day	58
CHAPTER IV.	
The Ceremonies of the Yaum Arafat, or the Second Day	72
CHAPTER V.	
The Ceremonies of the Yaum Nahr, or the Third Day	83
CHAPTER VI.	
The Three Days of Drying Flesh	100
CHAPTER VII.	
Life at Meccah, and Umrah, or the Little Pilgrimage	108
CHAPTER VIII.	
Places of Pious Visitation at Meccah	129
CHAPTER IX.	
To Jeddah	141
Remarks on the Map	163
The Mecca Pilgrimage	175
Index	185

A PILGRIMAGE TO
MECCA AND MEDINA.

CHAPTER I.

The Bayt Ullah.

THE House of Allah has been so fully described by my predecessors, that there is little inducement to attempt a new portrait. I will, therefore, do homage to the memory of the accurate Burckhardt, and extract from his pages a description which shall be illustrated by a few notes.

"The Ka'abah stands in an oblong square (enclosed by a great wall) 250 paces long, and 200 broad,* none of the sides of which run quite in a straight line, though at first sight the whole appears to be of a regular shape. This open square is enclosed on the eastern side by a colonnade. The pillars stand in a quadruple row; they are three deep on the other sides, and united by pointed arches, every four of which

---

* Ali Bey gives 536 feet 9 inches by 356 feet; my measurement 257 paces by 310. Most Moslem authors, reckoning by cubits, make the parallelogram 404 by 310.

support a small dome plastered and whitened on the outside. These domes, according to Kotobeddyn, are 152 in number.* The pillars are above twenty feet in height, and generally from one foot and a half to one foot and three quarters in diameter; but little regularity has been observed in regard to them. Some are of white marble, granite or porphyry; but the greater number are of common stone of the Meccah mountains.** El Fasy states the whole at 589, and says they are all of marble excepting 126, which are of common stone, and three of composition. Kotobeddyn reckons 555, of which, according to him, 311 are of marble, and the rest of the stone taken from the neighbouring mountains; but neither of the authors lived to see the latest repairs of the mosque, after the destruction occasioned by a torrent in A.D. 1626.*** Between every three or four columns stands an octagonal one, about four feet in thickness. On the east

* On each short side I counted 24 domes; on the long, 35. This would give a total of 118 along the cloisters. The Arabs reckon in all 152; viz. 24 on the east side, on the north 36, on the south 36; one on the mosque corner, near the Zarurah minaret; 16 at the porch of the Bab el Ziyadah; and 15 at the Bab Ibrahim. The shape of these domes is the usual "Media-Naranja," and the superstition of the Meccans informs the pilgrim that they cannot be counted. Books reckon 1352 pinnacles or battlements on the temple wall.

** The "common stone of the Meccah mountains" is a fine grey granite quarried principally from a hill near the Bab el Shabayki, which furnished materials for the Ka'abah. Eastern authors describe the pillars as consisting of three different substances, viz.: Rukham, white marble, not "alabaster," its general sense; Suwan, or granite (syenite?); and "Hajar Shumaysi," a kind of yellow sandstone, so called from "Bir Shumays," a place on the Jeddah road, near Haddah, the half-way station.

*** I counted in the temple 554 pillars. It is, however, difficult to be accurate, as the four colonnades and the porticos about the two great gates are irregular; topographical observations, moreover, must here be made under side are two shafts of reddish grey granite in one piece, and one fine grey porphyry with slabs of white feldspath. On the north side is one red granite column, and one of fine-grained red porphyry; these are probably the columns which Kotobeddyn states to have been brought from Egypt, and principally from Akhmim (Panopolis), when the chief (Caliph) El Mohdy enlarged the mosque, in A.H. 163. Among the 450 or 500 columns which form the enclosure I found not any two capitals or bases exactly alike. The capitals are of course Saracen workmanship; some of them, which had served for former buildings, by the ignorance of the workmen, have been placed upside down upon the shafts. I observed about half a dozen marble bases of good Grecian workmanship. A few of the marble columns bear Arabic or Cufic inscriptions, in which I read the dates 863 and 762 (A.H.).* A column on the east side exhibits a very ancient Cufic inscription, somewhat defaced, which I could neither read nor copy. Some of the columns are strengthened with broad iron rings or bands,** as in many other Saracen buildings of the East. They were first employed by

difficulties. Ali Bey numbers them roughly at "plus de 500 colonnes et pilastres."

[*] The author afterwards informs us, that "the temple has been so often ruined and repaired, that no traces of remote antiquity are to be found about it." He mentions some modern and unimportant inscriptions upon the walls and over the gates. Knowing that many of the pillars were sent in ships from Syria and Egypt by the Caliph El Mahdi, a traveller would have expected better things.

[**] The reason being, that "those shafts formed of the Meccan stone are mostly in three pieces; but the marble shafts are in one piece."

Ibn Dhaher Berkouk, king of Egypt, in rebuilding the mosque, which had been destroyed by fire in A.H. 802.*

"Some parts of the walls and arches are gaudily painted in stripes of yellow, red, and blue, as are also the minarets. Paintings of flowers, in the usual Muselman style, are nowhere seen; the floors of the colonnades are paved with large stones badly cemented together.

"Some paved causeways lead from the colonnades towards the Ka'abah, or Holy House, in the centre.** They are of sufficient breadth to admit four or five persons to walk abreast, and they are elevated about nine inches above the ground. Between these causeways, which are covered with fine gravel or sand, grass appears growing in several places, produced by the Zem Zem water oozing out of the jars which are placed in the ground in long rows during the day.*** There is a descent of eight or ten steps from the

---

* To this may be added, that the façades of the cloisters are twenty-four along the short walls, and thirty-six along the others; they have stone ornaments, not inaptly compared to the French "fleur de lis." The capital and bases of the outer pillars are grander and more regular than the inner; they support pointed arches, and the Arab secures his beloved variety by placing at every fourth arch a square pilaster. Of these there are on the long sides ten, on the short seven.

** I counted eight, not including the broad pavement which leads from the Bab el Ziyadah to the Ka'abah, or the four cross branches which connect the main lines. These "Firash el Hajar," as they are called, also serve to partition off the area. One space, for instance, is called "Haswat el Harim," or the "Women's sanded place," because appropriated to female devotees.

*** The jars are little amphoræ, each inscribed with the name of the donor and a peculiar cypher.

gates on the north side into the platform of the colonnade, and of three or four steps from the gates on the south side.

"Towards the middle of this area stands the Ka'abah; it is 115 paces from the north colonnade, and 88 from the south. For this want of symmetry we may readily account, the Ka'abah having existed prior to the mosque, which was built around it, and enlarged at different periods. The Ka'abah is an oblong massive structure, 18 paces in length, 14 in breadth, and from 35 to 40 feet in height.* It is constructed of the grey Mekka stone, in large blocks of different sizes joined together, in a very rough manner, with bad cement.** It was entirely rebuilt, as it now stands, in A.D. 1627. The torrent in the preceding year had thrown down three of its sides, and, preparatory to its re-erection, the fourth side was, according to Asamy, pulled down, after the Olemas, or learned divines, had been consulted on the question whether mortals might be permitted to destroy any part of the holy edifice without incurring the charge of sacrilege and infidelity.

"The Ka'abah stands upon a base two feet in

* My measurements give 22 paces or 55 feet in length by 18 (45), of breadth, and the height appeared greater than the length. Ali Bey makes the eastern side 37 French feet, 2 inches and 6 lines, the western 38, 4, 6, the northern 29 feet, the southern 31, 6, and the height 34, 4. He therefore calls it a "veritable trapezium." In El Idrisi's time it was 25 cubits by 24, and 27 cubits high.

** I would alter this sentence thus—"It is built of fine grey granite in horizontal courses of masonry of irregular depth; the stones are tolerably fitted together, and are held by excellent mortar like Roman cement." The lines are also straight.

height, which presents a sharp inclined plane.* Its roof being flat, it has at a distance the appearance of a perfect cube.** The only door which affords entrance, and which is opened but two or three times in the year,*** is on the north side, and about seven feet above the ground.† In the first periods of Islam,

* This base is called El Shazarwan, from the Persian Shadarwan, a cornice, eaves, or canopy. It is in pent-house shape, projecting about a foot beyond the wall, and composed of fine white marble slabs, polished like glass; there are two breaks in it, one opposite and under the doorway, and another in front of Ishmael's tomb. Pilgrims are directed, during circumambulation, to keep their bodies outside of the Shazarwan; this would imply it to be part of the building, but its only use appears in the large brass rings welded into it, for the purpose of holding down the Ka'abah covering.

** Ali Bey also errs in describing the roof as "plat en dessus." Were such the case, rain would not pour off with violence through the spout. Most Oriental authors allow a cubit of depression from south-west to north-west. In El Idrisi's day the Ka'abah had a double roof. Some say this is the case in the present building, which has not been materially altered in shape since its restoration by El Hajjaj A. H. 83. The roof was then eighteen cubits long by fifteen broad.

*** In Ibn Jubayr's time the Ka'abah was opened every day in Rajab, and in other months on every Monday and Friday. The house may now be entered ten or twelve times a year gratis; and by pilgrims as often as they can collect, amongst parties, a sum sufficient to tempt the guardians' cupidity.

† This mistake, in which Burckhardt is followed by all our popular authors, is the more extraordinary, as all Arabic authors call the door-wall Janib el Mashrik—the eastern side—or Wajh el Bayt, the front of the house, opposed to Zahr el Bayt, the back. Niebuhr is equally in error when he asserts that the door fronts to the south. Arabs always hold the "Rukn el Iraki" or Irak angle, to face the polar star, and so it appears in Ali Bey's plan. The Ka'abah, therefore, has no northern side. And it must be observed that Moslem writers make the length of the Ka'abah from east to west, whereas our travellers make it from north to south.

Ali Bey places the door only six feet from the pavement, but he calculates distances by the old French measure. It is about seven feet from the ground, and six from the corner of the Black Stone. Between the two the space of wall is called El Multazem (in Burckhardt, by a clerical error, "El Metzem," vol. I, p. 173). It derives its name, the "Attached-to," because here the circumambulator should apply his bosom, and beg pardon for his sins. El Multazem, according to M. de Perceval, following d'Ohsson, was formerly "le lieu des however, when it was rebuilt in A.H. 64 by Ibn Zebeyr (Zubayr), chief of Mecca, it had two doors even with the ground-floor of the mosque.* The present door (which, according to Azraky, was brought hither from Constantinople in A.D. 1633), is wholly coated with silver, and has several gilt ornaments; upon its threshold are placed every night various small lighted wax candles, and perfuming pans, filled with musk, aloe-wood, &c.**

engagements," whence, according to him, its name. "Le Moltexem," says M. Galland (Rits et Cérémonies du Pélerinage de la Mecque) "qui est entre la pierre noire et la porte, est l'endroit où Mahomet se réconcilia avec ses dix compagnons, qui disaient qu'il n'était pas véritablement Prophète."

* From the Bab el Ziyadah, or gate in the northern colonnade, you descend by two flights of steps, in all about twenty-five. This depression manifestly arises from the level of the town having been raised, like Rome, by successive layers of ruins; the most populous and substantial quarters (as the Shamiyah to the north) would, we might expect, be the highest, and this is actually the case. But I am unable to account satisfactorily for the second hollow within the temple, and immediately around the House of Allah, where the door, according to all historians, formerly on a level with the pavement, and now about seven feet above it, shows the exact amount of depression, which cannot be accounted for simply by calcation. Some chroniclers assert, that when the Kuraysh rebuilt the house they raised the door to prevent devotees entering without their permission. But seven feet would scarcely oppose an entrance, and how will this account for the floor of the building being also elevated to that height above the pavement? It is curious to observe the similarity between this inner hollow of the Meccan fane and the artificial depression of the Hindu pagoda, where it is intended to be flooded. The Hindus would also revere the form of the Meccan fane, exactly resembling their square temples, at whose corners are placed Brahma, Vishnu, Shiwa and Ganesha, who adore the Universal Generator in the centre.

The second door anciently stood on the side of the temple opposite the present entrance; inside, its place can still be traced. Ali Bey suspects its having existed in the modern building, and declares that the exterior surface of the wall shows the tracery of a blocked-up adit, similar to that still open. Some historians declare that it was closed by the Kuraysh when they rebuilt the house in Mohammed's day, and that subsequent erections have had only one. The general opinion is, that El Hajjaj finally closed up the western entrance. Doctors also differ as to its size; the popular measurement is three cubits broad and a little more than five in length.

** Pilgrims and ignorant devotees collect the drippings of wax, the ashes

"At the north-east* corner of the Ka'abah, near the door, is the famous 'Black Stone;'** it forms a

of the aloe-wood, and the dust from the "Atabah," or threshold of the Ka'abah, either to rub upon their foreheads or to preserve as relics. These superstitious practices are sternly rebuked by the Olema.

* For north-east read south-east.

** I will not enter into the fabulous origin of the Hajar el Aswad. Some of the traditions connected with it are truly absurd. "When Allah," says Ali, "made covenant with the Sons of Adam on the Day of Fealty, he placed the paper inside the stone;" it will, therefore, appear at the judgment, and bear witness to all who have touched it. Moslems agree that it was originally white, and became black by reason of men's sins. It appeared to me a common aërolite covered with a thick slaggy coating, glossy and pitch-like, worn and polished. Dr. Wilson of Bombay showed me a specimen in his possession, which externally appeared to be a black slag, with the inside of a bright and sparkling greyish-white, the result of admixture of nickel with the iron. This might possibly, as the learned Orientalist then suggested, account for the mythic change of color, its appearance on earth after a thunderstorm, and its being originally a material part of the heavens. Kutb el Din expressly declares that, when the Karamitah restored it after twenty-two years to the Meccans, men kissed it and rubbed it upon their brows; and remarked, that the blackness was only superficial, the inside being white. Some Greek philosophers, it will be remembered, believed the heavens to be composed of stones (Cosmos, "Shooting Stars"): and Sanconiathon, ascribing the aërolite-worship to the god Cœlus, declares them to be living or animated stones. "The Arabians," says Maximus of Tyre (Dissert. 38. p. 455), "pay homage to I know not what god, which they represent by a quadrangular stone." The gross fetishism of the Hindus, it is well known, introduced them to litholatry. At Jagannath they worship a pyramidal black stone, fabled to have fallen from heaven, or miraculously to have presented itself on the place where the temple now stands. Moreover, they revere the Salagram, as the emblem of Vishnu, the second person in their triad. The rudest emblem of the "Bonus Deus" was a round stone. It was succeeded in India by the cone and triangle; in Egypt by the pyramid; in Greece it was represented by cones of terra-cotta about three inches and a half long. Without going deep into theory, it may be said that the Ka'abah and the Hajar are the only two idols which have survived the 360 composing the heavenly host of the Arab pantheon. Thus the Hindu poet exclaims—

"Behold the marvels of my idol-temple, O Moslem!
That when its idols are destroy'd, it becomes Allah's House."

Wilford (As. Soc. vols. iii. and iv.) makes the Hindus declare that the Black Stone at Mokshesha, or Moksha-sthana (Meccah) was an incarnation of Moksheshwara, an incarnation of Shiwa, who with his consort visited El Hejaz. When the Ka'abah was rebuilt, this emblem was placed in the outer wall for part of the sharp angle of the building,* at four or five feet above the ground.** It is an irregular oval, about seven inches in diameter, with an undulating surface, composed of about a dozen smaller stones of different sizes and shapes, well joined together with a small quantity of cement, and perfectly well smoothed: it looks as if the whole had been broken into many pieces by a violent blow, and then united again. It is very difficult to determine accurately the quality of this stone, which has been worn to its present surface by the millions of touches and kisses it has received. It appeared to me like a lava, containing several small

contempt, but the people still respected it. In the Dabistan the Black Stone is said to be an image of Kaywan or Saturn; and El Shahristani also declares the temple to have been dedicated to the same planet Zuhal, whose genius is represented in the Puranas as fierce, hideous, four-armed, and habited in a black cloak, with a dark turban. Moslem historians are unanimous in asserting that Sasan, son of Babegan, and other Persian monarchs, gave rich presents to the Ka'abah; they especially mention two golden crescent moons, a significant offering. The Guebers assert that, among the images and relics left by Mahabad and his successors in the Ka'abah, was the Black Stone, an emblem of Saturn. They also call the city Mahgah—moon's place—from an exceedingly beautiful image of the moon; whence they say the Arabs derived "Meccah." And the Sabæans equally respect the Ka'abah and the pyramids, which they assert to be the tombs of Seth, Enoch (or Hermes), and Sabi the son of Enoch.

Meccah, then, is claimed as a sacred place, and the Hajar el Aswad, as well as the Ka'abah, are revered as holy emblems by four different faiths—the Hindu, Sabæan, Gueber, and Moslem. I have little doubt, and hope to prove at another time, that the Jews connected it with traditions about Abraham. This would be the fifth religion that looked towards the Ka'abah—a rare meeting-place of devotion.

* Presenting this appearance in profile. The Hajar has suffered from the iconoclastic principle of Islam, having once narrowly escaped destruction by order of El Hakim of Egypt. In these days the metal rim serves as a protection as well as an ornament.

** The height of the Hajar from the ground, according to my measurement, is four feet nine inches; Ali Bey places it forty-two inches above the pavement.

extraneous particles of a whitish and of a yellowish substance. Its colour is now a deep reddish brown, approaching to black. It is surrounded on all sides by a border composed of a substance which I took to be a close cement of pitch and gravel of a similar, but not quite the same, brownish colour.* This border serves to support its detached pieces; it is two or three inches in breadth, and rises a little above the surface of the stone. Both the border and the stone itself are encircled by a silver band,** broader below than above, and on the two sides, with a considerable swelling below, as if a part of the stone were hidden under it. The lower part of the border is studded with silver nails.

"In the south-east corner of the Ka'abah,*** or, as the Arabs call it, Rokn el Yemany, there is another

---

* The colour was black and metallic, and the centre of the stone was sunk about two inches below the metal circle. Round the sides was a reddish brown cement, almost level with the metal, and sloping down to the middle of the stone.

Ibn Jubayr declares the depth of the stone unknown, but that most people believe it to extend two cubits into the wall. In his day it was three "Shibr" (the large span from the thumb to the little finger tip) broad, and one span long, with knobs, and a joining of four pieces, which the Karamitah had broken. The stone was set in a silver band. Its softness and moisture were such, says Ibn Jubayr, "that the sinner never would remove his mouth from it, which phenomenon made the Prophet declare it to be the covenant of Allah on earth."

** The band is now a massive circle of gold or silver gilt. I found the aperture in which the stone is, one span and three fingers broad.

*** The "Rukn el Yemani" is the corner facing the south. The part alluded to in the text is the wall of the Ka'abah, between the Shami and Yemani angles, distant about three feet from the latter, and near the site of the old western door, long since closed. The stone is darker and redder than the rest of the wall. It is called El Mustajab (or Mustajab min el Zunub or Mustajab el Du'a, "where prayer is granted"). Pilgrims here extend their arms, press their bodies against the building, and beg forgiveness for their sins.

stone about five feet from the ground; it is one foot and a half in length, and two inches in breadth, placed upright, and of the common Meccah stone. This the people walking round the Ka'abah touch only with the right hand; they do not kiss it.*

"On the north side of the Ka'abah, just by its door, and close to the wall, is a slight hollow in the ground, lined with marble, and sufficiently large to admit of three persons sitting. Here it is thought meritorious to pray: the spot is called El Ma'ajan,** and supposed to be where Abraham and his son Ismael kneaded the chalk and mud which they used in building the Ka'abah; and near this Ma'ajan the former is said to have placed the large stone upon which he stood while working at the masonry. On the basis of the Ka'abah, just over the Ma'ajan, is an ancient Cufic inscription; but this I was unable to decipher, and had no opportunity of copying it.

"On the west (north-west) side of the Ka'abah,

---

* I have frequently seen it kissed by men and women.

** El Ma'ajan, the place of mixing or kneading, because the patriarchs here kneaded the mud used as cement in the holy building. Some call it El Hufrah (the digging), and it is generally known as Makam Jibrail (the place of Gabriel), because here descended the inspired order for the five daily prayers, and at this spot the Prophet and the Archangel performed their devotions, making it a most auspicious site. It is on the north of the door, from which it is distant about two feet; its length is seven spans and seven fingers; breadth five spans three fingers; and depth one span four fingers.

The following sentence from Herkler's "Qanoon e Islam" (ch. XII. sec. 5.) may serve to show the extent of error still popular. The author, after separating the Bayt Ullah from the Ka'abah, erroneously making the former the name of the whole temple, proceeds to say, "the rain water which falls on its (the Ka'abah's) *terrace* runs off through a golden spout on a stone near it, called *Rookn-e-Yemeni*, or *alabaster-stone*, and stands over the grave of Ishmael"——1 about two feet below its summit, is the famous Myzab, or water-spout,* through which the rain-water collected on the roof of the building is discharged, so as to fall upon the ground; it is about four feet in length, and six inches in breadth, as well as I could judge from below, with borders equal in height to its breadth. At the mouth hangs what is called the beard of the Myzab; a gilt board, over which the water flows. This spout was sent hither from Constantinople in A.H. 981, and is *reported* to be of pure gold. The pavement round the Ka'abah, below the Myzab, was laid down in A.H. 826, and consists of various coloured stones, forming a very handsome specimen of mosaic. There are two large slabs of fine *verde antico*** in the centre, which, according to Makrizi, were sent thither, as presents from Cairo, in A.H. 241. This is the spot where, according to Mohammedan tradition, Ismayl the son of Ibrahim, and his mother Hajirah, are buried; and here it is meritorious for the pilgrim to recite a prayer of two Rikats. On this side is a semi-circular wall, the two extremities of which are in a line with the sides of the Ka'abah, and distant from

* Generally called Mizab el Rahmah (of Mercy.) It carries rain from the roof, and discharges it upon Ishmael's grave, where pilgrims stand fighting to catch it. In El Idrisi's time it was of wood; now it is said to be gold, but it looks very dingy.

** Usually called the Hajar el Akhzar, or green stone. El Idrisi speaks of a white stone covering Ishmael's remains, Ibn Jubayr of "green marble, longish, in form of a Mihrab arch, and near it a white round slab, in both of which are spots that make them appear yellow." Near them, we are told, and towards the Iraki corner, is the tomb of Hagar, under a green slab one span and a half broad, and pilgrims used to pray at both places. Ali Bey erroneously applies the words El Hajar Ismail to the parapet about the slab.

it three or four feet,* leaving an opening, which leads to the burial-place of Ismayl. The wall bears the name of El Hatym;** and the area which it encloses is called Hedjer or Hedjer Ismael,*** on account of its being separated from the Ka'abah: the wall itself also is sometimes so called.

"Tradition says that the Ka'abah once extended as far as the Hatym, and that this side having fallen down just at the time of the Hadj, the expenses of repairing it were demanded from the pilgrims, under a pretence that the revenues of government were not acquired in a manner sufficiently pure to admit of their application towards a purpose so sacred. The sum, however, obtained proved very inadequate; all that could be done, therefore, was to raise a wall, which marked the space formerly occupied by the Ka'abah. This tradition, although current among the

---

* My measurements give five feet six inches. In El Idrisi's day the wall was fifty cubits long.

** El Hatim (الْحَطِيمُ) lit. the "broken"). Burckhardt asserts that the Mekkawi no longer apply the word, as some historians do, to the space bounded by the Ka'abah, the Partition, the Zem Zem, and the Makam of Ibrahim. I heard it, however, so used by learned Meccans, and they gave as the meaning of the name the break in this part of the oval pavement which surrounds the Ka'abah. Historians relate that all who rebuilt the "House of Allah" followed Abraham's plan till the Kuraysh, and after them El Hajjaj, curtailed it in the direction of El Hatim, which part was then first broken off, and ever since remained so.

*** El Hijr (الْحِجْرُ) is the space separated, as the name denotes, from the Ka'abah. Some suppose that Abraham here penned his sheep. Possibly Ali Bey means this part of the Temple when he speaks of El Hajar (الْحَجَرُ) Ismail—les pierres d'Ismail.

Metowefs (cicerones), is at variance with history; which declares that the Hedjer was built by the Beni Koreish, who contracted the dimensions of the Ka'abah; that it was united to the building by Hadjadj,* and again separated from it by Ibn Zebeyr. It is asserted by Fasy, that a part of the Hedjer as it now stands was never comprehended within the Ka'abah. The law regards it as a portion of the Ka'abah, inasmuch as it is esteemed equally meritorious to pray in the Hedjer as in the Ka'abah itself; and the pilgrims who have not an opportunity of entering the latter are permitted to affirm upon oath that they have prayed in the Ka'abah, although they have only prostrated themselves within the enclosure of the Hatym. The wall is built of solid stone, about five feet in height, and four in thickness, cased all over with white marble, and inscribed with prayers and invocations neatly sculptured upon the stone in modern characters.** These and the casing, are the work of El Ghoury, the Egyptian sultan, in A.H. 917. The walk round the Ka'abah is performed on the outside of the wall—the nearer to it the better.

"Round the Ka'abah is a good pavement of marble*** about eight inches below the level of the great square; it was laid in A.H. 981, by order of the

---

* "El Hajjaj;" this, as will afterwards be seen, is a mistake. He excluded the Hatim.

** As well as memory serves me, for I have preserved no note, the inscriptions are in the marble casing, and indeed no other stone meets the eye.

*** It is a fine, close, grey, polished granite; the walk is called El Mataf, or the place of circumambulation.

sultan, and describes an irregular oval; it is surrounded by thirty-two slender gilt pillars, or rather poles, between every two of which are suspended seven glass lamps, always lighted after sunset.* Beyond the poles is a second pavement, about eight paces broad, somewhat elevated above the first, but of coarser work; then another six inches higher, and eighteen paces broad, upon which stand several small buildings; beyond this is the gravelled ground; so that two broad steps may be said to lead from the square down to the Ka'abah. The small buildings just mentioned which surround the Ka'abah are the five Makams,** with the well of Zem Zem, the arch called Bab es Salam, and the Mambar.

"Opposite the four sides of the Ka'abah stand four other small buildings, where the Imaums of the orthodox Mohammedan sects, the Hanefy, Shafey, Hanbaly, and Maleky take their station, and guide the congregation in their prayers. The Makam el Maleky on the south, and that of Hanbaly opposite the Black

---

* These are now iron posts, very numerous, supporting cross rods, and of tolerably elegant shape. In Ali Bey's time there were "trente-une colonnes minces en piliers en bronze." Some native works say thirty-three, including two marble columns. Between each two hang several white or green glass globe-lamps, with wicks and oil floating on water; their light is faint and dismal. The whole of the lamps in the Haram is said to be more than 1000, yet they serve only to make "darkness visible."

** There are only four "Makams," the Hanafi, Maliki, Hanbali, and the Makam Ibrahim: and there is some error of diction below, for in these it is that the Imams stand before their congregations, and nearest the Ka'abah. In Ibn Jubayr's time the Zaydi sect was allowed an Imam, though known to be schismatics and abusers of the caliphs. Now, not being permitted to have a separate station for prayer, they suppose theirs to be suspended from heaven above the Ka'abah roof.

Stone, are small pavilions open on all sides, and supported by four slender pillars, with a light sloping roof, terminating in a point, exactly in style of Indian pagodas.* The Makam el Hanafy, which is the largest, being fifteen paces by eight, is open on all sides, and supported by twelve small pillars; it has an upper story, also open, where the Mueddin who calls to prayers takes his stand. This was first built in A.H. 923, by the Sultan Selim I.; it was afterwards rebuilt by Khoshgeldy, governor of Djidda, in 947; but all the four Makams, as they now stand, were built in A.H. 1074. The Makam-es'-Shafey is over the well Zem Zem, to which it serves as an upper chamber.**

"Near their respective Makams the adherents of the four different sects seat themselves for prayers. During my stay at Meccah the Hanefys always began their prayer first; but, according to Muselman custom, the Shafeys should pray first in the mosque; then the Hanefys, Malekys, and Hanbalys. The prayer of the Maghreb is an exception, which they are all enjoined to utter together.*** The Makam el Hanbaly is the

---

* The Makam el Maliki is on the west of, and thirty seven cubits from, the Ka'abah; that of the Hanbali forty-seven paces distant.

** Only the Muezzin takes his stand here, and the Shafe'is pray behind their Imam on the pavement round the Ka'abah, between the corner of the well Zem Zem, and the Makam Ibrahim. This place is forty cubits from the Ka'abah, that is to say, eight cubits nearer than the northern and southern "Makams." Thus the pavement forms an irregular oval ring round the house.

*** In Burckhardt's time the schools prayed according to the seniority of their founders, and they uttered the Azan of El Maghrib together, because that is a peculiarly delicate hour, which easily passes by unnoticed. In the twelfth century, at all times but the evening, the Shafe'i began, then came the Maliki and Hanbali simultaneously, and, lastly, the Hanafi. Now the Shaykh el Muezzin begins the call, which is taken up by the others. He is a Hanafi; as

place where the officers of government and other great people are seated during prayers; here the Pasha and the sheriff are placed, and in their absence the eunuchs of the temple. These fill the space under this Makam in front, and behind it the female Hadjys who visit the temple have their places assigned, to which they repair principally for the two evening prayers, few of them being seen in the mosque at the three other daily prayers: they also perform the Towaf, or walk round the Ka'abah, but generally at night, though it is not uncommon to see them walking in the day-time among the men.

"The present building which encloses Zem Zem stands close by the Makam Hanbaly, and was erected in A.H. 1072: it is of a square shape, and of massive construction, with an entrance to the north,* opening into the room which contains the well. This room is beautifully ornamented with marbles of various colours; and adjoining to it, but having a separate door, is a small room with a stone reservoir, which is always full of Zem Zem water. This the Hadjys get to drink by passing their hand with a cup through an iron grated opening, which serves as a window, into the reservoir, without entering the room. The mouth of the well is surrounded by a wall five feet in height and about ten feet in diameter. Upon this the people stand who draw up the water in leathern buckets, an iron railing

---

indeed are all the principal people at Meccah, only a few wild Sherifs of the hills being Shafe'i.
  * The door of the Zem Zem building opens to the south-east.

being so placed as to prevent their falling in. In El
Fasy's time there were eight marble basins in this
room, for the purpose of ablution.

"On the north-east (south-east) side of Zem Zem
stand two small buildings, one behind the other,*
called El Kobbateyn; they are covered by domes
painted in the same manner as the mosque, and in
them are kept water-jars, lamps, carpets, mats, brooms,
and other articles used in the very mosque.** These
two ugly buildings are injurious to the interior appearance of the building, their heavy forms and structure being very disadvantageously contrasted with the
light and airy shape of the Makams. I heard some
Hadjys from Greece, men of better taste than the
Arabs, express their regret that the Kobbateyn should
be allowed to disfigure the mosque. They were built
by Khoshgeldy, governor of Dijidda A.H. 947; one is
called Kobbet el Abbas, from having been placed on

---

* This is not exactly correct: the angle of one building fronts the angle of
its neighbour.

** Their names and offices are now changed. One is called the Kubbat el
Sa'at, and contains the clocks and chronometers (two of them English) sent as
presents to the mosque by the Sultan. The other, known as the Kubbat el
Kutub, is used as a store-room for manuscripts bequeathed to the mosque.
They still are open to Burckhardt's just criticism, being nothing but the common cupola springing from four walls, and vulgarly painted with bands of red,
yellow, and green. In Ibn Jubayr's time the two domes contained bequests of
books and candles. The Kubbat Abbas, or that further from the Ka'abah
was also called Kubbat el Sherab (the Dome of Drink), because Zem
Zem water was here kept cooling for the use of pilgrims in Daurak, or
earthen jars. The nearer was termed Kubbat el Yahudi; and the tradition
they told me was, that a Jew having refused to sell his house upon this spot, it
was permitted to remain *in loco* by the prophet, as a lasting testimony to his
regard for justice. A similar tale is told of an old woman's hut, which was
allowed to stand in the corner of the great Nushirawan's royal halls.

the site of a small tank said to have been formed by Abbas, the uncle of Mohammed.

"A few paces west (north-west) of Zem Zem, and directly opposite to the door of the Ka'abah, stands a ladder or staircase,* which is moved up to the wall of the Ka'abah on days when that building is opened, and by which the visitors ascend to the door. It is of wood, with some carved ornaments, moves on low wheels, and is sufficiently broad to admit of four persons ascending abreast. The first ladder was sent hither from Cairo in A.H. 818 by Moyaed Abou el Naser, king of Egypt.

"In the same line with the ladder and close by it stands a lightly built insulated and circular arch, about fifteen feet wide, and eighteen feet high, called Bab-es-Salam, which must not be confounded with the great gate of the mosque, bearing the same name. Those who enter the Bait Ullah for the first time are enjoined to do so by the outer and inner Bab-es-Salam; in passing under the latter they are to exclaim, 'O God, may it be a happy entrance.' I do not know by whom this arch was built, but it appears to be modern.**

"Nearly in front of the Bab-es-Salam and nearer the Ka'abah than any of the other surrounding buildings, stands the Makam Ibrahim.*** This is a small

---

* Called "El Daraj." A correct drawing of it may be found in Ali Bey's work.
** The Bab el Salam, or Bab el Naby, or Bab beni Shaybah, resembles in its isolation a triumphal arch, and is built of cut stone.
*** "The (praying) place of Abraham." Readers will remember that the

building supported by six pillars about eight feet high, four of which are surrounded from top to bottom by a fine iron railing, while they leave the space beyond the two hind pillars open; within the railing is a frame about five feet square, terminating in a pyramidal top, and said to contain the sacred stone upon which Ibrahim stood when he built the Ka'abah, and which with the help of his son Ismayl he had removed from hence to the place called Ma'ajen, already mentioned. The stone is said to have yielded under the weight of the Patriarch, and to preserve the impression of his foot still visible upon it; but no Hadjy has ever seen it,[*] as the frame is always entirely covered with a

---

Meccan Mosque is peculiarly connected with Ibrahim, whom Moslems prefer to all prophets and apostles except Mohammed.

[*] This I believe to be incorrect. I was asked five dollars for permission to enter; but the sum was too high for my finances. Learned men told me that the stone shows the impress of two feet, especially the big toes, and devout pilgrims fill the cavities with water, which they rub over their eyes and faces. When the Caliph el Mahdi visited Meccah, one Abdullah bin Usman presented himself at the unusual hour of noon and, informing the prince that he had brought him a relic which no man but himself had yet seen, produced this celebrated stone. El Mahdi, rejoicing greatly, kissed it, rubbed his face against it, and pouring water upon it, drank the draught. Kutb el Din, one of the Meccan historians, says that it was visited in his day. In Ali Bey's time it was covered with "un magnifique drap noir brodé en or et en argent avec de gros glands en or;" he does not say, however, that he saw the stone. Its veils, called Sitr Ibrahim el Khalil, are of green "Ibrisham," or silk mixed with cotton and embroidered with gold. They are made at Cairo of three different colours, black, red, and green; and one is devoted to each year. The gold embroidery is in the Sulsi character, and expresses the Throne-verse, the Chapter of the Cave, and the name of the reigning Sultan; on the top is "Allah," below is "Mohammed;" beneath this is "Ibrahim el Khalil;" and at each corner is the name of one of the four caliphs.

In a note to the "Dabistan" (vol. II. page 410) we find two learned Orientalists confounding the Black Stone with Abraham's Station or Platform. "The Prophet honoured the Black Stone, upon which Abraham conversed with Hagar, to which he tied his camels, and upon which the traces of his feet are still seen."

brocade of red silk richly embroidered. Persons are constantly seen before the railing invoking the good offices of Ibrahim; and a short prayer must be uttered by the side of the Makam after the walk round the Ka'abah is completed. It is said that many of the Sahaba, or first adherents of Mohammed, were interred in the open space between this Makam and Zem Zem;* from which circumstance it is one of the most favorite places of prayers in the mosque. In this part of the area the Khalif Soleyman Ibn Abd el Melek, brother of Wolyd (El Walid), built a fine reservoir in A.H. 97, which was filled from a spring east of Arafat;** but the Mekkawys destroyed it after his death, on the pretence that the water of Zem Zem was preferable.

"On the side of Makam Ibrahim, facing the middle part of the front of the Ka'abah, stands the Mambar, or pulpit of the mosque; it is elegantly formed of fine white marble, with many sculptured ornaments; and was sent as a present to the mosque in A.H. 969 by Sultan Soleyman Ibn Selym.*** A straight, narrow staircase leads up to the post of the Khatyb, or preacher, which is surmounted by a gilt polygonal pointed steeple, resembling an obelisk. Here a sermon is preached on Fridays and on certain festivals.

---

* Not only here, I was told by learned Meccans, but under all the oval pavements surrounding the Ka'abah.

** The spring gushes from the southern base of Mount Arafat, as will afterwards be noticed. It is exceedingly pure.

*** The author informs us that "the first pulpit was sent from Cairo in A.H. 818, together with the staircase, both being the gifts of Moayed, caliph of Egypt." Ali Bey accurately describes the present Mambar.

22   A PILGRIMAGE TO MECCA AND MEDINA.

These, like the Friday sermons of all mosques in the Mohammedan countries, are usually of the same turn, with some slight alterations upon extraordinary occasions.*

"I have now described all the buildings within the inclosure of the temple.

"The gates of the mosque are nineteen in number, and are distributed about it without any order or symmetry."**

---

* The curious will find a specimen of a Moslem sermon in Lane's Mod. Egypt, vol. 1. ch. 3.

** Burckhardt "subjoins their names as they are usually written upon small cards by the Metowefs: in another column are the names by which they were known in more ancient times, principally taken from Azraky and Kotoby." I have added a few remarks in brackets.

Modern names.	Arches.	Ancient names.
1. Bab el Salam, composed of smaller gates or arches	3	Bab Beni Shaybah (this is properly applied to the inner, not the outer Salam Gate).
2. Bab el Neby	2	Bab el Jenaiz, Gate of Biers, the dead being carried through it to the mosque.
3. Bab el Abbas, opposite to this the house of Abbas once stood	3	Bab Sertakat (some Moslem authors confound this Bab el Abbas with the Gate of Biers).
4. Bab Aly	3	Bab Beni Hashem.
5. Bab el Zayt / Bab el Ashra	2	Bab Razan (so called from a neighbouring hill).
6. Bab el Baghlah	2	
7. Bab el Szafa (Safa)	5	Bab Beni Makhzoum.
8. Bab Sherif	2	Bab el Djiyad (so called because leading to the hill Jiyad).
9. Bab Medjahed	2	Bab el Dokhmah.
10. Bab Zoleykha	2	Bab Sherif Adjelan, who built it.
11. Bab Om Hany, so called from the daughter of Aby Taleb	2	
Carry forward	28	

Burckhardt's description of the gates is short and imperfect. On the eastern side of the Mosque there are four principal entrances, seven on the southern side, three in the western, and five in the northern wall.

The eastern gates are the Greater Bab el Salam, through which the pilgrim enters the temple; it is close to the north-east angle. Next to it the Lesser Bab el Salam, with two small arches; thirdly, the Bab el Nabi, where the Prophet used to pass through from Khadijah's house; and, lastly, near the south-east

Modern names.	Arches.	Ancient names.
Brought forward	28	
12. Bab el Woda'a (El Wida'a) through which the pilgrim passes when taking his final leave of the temple	2	Bab el Hazoura (some write this Bab el Zarurah).
13. Bab Ibrahim, so called from a tailor who had a shop near it	1	Bab el Kheyatyn or Bab Djomah.
14. Bab el Omra, through which pilgrims issue to visit the Omra. Also called Benu Saham	1	
15. Bab Atech	1	Bab Amer Ibn el Aas, or Bab el Sedra.
16. Bab el Bastye	1	Bab el Adjale.
17. Bab el Kotoby, so called from an historian of Mekka who lived in an adjoining lane and opened this small gate into the mosque	1	Bab Zyade Dar el Nedoua.
18. Bab Zyade	3	(It is called Bab Ziyadah—Gate of Excess -because it is a new structure thrown out into the Shamiyah, or Syrian quarter).
19. Bab Dereybe	1	Bab Medrese.
Total	39	

corner, the Bab Ali, or of the Benú Hashim, opening upon the street between Safa and Marwah.

Beyond the north-eastern corner, in the northern wall, is the Bab Duraybah, a small entrance with one arch. Next to it, almost fronting the Ka'abah, is the grand adit, Bab el Ziyadah, also known as Bab el Nadwah. Here the colonnade, projecting far beyond the normal line, forms a small square or hall supported by pillars, and a false colonnade of sixty-one columns leads to the true cloister of the Mosque. This portion of the building, being cool and shady, is crowded by the poor, the diseased, and the dying, during divine worship, and at other times by idlers, schoolboys, and merchants. Passing through three external arches, pilgrims descend by a flight of steps into the hall, where they deposit their slippers, it not being considered decorous to hold them when circumambulating the Ka'abah. A broad pavement, in the shape of an irregular triangle, whose base is the cloister, leads to the circuit of the house. Next to the Ziyadah Gate is a small, single-arched entrance, "Bab Kutubi," and beyond it one similar, the Bab el Ajlah (عجلة), also named El Basitiyah, from its proximity to the college of Abd el Basitah. Close to the north-west angle of the cloister is the Bab el Nadwah, anciently called Bab el Umrah, and now Bab el Atik, the Old Gate. Near this place and opening into the Ka'abah, stood the "Town Hall" (Dar el Nadwah), built by Kusay, for containing the oriflamme "El Liwa," and as a council-chamber for the ancients of the city.

In the western wall are three entrances. The single-arched gate nearest to the north angle is called Bab Beni Saham or Bab el Umrah, because pilgrims pass through it to the Tanim and the ceremony El Umrah (Little Pilgrimage). In the centre of the wall is the Bab Ibrahim, or Bab el Khayyatin (the Tailors' Gate); a single arch leading into a large projecting square, like that of the Ziyadah entrance, but somewhat smaller. Near the south-west corner is a double-arched adit, the Bab el Wida'a ("of Farewell"): hence departing pilgrims issue forth from the temple.

At the western end of the southern wall is the two-arched Bab Umm Hani, so called after the lady's residence, when included in the Mosque. Next to it is a similar building, "Bab Ujlan" (عُجْلان), which derives its name from the large college "Madrasat Ujlan;" some term it Bab el Sherif, because it is opposite one of the palaces. After which, and also pierced with two arches, is the Bab el Jiyad (some erroneously spell it El Jihad, "of Religious War"), the gate leading to Jebel Jiyad. The next is also double arched, and called the Bab el Mujahid or El Rahmah ("of Mercy"). Nearly opposite the Ka'abah, and connected with the pavement by a raised line of stone, is the Bab el Safa, through which pilgrims now issue to perform the ceremony "El Sa'i;" it is a small and unconspicuous erection. Next to it is the Bab el Baghlah, with two arches; and close to the south-east angle of the Mosque the Bab Yunus, alias Bab Bazan, alias

Bab el Zayt, alias Bab el Asharah, "of the Ten," because a favorite with the ten first Sahabah, or Companions of the Prophet. "Most of these gates," says Burckhardt, "have high pointed arches; but a few round arches are seen among them, which, like all arches of this kind in the Hejar, are nearly semicircular. They are without ornament, except the inscription on the exterior, which commemorates the name of the builder, and they are all posterior in date to the fourteenth century. As each gate consists of two or three arches, or divisions, separated by narrow walls, these divisions are counted in the enumeration of the gates leading into the Ka'abah, and they make up the number thirty-nine. There being no doors to the gates, the Mosque is consequently open at all times. I have crossed at every hour of the night, and always found people there, either at prayers or walking about.*

"The outside walls of the mosques are those of the houses which surround it on all sides. These houses belonged originally to the Mosque; the greater part are now the property of individuals. They are let out to the richest Hadjys, at very high prices, as much as 500 piastres being given during the pilgrimage for a good apartment with windows opening into the Mosque.**

---

* The Meccans love to boast that at no hour of the day or night is the Ka'abah ever seen without a devotee to perform "Tawaf."

** This would be about 50 dollars, whereas 25 is a fair sum for a single apartment. Like English lodging-house keepers, the Meccans make the season pay for the year. In Burckhardt's time the colonnato was worth from 9 to 12 piastres: the value of the latter coin is now greatly decreased, for 28 go to the Spanish dollar all over El Hejaz.

Windows have in consequence been opened in many parts of the walls on a level with the street, and above that of the floor of the colonnades. Hadjys living in these apartments are allowed to perform the Friday's prayers at home; because, having the Ka'abah in view from the windows, they are supposed to be in the Mosque itself, and to join in prayer those assembled within the temple. Upon a level with the ground floor of the colonnades and opening into them are small apartments formed in the walls, having the appearance of dungeons; these have remained the property of the Mosque while the houses above them belong to private individuals. They are let out to watermen, who deposit in them the Zem Zem jars, or to less opulent Hadjys who wish to live in the Mosque.* Some of the surrounding houses still belong to the Mosque, and were originally intended for public schools as their names of Medresa implies; they are now all let out to Hadjys.

"The exterior of the Mosque is adorned with seven minarets irregularly distributed:—1. Minaret of Bab el Omra (Umrah); 2. of Bab el Salam; 3. of Bab Aly; 4. of Beb el Wodaa (Wida'a); 5. of Medesa Kail (Kait) Bey; 6. of Beb el Zyadi; 7. of Medreset Sultan Soleyman.** They are quadrangular or round steeples, in

* I entered one of these caves, and never experienced such a sense of suffocation even in that favourite spot for Britons to asphixiate themselves —the Baths of Nero.

** The Magnificent (son of Selim I.), who built at El Medinah the minaret bearing his name. The minarets at Meccah are far inferior to those of her rival, and their bands of gaudy colours give them an appearance of tawdry vulgarity.

no way differing from other minarets. The entrance to them is from the different buildings round the Mosque, which they adjoin.* A beautiful view of the busy crowd below is attained by ascending the most northern one."**

Having described at length the establishment attached to the Mosque of El Medinah, I spare my readers a detailed account of the crowd of idlers that hang about the Meccan temple. The Naib el Haram, or vice-intendant, is one Sayyid Ali, said to be of Indian extraction; he is superior to all the attendants. There are about eighty eunuchs, whose chief, Serur Agha, was a slave of Mohammed Ali Pasha. Their pay varies from 100 to 1000 piastres per mensem; it is, however, inferior to the Medinah salaries. The Imams, Muezzins, Khatibs, Zem Zemis, &c. &c., are under their respective Shaykhs who are of the Olema.

Briefly to relate the history of the Ka'abah.

The "House of Allah" is supposed to have been built and rebuilt ten times.

The first origin of the idea is manifestly a symbolical allusion to the angels standing before the Almighty and praising His name. When Allah, it is said,

---

* Two minarets, namely, those of the Bab el Salam and the Bab el Safa, are separated from the Mosque by private dwelling-houses, a plan neither common nor regular.

** A stranger must be careful how he appears at a minaret window, unless he would have a bullet whizzing past his head. Arabs are especially jealous of being overlooked, and have no fellow-feeling for votaries of "beautiful views." For this reason here, as in Egypt, a blind Muezzin is preferred, and many ridiculous stories are told about men who for years have counterfeited cecity to live in idleness.

informed the celestial throng that he was about to send a vicegerent on earth, they deprecated the design. Being reproved with these words, "God knoweth what ye know not," and dreading the eternal anger, they compassed the Arsh, or throne, in adoration. Upon this Allah created the Bayt el Ma'amur, four jasper pillars with a ruby roof, and the angels circumambulated it, crying, "Praise be to Allah, and exalted be Allah, and there is no god but Allah, and Allah is omnipotent!" The Creator then ordered them to build a similar house for man on earth. This, according to Ali, took place 40, according to Abu Hurayrah, 2000 years before the creation; both authorities, however, are agreed that the firmaments were spread above and the seven earths beneath this Bayt el Ma'amur.

There is considerable contradiction concerning the second house. Ka'ab related that Allah sent down with Adam[*] a Khaymah, or tabernacle of hollow ruby, which the angels raised on stone pillars. This was also called Bayt el Ma'amur. Adam received an order to compass it about; after which he begged a reward for obedience, and was promised a pardon to himself and to all his progeny who repent.

Others declare that Adam, expelled from Paradise, and lamenting that he no longer heard the prayers of the angels, was ordered by Allah to take the stones of five hills, Lebanon, Sinai, Tur Zayt (Olivet), Ararat,

[*] It must be remembered that the Moslems, like many of the Jews, hold that Paradise was not on earth, but in the lowest firmament, which is, as it were, a reflection of earth.

and Hira, which afforded the first stone. Gabriel, smiting his wing upon earth, opened a foundation to the seventh layer, and the position of the building is exactly below the heavenly Bayt el Ma'amur—a Moslem corruption of the legends concerning the heavenly and the earthly Jerusalem. Our First Father circumambulated it as he had seen the angels do, and was by them taught the formula of prayer and the number of circuits.

According to others, again, this second house was not erected till after the "Angelic Foundation" was destroyed by time.

The history of the third house is also somewhat confused. When the Bayt el Ma'amur, or, as others say, the tabernacle, was removed to heaven after Adam's death, a stone-and-mud building was placed in its stead by his son Shays (Seth). For this reason it is respected by the Sabæans, or Christians of St. John, as well as by the Moslems. This Ka'abah, according to some, was destroyed by the deluge, which materially altered its site. Others believe that it was raised to heaven. Others, again, declare that only the pillars supporting the heavenly tabernacle were allowed to remain. Most authorities agree in asserting that the Black Stone was stored up in Abu Kubays, whence that "first created of mountains" is called El Amin, "the Honest."

Abraham and his son were ordered to build the fourth house upon the old foundations: its materials, according to some, were taken from the five hills which supplied the second; others give the names Ohod, Kuds, Warka, Sinai, Hira, and a sixth, Abu Kubays. It was of irregular shape: 32 cubits from the eastern to the northern corner; 32 from north to west; 31 from west to south; 20 from south to east; and only 9 cubits high. There was no roof; two doors, level with the ground, were pierced in the eastern and western walls; and inside, on the right hand, near the present entrance, a hole for treasure was dug. Gabriel restored the Black Stone, which Abraham, by his direction, placed in its present corner, as a sign where circumambulation is to begin; and the patriarch then learned all the complicated rites of pilgrimage. When this house was completed, Abraham, by Allah's order, ascended Jebel Sabir, and called the world to visit the sanctified spot; and all earth's sons heard him, even those "in their father's loins or in their mother's womb, from that day unto the day of resurrection."

The Amalikah (descended from Imlik, great grandson of Sam, son of Noah), who first settled near Meccah, founded the fifth house. El Tabari and the Moslem historians generally made the erection of the Amalikah to precede that of the Jurham; these, according to others, repaired the house which Abraham built.

The sixth Ka'abah was built about the beginning of the Christian era by the Beni Jurham, the children of Kahtan, fifth descendant from Noah. Ismael married, according to the Moslems, a daughter of this tribe,

Da'alah bint Muzaz (مضاض) bin Umar, and abandoning Hebrew, he began to speak Arabic (Ta'arraba). Hence his descendants are called Arabicized Arabs. After Ismail's death, which happened when he was 130 years old, Sabit, the eldest of his twelve sons, became "Lord of the house." He was succeeded by his maternal grandfather Muzaz, and afterwards by his children. The Jurham inhabited the higher parts of Meccah, especially Jebel Ka'aka'an, so called from their clashing arms; whereas the Amalikah dwelt in the lower grounds, which obtained the name of Jiyad, from their generous horses.

Kusay bin Kilab, governor of Meccah, and fifth forefather of the Prophet, built the seventh house, according to Abraham's plan. He roofed it over with palm-leaves, stocked it with idols, and persuaded his tribe to settle near the Haram.

Kusay's house was burnt down by a woman's censer, which accidentally set fire to the Kiswat, or covering, and the walls were destroyed by a torrent. A merchant-ship belonging to a Greek trader, called "Bakum" (باقوم), being wrecked at Jeddah, afforded material for the roof, and the crew were employed as masons. The Kuraysh tribe, who rebuilt the house, failing in funds of pure money, curtailed its proportions by nearly seven cubits, and called the omitted portion El Hatim. In digging the foundation they came to a green stone, like a camel's hunch, which, struck with a pickaxe, sent forth blinding lightning, and prevented further excavation. The Kuraysh, amongst other alterations, raised the walls from nine to eighteen cubits, built a staircase in the northern breadth, closed the western door, and placed the eastern entrance above the ground, to prevent men entering without their leave.

When the eighth house was being built, Mohammed was in his twenty-fifth year. His surname of El Amin, the Honest, probably induced the tribes to make him their umpire for the decision of a dispute about the position of the Black Stone, and who should have the honour of raising it to its place. Others derive the surname from this affair. He decided for the corner chosen by Abraham, and distributed the privilege amongst the clans. The Benú Zahrah and Benú Abd Manaf took the front wall and the door; to the Benú Jama and the Benú Sahm was allotted the back wall; the Benú Makhzum and their Kuraysh relations stood at the southern wall; and at the "Stone" corner were posted the Benú Abd el Dar, the Benú Asad, and the Benú Ada.

Abdullah bin Zubayr, nephew of Ayisha, rebuilt the Ka'abah in A.H. 64. It had been weakened by fire, which burnt the covering, besides splitting the Black Stone into three pieces, and by the Manjanik (catapults) of Husayn (حصين) bin Numayr, general of Yezid, who obstinately besieged Meccah till he heard of his sovereign's death. Abdullah, hoping to fulfil a prophecy, and seeing that the people of Meccah fled in alarm, pulled down the building by means of "thin-calved Abyssinian slaves:" when they came to Abraham's foundation he saw that it included the Hijr, which part the Kuraysh had been unable to build. This house was made of cut stone and fine lime brought from Yemen. Abdullah, taking in the Hatim, lengthened the building by seven cubits, and added to its former height nine cubits, thus making a total of twenty-seven. He roofed over the whole, or a part; re-opened the western door, to serve as an exit; and, following the advice of his aunt, who quoted the Prophet's words, he supported the interior with a single row of three columns, instead of the double row of six placed there by the Kuraysh. Finally, he paved the Mataf, or circuit, ten cubits round with the remaining slabs, and increased the Haram by taking in the nearer houses. During the building, a curtain was stretched round the walls, and pilgrims compassed them externally. When finished, it was perfumed inside and outside, and invested with brocade. Then Abdullah and all the citizens went forth in procession to the Tanim, a reverend place near Meccah, returned to perform Umrah (the lesser pilgrimage), slew 100 victims, and rejoiced with great festivities.

The Caliph Abd el Malik bin Marwan besieged Abdullah bin Zubayr, who, after a brave defence, was slain. In A.H. 74 Hajjaj bin Yusuf, general of Abd el Malik's troops, wrote to the prince, informing him that Abdullah had made unauthorised additions to and changes in the Haram: the reply brought an order to rebuild the house. Hajjaj again excluded the Hatim, and retired the northern wall six cubits and a span, making it twenty-five cubits long by twenty-four broad: the other three sides were allowed to remain as built by the son of Zubayr. He gave the house a double roof, closed the western door, and raised the eastern four cubits and a span above the Mataf, or circuit, which he paved over. The Haram was enlarged and beautified by the Abbasides, especially by El Mehdi, El Mutamid, and El Mutazid. Some authors reckon, as an eleventh house, the repairs made by Sultan Murad Khan. On the night of Tuesday, 20th Sha'aban, A.H. 1030, a violent torrent swept the Haram; it rose one cubit above the threshold of the Ka'abah, carried away the lamp-posts and the Makam Ibrahim, all the northern wall of the house, half of the eastern, and one-third of the western side. It subsided on Wednesday night. The repairs were not finished till A.H. 1040. The greater part, however, of the building dates from the time of El Hajjaj; and Moslems, who never mention his name without a curse, knowingly circumambulate his work. The Olema indeed have insisted upon its remaining untouched, lest kings in wantonness should change its form: Harun el Rashid desired to rebuild it, but was forbidden by the Imam Malik.

The present proofs of the Ka'abah's sanctity, as adduced by the learned, are puerile enough, but curious. The Olema have made much of the verselet: "Verily the first house built for mankind (to worship in) is that in Bakkah* (Meccah), blessed and a salvation to the three worlds. Therein (fihi) are manifest signs, the standing-place of Abraham, which whoso entereth shall be safe." (Kor. ch. 3.) The word "therein" is interpreted to mean Meccah, and the "manifest signs" the Ka'abah, which contains such marvels as the footprints on Abraham's platform, and the spiritual safeguard of all who enter the Sanctuary. The other "signs"—historical, psychical, and physical—are briefly these:—

The preservation of the Hajar el Aswad and the Makam Ibrahim from many foes, and the miracles put forth (as in the War of the Elephant) to defend the house; the violent and terrible deaths of the sacrilegious; and the fact that, in the Deluge, the large fish did not eat the little fish in the Haram. A wonderful desire and love impel men from distant regions to visit the holy spot; and the first sight of the Ka'abah causes awe and fear, horripilation and tears. Furthermore, ravenous beasts will not destroy their prey in the Sanctuary land, and the pigeons and other birds never perch upon the house, except to be cured of sickness, for fear of defiling the roof. The Ka'abah, though small, can contain any number of devotees: no

---

* Makkah (our Mecca) is the common word; Bakkah is a synonyme never used but in books. The former means "a concourse of people." But why derive it from the Hebrew and translate it "a slaughter?" Is this a likely name for a Holy Place? Dr. Colenso actually turns the Makorabe of Ptolemy into "Makkahrabbah"—plentiful slaughter. But if Makorabe be Mecca it is evidently a corruption of "Makkah" and "Arabah"—the Arab race.

Again supposing the Meccan temple to be originally dedicated to the Sun, why should the pure Arab word "Ba'al" become Hobal with the Hebrew article; that deity being only one of the 360 that formed the Pantheon?

one is ever hurt in it,—this is an audacious falsehood the Ka'abah is scarcely ever opened without some accident happening—and invalids recover their health by rubbing themselves against the Kiswah and the Black Stone. Finally, it is observed that every day 100,000 mercies descend upon the house; and especially that if rain come up from the northern corner, there is plenty in Irak; if from the south, there is plenty in Yemen; if from the east, plenty in India; if from the western, there is plenty in Syria; and if from all four angles, general plenty is presignified.

CHAPTER II.

The first Visit to the House of Allah.

THE boy Mohammed left me in the street, and having at last persuaded the sleepy and tired Indian porter, by violent kicks and testy answers to twenty cautious queries, to swing open the huge gate of his fortress, he rushed up stairs to embrace his mother. After a minute I heard the Zaghritah, lululú or shrill cry which in these lands welcomes the wanderer home; the sound so gladdening to the returner sent a chill to the stranger's heart.

Presently the youth returned. His manner had changed from a boisterous and jaunty demeanour to one of grave and attentive courtesy—I had become his guest. He led me into the gloomy hall, seated me upon a large carpeted Mastabah, or platform, and told his "bara Miyan" (great sir), the Hindostani porter, to bring a light. Meanwhile a certain shuffling of slippered feet above informed my hungry ears that the "Kabirah," the mistress of the house, was intent on hospitable thoughts. When the camels were unloaded appeared a dish of fine vermicelli, browned and powdered with loaf-sugar. The boy Mohammed, I, and Shaykh Nur, lost no time in exerting our right hands: and truly, after our hungry journey, we found the "Kunafah" delicious. After the meal we procured cots from a neighbouring coffee-house, and we lay down, weary, and anxious to snatch an hour or two of repose. At dawn we were expected to perform our "Tawaf el Kudum," or "Circumambulation of Arrival," at the Haram.

Scarcely had the first smile of morning beamed upon the rugged head of the Eastern hill, Abu Kubays, when we arose, bathed, and proceeded in our pilgrim-garb to the Sanctuary. We entered by the Bab el Ziyadah, or principal northern door, descended two long flights of steps, traversed the cloister, and stood in sight of the Bayt Allah.

* * * * * *

There at last it lay, the bourn of my long and weary pilgrimage, realising the hopes and plans of many and many a year. The mirage medium of Fancy invested the huge catafalque and its gloomy pall with peculiar charms. There were no giant fragments of hoar antiquity as in Egypt, no remains of graceful and harmonious beauty as in Greece and Italy, no barbaric gorgeousness as in the buildings of India; yet the view was strange, unique—and how few have looked upon the celebrated shrine! I may truly say that, of all the worshippers who clung weeping to the curtain, or who pressed their beating hearts to the stone, none felt for the moment a deeper emotion than did the Haji from the far north. It was as if the poetical legends of the Arab spoke truth, and that the waving wings of angels, not the sweet breeze of morning, were agitating and swelling the black covering of the shrine.

Few Moslems contemplate for the first time the Ka'abah, without fear and awe: there is a popular jest against new comers, that they generally inquire the direction of prayer. This being the Kiblah, or fronting place, Moslems pray all around it; a circumstance which of course cannot take place in any spot of El Islam but the Haram. The boy Mohammed therefore, left me for a few minutes to myself; but presently he warned me that it was time to begin. Advancing, we entered through the Bab Beni Shaybah, "Gate of the Sons of the Shaybah" (old woman). There we raised our hands, repeated the Labbayk, the Takbir, and the Tahlil; after which we uttered certain supplications, and drew our hands down our faces. Then we proceeded to the Shafe'i place of worship—the open pavement between the Makam Ibrahim and the well Zem Zem—here we performed the usual two-prostration prayer in honour of the Mosque. This was followed by a cup of holy water and a present to the Sakkas, or carriers, who for the consideration distributed a large earthen vaseful in my name to poor pilgrims.

The word Zem Zem has a doubtful origin. Some derive it from the Zam Zam, or murmuring of its waters, others from Zam! Zam! (fill! fill! *i. e.* the bottle), Hagar's impatient exclamation when she saw the stream. Sale translates it stay! stay! and says, that Hagar called out in the Egyptian language, to prevent her son wandering. The Hukama, or Rationalists of El Islam, who invariably connect their faith with the worship of Venus especially, and the heavenly bodies generally, derive Zem Zem from the Persian, and make it signify the "great luminary." Hence they say the Zem Zem, as well as the Ka'abah, denoting the Cuthite or Ammonian worship of sun and fire, deserve man's reverence. So the Persian poet Khakani addresses these two buildings—

> "O Ka'abah, thou traveller of the heavens!"
> O Venus, thou fire of the world!"

Thus Wahid Mohammed, founder of the Wahidiyah sect, identifies the Kiblah and the sun; wherefore he says the door fronts the east. By the names Yemen ("right-hand"), Sham ("left-hand"), Kubul, or the east wind ("fronting"), and Dubur, or the west wind ("from the back"), it is evident that worshippers fronted the rising sun. According to the Hukama, the original Black Stone represents Venus, "which in the border of the heavens is a star of the planets," and symbolical of the power of nature, "by whose passive energy the universe was warmed into life and motion." The Hindus accuse the Moslems of adoring the Bayt Ullah—

> "O Moslem, if thou worship the Ka'abah,
> Why reproach the worshippers of idols?"

Says Rai Manshar. And Musaylimah, who in his attempt to found a fresh faith, gained but the historic epithet of "Liar," allowed his followers to turn their faces in any direction, mentally ejaculating, "I address myself to thee, who hast neither side nor figure;" a doctrine which might be sensible in the abstract, but certainly not material enough and pride-flattering to win him many converts in Arabia.

The produce of Zem Zem is held in great esteem. It is used for drinking and religious ablution, but for no baser purposes; and the Meccans advise pilgrims always to break their fast with it. It is apt to cause diarrhœa and boils, and I never saw a stranger drink it without a wry face. Sale is decidedly correct in his assertion: the flavour is a salt-bitter, much resembling an infusion of a tea-spoonful of Epsom salts in a large tumbler of tepid water. Moreover, it is exceedingly "heavy" to digest. For this reason Turks and other strangers prefer rain-water, collected in cisterns and sold for five farthings a gugglet. It was a favorite amusement with me to watch them whilst they drank the holy water, and to taunt their scant and irreverent potations.*

The water is transmitted to distant regions in glazed earthen jars covered with basket-work, and sealed by the Zem Zemis. Religious men break their lenten fast with it; apply it to their eyes to brighten vision, and imbibe a few drops at the hour of death, when Satan stands by holding a bowl of purest water, the price of the departing soul. Of course modern

---

* The strictures of the Calcutta Review (No. 41. art 1.) based upon the taste of Zem Zem, are unfounded. In these days a critic cannot be excused for such hasty judgments; at Calcutta or Bombay he would easily find a jar of Zem Zem water, which he might taste for himself.

superstition is not idle about the waters of Zem Zem. The copious supply of the well is considered at Meccah miraculous; in distant countries it facilitates the pronunciation of Arabic to the student, and everywhere the nauseous draught is highly meritorious in a religious point of view.

We then advanced towards the eastern angle of the Ka'abah, in which is inserted the Black Stone, and, standing about ten yards from it, repeated with upraised hands, "There is no god but Allah alone, Whose Covenant is Truth, and Whose Servant is victorious. There is no god but Allah, without Sharer; His is the Kingdom, to Him be Praise, and He over all Things is potent." After which we approached as close as we could to the stone. A crowd of pilgrims preventing our touching it that time, we raised our hands to our ears, in the first position of prayer, and then lowering them, exclaimed, "O Allah (I do this), in Thy Belief, and in Verification of Thy Book, and in Pursuance of Thy Prophet's Example—may Allah bless Him and preserve! O Allah, I extend my Hand to Thee, and great is my Desire to Thee! O accept Thou my Supplication, and diminish my Obstacles, and pity my Humiliation and graciously grant me Thy Pardon!" After which, as we were still unable to reach the stone, we raised our hands to our ears, the palms facing the stone as if touching it, recited the various religious formulæ, the Takbir, the Tahlil, and the Hamdilah, blessed the Prophet, and kissed the finger-tips of the right hand.

The Prophet used to weep when he touched the Black Stone, and said that it was the place for the pouring forth of tears. According to most authors, the second Caliph also used to kiss it. For this reason most Moslems, except the Shafe'i school, must touch the stone with both hands and apply their lips to it, or touch it with the fingers, which should be kissed, or rub the palms upon it, and afterwards draw them down the face. Under circumstances of difficulty, it is sufficient to stand before the stone, but the Prophet's Sunnat, or practice, was to touch it. Lucian mentions adoration of the sun by kissing the hand.

Then commenced the ceremony of "Tawaf," or circumambulation, our route being the "Mataf"—the low oval of polished granite immediately surrounding the Ka'abah. I repeated, after my Mutawwif, or cicerone, "In the Name of Allah, and Allah is omnipotent! I purpose to circuit seven Circuits unto Almighty Allah, glorified and exalted!" This is technically called the Niyat (intention) of Tawaf.

Then we began the prayer, "O Allah (I do this) in Thy Belief, and in Verification of Thy Book, and in Faithfulness to Thy Covenant, and in Perseverance of the Example of the Prophet Mohammed—may Allah bless Him and preserve!" till we reached the place El Multazem, between the corner of the Black Stone and the Ka'abah door.

Here we ejaculated, "O Allah, Thou hast Rights, so pardon my transgressing them!" Opposite the door we repeated, "O Allah, verily the House is Thy House, and the Sanctuary Thy Sanctuary, and the Safeguard Thy Safeguard, and this is the Place of him who flies to Thee from (hell) Fire!"

At the little building called Makam Ibrahim we said, "O Allah, verily this is the Place of Abraham, who took Refuge with and fled to Thee from the Fire! —O deny my Flesh and Blood, my Skin and Bones to the (eternal) Flames!"

As we paced slowly round the north or Irak corner of the Ka'abah we exclaimed, "O Allah, verily I take Refuge with Thee from Polytheism, and Disobedience, and Hypocrisy, and evil Conversation, and evil Thoughts concerning Family, and Property, and Progeny!"

When fronting the Mizab, or spout, we repeated the words, "O Allah, verily I beg of Thee Faith which shall not decline, and a Certainty which shall not perish, and the good Aid of Thy Prophet Mohammed —may Allah bless Him and preserve! O Allah, shadow me in Thy Shadow on that Day when there is no Shade but Thy Shadow, and cause me to drink from the Cup of Thy Prophet Mohammed—may Allah bless Him and preserve!—that pleasant Draught after which is no Thirst to all Eternity, O Lord of Honour and Glory!"

Turning the west corner, or the Rukn el Shami, we exclaimed, "O Allah, make it an acceptable Pilgrimage, and a Forgiveness of Sins, and a laudable Endeavour, and a pleasant Action (in Thy Sight), and a Store which perisheth not, O Thou Glorious! O Thou Pardoner!"

This was repeated thrice, till we arrived at the Yemani, or south corner, where, the crowd being less importunate, we touched the wall with the right hand, after the example of the Prophet, and kissed the finger-tips.

Finally between the south angle and that of the Black Stone, where our circuit would be completed, we said, "O Allah, verily I take Refuge with Thee from Infidelity, and I take Refuge with Thee from Want, and from the Tortures of the Tomb, and from the Troubles of Life and Death. And I fly to Thee from Ignominy in this World and the next, and I implore Thy Pardon for the Present and for the Future. O Lord, grant to me in this Life Prosperity; and in the next Life Prosperity, and save me from the Punishment of Fire."

Thus finished a Shaut, or single course round the house. Of these we performed, the three first at the pace called Harwalah, very similar to the French "pas gymnastique," or Tarammul, that is to say, "moving the shoulders as if walking in sand." The four latter are performed in Ta'ammul, slowly and leisurely; the reverse of the Sa'i, or running. These seven Ashwat, or courses, are called collectively one Usbu. The Moslem origin of this custom is too well known to require mention. After each Taufah, or circuit, we being unable to kiss or even to touch the Black Stone, fronted towards it, raised our hands to our ears, exclaimed "In the Name of Allah, and Allah is omnipotent!" kissed fingers, and resumed the ceremony of circumambulation, as before, with "Allah, in Thy Belief," &c.

At the conclusion of the Tawaf it was deemed advisable to attempt to kiss the stone. For a time I stood looking in despair at the swarming crowd of Bedawin and other pilgrims that besieged it. But the boy Mohammed was equal to the occasion. During our circuit he had displayed a fiery zeal against heresy and schism, by foully abusing every Persian in his path; and the inopportune introduction of hard words into his prayers made the latter a strange patchwork; as "Ave Maria purissima,—arrah, don't ye be letting the pig at the pot!—sanctissima," and so forth. He might, for instance, be repeating "and I take Refuge with Thee from Ignominy in this World," when, "O thou rejected one, son of the rejected!" would be the interpolation addressed to some long-bearded Khorasani —"and in that to come"—"O hog and brother of a hoggess!" And so he continued till I wondered that none dared to turn and rend him. After vainly addressing the pilgrims, of whom nothing could be seen but a mosaic of occiputs and shoulder-blades, the boy Mohammed collected about half a dozen stalwart Meccans, with whose assistance, by sheer strength, we wedged our way through the thin and light-legged crowd. The Bedawin turned round upon us like wild cats, but they had no daggers. The season being autumn, they had not swelled themselves with milk for six months; and they had become such living mummies, that I could have managed single-handed half a dozen of them. After thus reaching the stone, despite popular indignation testified by impatient shouts, we monopolised the use of it for at least ten minutes. Whilst kissing it and rubbing hands and forehead upon it I narrowly observed it, and came away persuaded that it is an aërolite.

It is curious that almost all travellers agree upon one point, namely, that the stone is volcanic. Ali Bey calls it "mineralogically" a "block of volcanic basalt, whose circumference is sprinkled with little crystals, pointed and straw-like, with rhombs of tile-red feldspath upon a dark background, like velvet or charcoal, except one of its protuberances, which is reddish." Burckhardt thought it was "a lava containing several small extraneous particles of a whitish and of a yellowish substance."

Having kissed the stone, we fought our way through the crowd to the place called El Multazem. Here we pressed our stomachs, chests, and right cheeks to the Ka'abah, raising our arms high above our heads, and exclaiming, "O Allah! O Lord of the Ancient House, free my Neck from Hell-fire, and preserve me from every ill Deed, and make me contented with that daily Bread which Thou hast given to me, and bless me in all Thou hast granted!" Then came the Istighfar, or begging of pardon: "I beg Forgiveness of Allah the most high, who, there is no other god but He, the Living, the Eternal, and unto Him I repent myself!" After which we blessed the Prophet, and then asked for ourselves all that our souls most desired.

After embracing the Multazem we repaired to the Shafe'i place of prayer near the Makám Ibrahim, and there recited two prostrations, technically called "Sunnat el Tawaf," or the (Prophet's) practice of circumambulation. The chapter repeated in the first was "Say thou, O Infidels:" in the second, "Say thou He is the one God." We then went to the door of the building in which is Zem Zem: there I was condemned to another nauseous draught, and was deluged with two or three skinfuls of water dashed over my head en douche. This ablution causes sins to fall from the spirit like dust. During the potation we prayed, "O Allah, verily I beg of Thee plentiful daily Bread, and profitable Learning, and the Healing of every Disease!" Then we returned towards the Black Stone, stood far away opposite, because unable to touch it, ejaculated the Takbir, the Tahlil, and the Hamdilah, and thoroughly worn out with scorched feet and a burning head—both extremities, it must be remembered, were bare, and various delays had detained us till ten A.M. —I left the Mosque.

The boy Mohammed had miscalculated the amount of lodging in his mother's house. She, being a widow and a lone woman, had made over for the season all the apartments to her brother, a lean old Meccan, of true ancient type, vulture-faced, kite-clawed, with a laugh like a hyena, and a mere shell of body. He regarded me with no favoring eye when I insisted as a guest upon having some place of retirement; but he promised that, after our return from Arafat, a little store-room should be cleared out for me. With this I was obliged to be content and pass that day in the common male drawing-room of the house, a vestibule on the ground-floor, called in Egypt a "Takhta-bush." Entering, to the left was a large Mastabah, or platform, and at the bottom a second, of smaller dimensions and foully dirty. Behind this was a dark and unclean store-room containing the Hajis' baggage. Opposite the Mastabah stood a firepan for pipes and coffee, superintended by a family of lean Indians; and by the side a doorless passage led to a bathing-room and staircase.

I had scarcely composed myself upon the comfortably carpeted Mastabah, when the remainder of it was suddenly invaded by the Turkish pilgrims inhabiting the house, and a host of their visitors. They were large, hairy men with gruff voices and square figures; they did not take the least notice of me, although, feeling the intrusion, I stretched out my legs with a provoking nonchalance. At last one of them addressed me in Turkish, to which I replied by shaking my head. His question being interpreted to me in Arabic, I drawled out, "My native place is the land of Khorasan." This provoked a stern and stony stare from the Turks, and an "ugh," which said plainly enough, "Then you are a pestilent heretic." I surveyed them with a self-satisfied simper, stretched my legs a trifle farther, and conversed with my water-pipe.

Presently, when they all departed for a time, the boy Mohammed raised, by request, my green box of medicines, and deposited it upon the Maṣtabah; thus defining, as it were, a line of demarcation, and asserting my privilege to it before the Turks. Most of these men were of one party, headed by a colonel of Nizam, whom they called Bey. My acquaintance with them began roughly enough, but afterwards, with some exceptions, who were gruff as an English butcher when accosted by a wretched foreigner, they proved to be kind-hearted and not unsociable men. It often happens to the traveller, as the charming Mrs. Malaprop observes, to find intercourse all the better for beginning with a little aversion.

In the evening, accompanied by the boy Mohammed, and followed by Shaykh Nur, who carried a lantern and a praying-rug, I again repaired to the "Navel of the World;" this time æsthetically, to enjoy the delights of the hour after the "gaudy, babbling and remorseful day." The moon, now approaching the full, tipped the brow of Abu Kubays, and lit up the spectacle with a more solemn light. In the midst stood the huge bier-like erection—

> "Black as the wings
> Which some spirit of ill o'er a sepulchre flings,"—

except where the moonbeams streaked it like jets of silver falling upon the darkest marble. It formed the point of rest for the eye; the little pagoda-like buildings and domes around it, with all their gilding and fretwork, vanished. One object, unique in appearance, stood in view—the temple of the one Allah, the God of Abraham, of Ishmael, and of their posterity. Sublime it was, and expressing by all the eloquence of fancy the grandeur of the One Idea which vitalised El Islam, and the strength and steadfastness of its votaries.

The oval pavement around the Ka'abah was crowded with men, women, and children, mostly divided into parties, which followed a Mutawwif; some walking staidly, and others running, whilst many stood in groups to prayer. What a scene of contrast! Here stalked the Bedawi woman, in her long black robe like a nun's serge, and poppy-coloured face-veil, pierced to show two fiercely-flashing orbs. There an Hindi woman, with her semi-Tartar features, nakedly hideous, and her thin legs, encased in wrinkled tights, hurried round the fane. Every now and then a corpse, borne upon its wooden shell, circuited the shrine by means of four bearers, whom other Moslems, as is the custom, occasionally relieved. A few fair-skinned Turks lounged about, looking cold and repulsive, as is their wont. In one place a fast Calcutta "Khitmugar" stood, with turban awry and arms akimbo, contemplating the view jauntily, as those "gentlemen's gentlemen" will do. In another, some poor wretch, with arms thrown on high, so that every part of his person might touch the Ka'abah, was clinging to the curtain and sobbing as though his heart would break.

From this spectacle my eyes turned towards Abu Kubays. The city extends in that direction half way up the grim hill: the site might be compared, at an humble distance, to Bath. Some writers liken it to Florence; but conceive a Florence without beauty! To the south lay Jebel Jiyad the Greater, also partly built over and crowned with a fort, which at a distance looks less useful than romantic: a flood of pale light was sparkling upon its stony surface. Below, the minarets became pillars of silver, and the cloisters, dimly streaked by oil lamps, bounded the view of the temple with horizontal lines of shade.

Before nightfall the boy Mohammed rose to feed the Mosque pigeons, for whom he had brought a pocketful of barley. He went to the place where these birds flock; the line of pavement leading from the isolated arch to the eastern cloisters. During the day women and children are to be seen sitting here, with small piles of grain upon little plaited trays of basket-work. For each they demand a copper piece; and religious pilgrims consider it their duty to provide the reverend volatiles with a plentiful meal.

The Hindu Pandits assert that Shiwa and his spouse, under the forms and names of Kapot-Eshwara (pigeon god) and Kapoteshi, dwelt at Meccah. The dove was the device of the old Assyrian Empire, because it is supposed Semiramis was preserved by that bird. The Meccan pigeons — large blue rocks — are held sacred probably in consequence of the wild traditions of the Arabs about Noah's dove. Some authors declare that, in Mohammed's time, among the idols of the Meccan Pantheon, was a pigeon carved in wood, and above it another, which Ali, mounting upon the Prophet's shoulder, pulled down. This might have been a Hindu, a Jewish, or a Christian symbol. The Moslems connect the pigeon on two occasions with their faith: first, when that bird appeared to whisper in Mohammed's ear; and, secondly, during the flight to El Medinah. Moreover, in many countries they are called "Allah's Proclaimers," because their movement when cooing resembles inclination.

Almost everywhere the pigeon has entered into the history of religion; which probably induced Mr. Lascelles to incur the derision of our grandfathers by pronouncing it a "holy bird." At Meccah they are called the doves of the Ka'abah, and never appear at table. They are remarkable for propriety when sitting upon the holy building. This may be a minor miracle: I would rather believe that there is some contrivance on the roof. My friend Mr. Bicknell remarks "This marvel, however, having of late years been suspended, many discern another omen of the approach of the long-predicted period when unbelievers shall desecrate the Sacred Soil."

Late in the evening I saw a negro in the state called Malbus—religious frenzy. To all appearance a Takruri, he was a fine and a powerful man, as the numbers required to hold him testified. He threw his arms wildly about him, uttering shrill cries, which sounded like lé lé lé lé! and when held, he swayed his body, and waved his head from side to side, like a chained and furious elephant, straining out the deepest groans. The Africans appear unusually subject to this nervous state, which, seen by the ignorant, and the imagination, would at once suggest a "demoniacal possession." Either their organisation is more impressionable, or more probably the hardships, privations, and fatigues endured whilst wearily traversing perilous seas and inhospitable wilds have exalted their imaginations to a pitch bordering upon frenzy. Often they are seen prostrate on the pavement, or clinging to the curtain, or rubbing their foreheads upon the stones, weeping bitterly, and pouring forth the wildest ejaculations.

That night I stayed in the Haram till 2 A.M., wishing to see if it would be empty. But the morrow was to witness the egress to Arafat; many, therefore, passed the hours of darkness in the Haram. Numerous parties of pilgrims sat upon their rugs, with lanterns in front of them, conversing, praying, and contemplating the Ka'abah. The cloisters were full of merchants, who resorted there to "talk shop" and to vend such holy goods as combs, tooth-sticks, and rosaries. Before 10 P.M. I found no opportunity of praying the usual two prostrations over the grave of Ishmael. After waiting long and patiently, at last I was stepping into the vacant place, when another pilgrim rushed forward; the boy Mohammed, assisted by me, instantly seized him, and, despite his cries and struggles, taught him to wait. Till midnight we sat chatting with the different ciceroni, who came up to offer their services. I could not help remarking their shabby and dirty clothes, and was informed that, during pilgrimage, when splendor is liable to be spoiled, they wear out old dresses, and appear "endimanchés" for the Muharram fête, after most travellers have left the city. Presently my two companions, exhausted with fatigue, fell asleep; I went up to the Ka'abah, with the intention of "annexing" a bit of the torn old Kiswat or curtain, but too many eyes were looking on. At this season of the year the veil is much tattered at the base, partly by pilgrims' fingers, and partly by the strain of the cord which confines it when the wind is blowing. It is considered a mere peccadillo to purloin a bit of the venerable stuff; but as the officers of the temple make money by selling it, they certainly would visit detection with an unmerciful application of the quarter-staff. The piece in my possession was given to me by the boy Mohammed before I left Meccah. Waistcoats cut out of the Kiswat still make the combatant invulnerable in battle, and are considered presents fit for princes. The Moslems generally try to secure a strip of this cloth as a mark for the Koran, or some such purpose.

At last sleep began to weigh heavily upon my eyelids. I awoke my companions, and in the dizziness of slumber they walked with me through the tall, narrow street from the Bab el Ziyadah to our home in the Shamiyah. The brilliant moonshine prevented our complaining, as other travellers have had reason to do, of the darkness and the difficulty of Meccan streets. The town, too, appeared safe; there were no watchmen, and yet people lay everywhere upon cots placed opposite their open doors. Arrived at the house, we made some brief preparations for snatching a few hours' sleep upon the Mastabah—a place so stifling, that nothing but utter exhaustion could induce lethargy there.

CHAPTER III.

The Ceremonies of the Yaum el Tarwiyah, or the First Day.

AT 10 A.M. on the 8th Zu'l Hijjah, A.H. 1269 (Monday, 12th Sept. 1853), habited in our Ihram, or pilgrim garbs, we mounted the litter. Shaykh Mas'ud had been standing at the door from dawn-time, impatient to start before the Damascus and the Egyptian caravans made the road dangerous. Our delay arose from the tyrannical conduct of the boy Mohammed, who insisted upon leaving his little nephew behind. It was long before he yielded. I then placed the poor child, who was crying bitterly, in the litter between us, and at last we started.

We followed the road by which the Caravans entered Meccah. It was covered with white-robed pilgrims, some few wending their way on foot, others riding, and all men barefooted and bareheaded. Most of the wealthier classes mounted asses. The scene was, as usual, one of strange contrasts; Bedawin bestriding swift dromedaries; Turkish dignitaries on fine horses; the most picturesque beggars, and the most uninteresting Nizam. Not a little wrangling mingled with the loud bursts of "Talbyat." Dead animals dotted the ground, and carcasses had been cast into a dry tank, the "Birkat el Shami," which caused every

Bedawi to hold his nose. Here, on the right of the road, the poorer pilgrims, who could not find houses, had erected huts, and pitched their ragged tents.

Traversing the suburb El Ma'b'dah (Ma'abadah), in a valley between the two barren prolongations of Kayka'an and Khandamah, we turned to the north-east, leaving on the left certain barracks of Turkish soldiery, and the negro militia here stationed, with the "Saniyat Kuda'a" in the background.

Then advancing about 3000 paces over rising ground, we passed by the conical head of Jebel Nur (anciently Hira), and entered the plain of many names. It contained nothing but a few whitewashed walls, surrounding places of prayer, and a number of stone cisterns, some well preserved, others in ruins. All, however, were dry, and water vendors crowded the roadside. Gravel and lumps of granite there grew like grass, and from under every large stone, as Shaykh Mas'ud took a delight in showing, a small scorpion, with tail curled over its back, fled, Parthian-like, from the invaders of its home. At 11 A.M. ascending a Mudarraj, or flight of stone steps, about thirty yards broad, we passed without difficulty, for we were in advance of the caravans, over the Akabah, or Steeps, and the narrow, hill-girt entrance, to the low gravel basin in which Muna lies.

Muna, more classically called Mina, is a place of considerable sanctity. Its three standing miracles are these—The pebbles thrown at "the Devil" return by angelic agency to whence they came; during the three

Days of Drying Meat rapacious beasts and birds cannot prey there; and flies do not settle upon the articles of food exposed so abundantly in the bazars.* During pilgrimage houses are let for an exorbitant sum, and it becomes a "World's Fair" of Moslem merchants. At all other seasons it is almost deserted, in consequence, says popular superstition, of the Rajm or (diabolical) lapidation. Distant about three miles from Meccah, it is a long, narrow, straggling village, composed of mud and stone houses of one or two stories, built in the common Arab style. Traversing a narrow street, we passed on the left the Great Devil, which shall be described at a future time. After a quarter of an hour's halt, spent over pipes and coffee, we came to an open space, where stands the mosque "El Khayf." Here, according to some Arabs, Adam lies, his head being at one end of the long wall, and his feet at another, whilst the dome covers his omphalic region. Grand preparations for fireworks were being made in this square; I especially remarked a fire-ship, which savoured strongly of Stambul. After passing through the town, we came to Batn el Muhassir, "the Basin of the Troubler" (Satan), at the beginning of a descent leading to Muzdalifah (the Approacher), where the road falls into the valley of the Arafat torrent.

At noon we reached the Muzdalifah, also called Mashar el Haram, the "Place dedicated to Religious

* According to Mohammed the pebbles of the accepted are removed by angels; as, however, each man and woman must throw 49 or 70 stones, it is fair to suspect the intervention of something more material. Animals are frightened away by the bustling crowd, and flies are found in myriads.

Ceremonies."* It is known in El Islam as "the Minaret without the Mosque," opposed to Masjid Nimrah, which is the "Mosque without the Minaret." Half way between Muna and Arafat it is about three miles from both. There is something peculiarly striking in the distant appearance of the tall, solitary tower, rising abruptly from the desolate valley of gravel, flanked with buttresses of yellow rock. No wonder that the ancient Arabs loved to give the high-sounding name of this oratory to distant places in their giant Caliph-empire.

Here, as we halted to perform the midday prayer, we were overtaken by the Damascus Caravan. It was a grand spectacle. The Mahmal, no longer naked as upon the line of march, flashed in the sun all green and gold. Around the moving host of white-robed pilgrims hovered a crowd of Bedawin, male and female, all mounted on swift dromedaries, and many of them armed to the teeth. As their drapery floated in the wind, and their faces were veiled with the "Lisam," it was frequently difficult to distinguish the sex of the wild being flogging its animal to speed. These people, as has been said, often resort to Arafat for blood-revenge, in hopes of finding the victim unprepared. Nothing can be more sinful in El Islam than such deed — it is murder, "made sicker" by sacrilege; yet the prevalence of the practice proves how feeble is the religion's hold upon the race. The women are as

* Many, even since Sale corrected the error, have confounded this Mashar el *Harám* with the Masjid el *Harím* of Meccah.

unscrupulous: I remarked many of them emulating the men in reckless riding, and striking with their sticks every animal in the way.

Travelling eastward up the Arafat Fiumara, after about half an hour we came to a narrow pass called El Akhshabayn, or the "Two Rugged Hills." Here the spurs of the rock limit the road to about 100 paces, and it is generally a scene of great confusion. After this we arrived at El Bazan (the Basin), a widening of the plain, and another half-hour brought us to the Alamayn (the "Two Signs"), whitewashed pillars, or rather thin, narrow walls, surmounted with pinnacles, which denote the precincts of the Arafat plain.

Here, in full sight of the Holy Hill, standing quietly out from the deep blue sky, the host of pilgrims broke into loud Labbayks. A little beyond, and to our right, was the simple enclosure called the Masjid Nimrah. We then turned from our eastern course northwards, and began threading our way down the main street of the town of tents which clustered about the southern foot of Arafat. At last, about 3 P.M. we found a vacant space near the Matbakh, or kitchen, formerly belonging to a Sherif's palace, but now a ruin with a few shells of arches.

Arafat is about six hours' very slow march, or twelve miles, on the Taif road, due east of Meccah. We arrived there in a shorter time, but our weary camels, during the last third of the way, frequently threw themselves upon the ground. Human beings suffered more. Between Muna and Arafat I saw no less than five men fall down and die upon the highway: exhausted and moribund, they had dragged themselves out to give up the ghost where it departs to instant beatitude. The spectacle showed how easy it is to die in these latitudes; each man suddenly staggered, fell as if shot, and after a brief convulsion, lay still as marble. The corpses were carefully taken up, and carelessly buried that same evening, in a vacant space amongst the crowds encamped upon the Arafat plain.

The boy Mohammed, who had long chafed at my pertinacious claim to dervishhood, resolved on this occasion to be grand. To swell the party, he had invited Umar Effendi, whom we accidentally met in the streets of Meccah, to join us: but failing therein, he brought with him two cousins, fat youths of sixteen and seventeen, and his mother's ground-floor servants. These were four Indians; an old man; his wife, a middle-aged woman of the most ordinary appearance, their son, a sharp boy, who spoke excellent Arabic; and a family friend, a stout fellow about thirty years old. They were Panjabis, and the bachelor's history was instructive. He was gaining an honest livelihood in his own country, when suddenly one night Hazrat Ali, dressed in green, and mounted upon his charger Duldul—at least, so said the narrator—appeared, crying in a terrible voice, "How long wilt thou toil for this world, and be idle about the life to come?" From that moment, like an English murderer, he knew no peace, Conscience and Hazrat Ali haunted him.

Finding life unendurable at home, he sold everything, raised the sum of 20*l.*, and started for the Holy Land. He reached Jeddah with a few rupees in his pocket, and came to Meccah where, everything being exorbitantly dear and charity all but unknown, he might have starved, had he not been received by his old friend. The married pair and their son had been taken as house-servants by the boy Mohammed's mother, who generously allowed them shelter and a pound of rice per diem to each, but not a farthing of pay. They were even expected to provide their own turmeric and onions. Yet these poor people were anxiously awaiting the opportunity to visit El Medinah, without which their pilgrimage would not, they believed, be complete. They would beg their way through the terrible Desert and its Bedawin—an old man, a boy, and a woman! What were their chances of returning to their homes?

Such, I believe, is too often the history of those wretches, whom a fit of religious enthusiasm, likest to insanity, hurries away to the Holy Land. I strongly recommend the subject to the consideration of our Indian government as one that calls loudly for their interference. No Eastern ruler parts, as we do, with his subjects; all object to lose productive power. To an "Empire of Opinion" this emigration is fraught with evils. It sends forth a horde of malcontents that ripen into bigots; it teaches foreign nations to despise our rule; and it unveils the present nakedness of once wealthy India. And, we have both prevention and cure in our own hands.

As no Moslem, except the Maliki, is bound to pilgrimage without a sum sufficient to support himself and his family, all who embark at the different ports of India should be obliged to prove their solvency before being provided with a permit. Arrived at Jeddah, they should present the certificate at the British vice-consulate, where they would become entitled to assistance in case of necessity.

The vice-consul at Jeddah ought also be instructed to assist our Indian pilgrims. Mr. Cole, when holding that appointment, informed me that, though men die of starvation in the streets, he was unable to relieve them. The streets of Meccah abound in pathetic Indian beggars, who affect lank bodies, shrinking frames, whining voices, and all the circumstance of misery, because it supports them in idleness.

There are no less than 1500 Indians at Meccah and Jeddah, besides 700 or 800 in Yemen. Such a body requires a consul. By the representation of a vice-consul when other powers send an officer of superior rank to El Hejaz, we voluntarily place ourselves in an inferior position. And although the Meccan Sherif might for a time object to establishing a Moslem agent at the Holy City with orders to report to the consul at Jeddah, his opposition would soon fall to the ground.

With the Indians' assistance the boy Mohammed removed the handsome Persian rugs with which he had covered the Shugduf, pitched the tent, carpeted the ground, disposed a Diwan of silk and satin cushions round the interior, and strewed the centre with new Chibouques, and highly polished Shishahs. At the doorway was placed a large copper fire-pan, with coffee pots singing a welcome to visitors. In front of us were the litters, and by divers similar arrangements our establishment was made to look fine. The youth also insisted upon my removing the Rida, or upper cotton cloth, which had become way-soiled, and he supplied its place by a rich cashmere, left with him, some years before, by a son of the king of Delhi.

Arafat, anciently called Jebel Ilal (الال), "the Mount of Wrestling in Prayer," and now Jebel el Rahmah, the "Mount of Mercy," is a mass of coarse granite split into large blocks, with a thin coat of withered thorns. About one mile in circumference it rises abruptly, to the height of 180 or 200 feet, from the low gravelly plain—a dwarf wall at the southern base forming the line of demarcation. It is separated by Batn Arnah (عرنة), a sandy vale, from the spurs of the Taif hills. Nothing can be more picturesque than the view it affords of the azure peaks behind, and the vast encampment scattered over the barren yellow plain below. On the north lay the regularly pitched camp of the guards that defend the unarmed pilgrims. To the eastward was the Sherif's encampment with the bright Mahmals and the gilt knobs of the grandees' pavilions; whilst, on the southern and western sides, the tents of the vulgar crowded the ground, disposed in Dowars, or circles. After many calculations, I estimated the number to be not less than 50,000, of all ages and sexes; a sad falling off, it is true, but still considerable.

Ali Bey (A.D. 1807) calculates 83,000 pilgrims; Burckhardt (1814), 70,000. I reduce it, in 1853, to 50,000, and in A.D. 1854, owing to political causes, it fell to about 25,000. Of these at least 10,000 are Meccans, as every one who can leave the city does so at pilgrimage-time. The Arabs have a superstition that the numbers at Arafat cannot be counted, and that if less than 600,000 mortals stand upon the hill to hear the sermon, the angels descend and complete the number. Even this year my Arab friends declared that 150,000 spirits were present in human shape. It may be observed, that when the good old Bertrand de la Brocquière, esquire-carver to Philip of Burgundy, declares that the yearly Caravan from Damascus to El Medinah must always be composed of 700,000 persons, and that this number being incomplete, Allah sends some of his angels to make it up, he probably confounds the Caravan with the Arafat multitude.

The Holy Hill owes its name* and honours to a well-known legend. When our first parents forfeited heaven by eating wheat, which deprived them of their primeval purity, they were cast down upon earth. The serpent descended at Ispahan, the peacock at Cabul, Satan at Bilbays (others say Semnan and Seistan), Eve upon Arafat, and Adam at Ceylon. The latter,

* The word is explained in many ways One derivation has already been mentioned. Others assert that when Gabriel taught Abraham the ceremonies, he ended by saying "A '*arafta* manásik'ak?"—Hast thou learned thy pilgrim rites? To which the friend of Allah replied, "*Araftu!*"—I have learned them.

determining to seek his wife, began a journey, to which earth owes its present mottled appearance. Wherever our first father placed his foot—which was large—a town afterwards arose; between the strides will always be "country." Wandering for many years, he came to the Mountain of Mercy, where our common mother was continually calling upon his name, and their *recognition* gave the place the name of Arafat. Upon its summit Adam, instructed by the archangel Gabriel, erected a "Mada'a," or place of prayer; and between this spot and the Nimrah mosque the couple abode till death. Others declare that, after recognition, the first pair returned to India, whence for forty-four years in succession they visited the Sacred City at pilgrimage-time.

From the Holy Hill I walked down to look at the camp arrangements. The main street of tents and booths, huts and shops, was bright with lanterns, and the bazars were crowded with people and stocked with all manner of eastern delicacies. Some anomalous spectacles met the eye. Many pilgrims, especially the soldiers, were in laical costume. In one place a half-drunken Arnaut stalked down the road, elbowing peaceful passengers and frowning fiercely in hopes of a quarrel. In another part, a huge dimly-lit tent, reeking hot, and garnished with cane-seats, contained knots of Egyptians, as their red Tarbushes, white turbans, and black Za'abuts showed, noisily intoxicating themselves with forbidden hemp. There were frequent brawls and great confusion; many men had lost their parties, and, mixed with loud Labbayks, rose the shouted names of women as well as men. I was surprised at the disproportion of female nomenclature—the missing number of fair ones seemed to double that of the other sex—and at a practice so opposed to the customs of the Moslem world. At length the boy Mohammed enlightened me. Egyptian and other bold women, when unable to join the pilgrimage, will pay or persuade a friend to shout their names in hearing of the Holy Hill, with a view of ensuring a real presence at the desired spot next year. So the welkin rang with the indecent sounds of O Fat'imah! O Zaynab! O Khayz'ran!* Plunderers, too, were abroad. As we returned to the tent we found a crowd assembled near it; a woman had seized a thief as he was beginning operations, and had the courage to hold his beard till men ran to her assistance. And we were obliged to defend by force our position against a knot of gravediggers, who would bury a little heap of bodies within a yard or two of our tent.

One point struck me at once, the difference in point of cleanliness between an encampment of citizens and Bedawin. Poor Mas'ud sat holding his nose in ineffable disgust; for which he was derided by the Meccans. I consoled him with quoting the celebrated

* The latter name, "Ratan," is servile. Respectable women are never publicly addressed by Moslems except as "daughter," "female pilgrim," after some male relation, "O mother of Mohammed," "O sister of Umar," or "tout bonnement," by a man's name. It would be ill-omened and dangerous were the true name known. So most women, when travelling, adopt an alias. Whoever knew an Afghan fair who was not "Nur Jan," or "Sahib Jan?"

song of Maysunah, the beautiful Bedawi wife of the Caliph Muawiyah. Nothing can be more charming in its own Arabic than this little song: the Bedawin never hear it without screams of joy.

> "O take these purple robes away,
>   Give back my cloak of camel's hair,
> And bear me from this tow'ring pile
>   To where the Black Tents flap i' the air.
> The camel's colt with falt'ring tread,
>   The dog that bays at all but me,
> Delight me more than ambling mules—
>   Than every art of minstrelsy.
> And any cousin, poor but free,
>   Might take me, fatted ass! from thee." *

The old man, delighted, clapped my shoulder, and exclaimed "Verily, O Father of Mustachios, I will show thee the black tents of my tribe this year!"

At length night came, and we threw ourselves upon our rugs, but not to sleep. Close by, to our bane, was a prayerful old gentleman, who began his devotions at a late hour and concluded them not before dawn. He reminded me of the undergraduate my neighbour at Trinity College, Oxford, who would spout Æschylus at 2 A.M. Sometimes the chaunt would grow drowsy,

---

* The British reader will be shocked to hear that by the term "fatted ass" the intellectual lady alluded to her husband. The story is, that Muawiyah, overhearing the song, sent back the singer to her cousins and beloved wilds. Maysunah departed with her son Yezid, and did not return to Damascus till the "fatted ass" had joined his forefathers.

Yezid inherited, with his mother's talents, all her contempt for his father: at least the following quatrain, addressed to Muawiyah, and generally known in El Islam, would appear to argue anything but reverence—

> "I drank the water of the vine; that draught had power to rouse
> Thy wrath, grim father! now, indeed, 'tis joyous to carouse!
> I'll drink!—Be wrath!—I reck not!—Ah! dear to this heart of mine
> It is to scoff a sire's command—to quaff forbidden wine."

and my ears would hear a dull retreating sound; presently, as if in self-reproach, it would rise to a sharp treble, and proceed at a rate perfectly appalling. The coffee-houses, too, were by no means silent; deep into the night I heard the clapping of hands accompanying merry Arab songs, and the loud shouts of laughter of the Egyptian hemp-drinkers. And the guards and protectors of the camp were not "Charleys" or night-nurses.

CHAPTER IV.

The Ceremonies of the Yaum Arafat, or the Second Day.

THE morning of the ninth Zu'l Hijjah (Tuesday, 13th Sept.) was ushered in by military sounds: a loud discharge of cannon warned us to arise and to prepare for the ceremonies of this eventful day.

After ablution and prayer, I proceeded with the boy Mohammed to inspect the numerous consecrated sites on the "Mountain of Mercy." In the first place, we repaired to a spot on rising ground to the southeast, and within a hundred yards of the hill. It is called "Jami el Sakhrah"—the Assembling Place of the Rock—from two granite boulders upon which the Prophet stood to perform "Talbiyat." There is nothing but a small inclosure of dwarf and whitewashed stone walls, divided into halves by a similar partition, and provided with a niche to direct prayer towards Meccah. Entering by steps we found crowds of devotees and guardians, who for a consideration offered mats and carpets. After a two-bow prayer and a long supplication opposite the niche, we retired to the inner compartment, stood upon a boulder and shouted the "Labbayk."

Thence, threading our way through many obstacles of tent and stone, we ascended the broad flight of rugged steps which winds up the southern face of the rocky hill. Even at this early hour it was crowded with pilgrims, principally Bedawin and Wahhabis, who had secured favorable positions for hearing the sermon. Already their green flag was planted upon the summit close to Adam's Place of Prayer. The wilder Arabs insist that "Wukuf" (standing) should take place upon the Hill. This is not done by the more civilised, who hold that all the plain within the Alamayn ranks as Arafat. About half-way up I counted sixty-six steps, and remarked that they became narrower and steeper. Crowds of beggars instantly seized the pilgrims' robes and strove to prevent our entering a second enclosure. This place, which resembles the former, except that it has but one compartment and no boulders, is that whence Mohammed used to address his followers, and here, to the present day, the Khatib, or preacher, in imitation of the "Last of the Prophets," sitting upon a dromedary, recites the Arafat sermon. Here, also, we prayed a two-bow prayer, and gave a small sum to the guardian.

Thence ascending with increased difficulty to the hill-top, we arrived at a large stuccoed platform, with prayer-niche and a kind of obelisk, mean and badly built of lime and granite stone, whitewashed, and conspicuous from afar. It is called the Makam, or Mada'a Sayyidna Adam. Here we performed the customary ceremonies amongst a crowd of pilgrims, and then we walked down the little hill. Close to the plain we saw the place where the Egyptian and

Damascus Mahmals stand during the sermon; and, descending the wall that surrounds Arafat by a steep and narrow flight of coarse stone steps, we found on our right the fountain which supplies the place with water. It bubbles from the rock, and is exceedingly pure, as such water generally is in El Hejaz.

Our excursion employed us longer than the description requires — nine o'clock had struck before we reached the plain. All were in a state of excitement. Guns fired incessantly. Horsemen and camel-riders galloped about without apparent object. Even the women and the children stood and walked, too restless even to sleep. Arrived at the tent, I was unpleasantly surprised to find a new visitor in an old acquaintance, Ali ibn Ya Sin the Zem Zemi. He had lost his mule, and, wandering in search of its keeper, he unfortunately fell in with our party. I had solid reasons to regret the mishap — he was far too curious and observant to suit my tastes. On the present occasion he, being uncomfortable, made us equally so. Accustomed to all the terrible "neatness" of an elderly damsel in Great Britain, a few specks of dirt upon the rugs, and half-a-dozen bits of cinder upon the ground, sufficed to give him attacks of "nerves."

That day we breakfasted late, for night must come before we could eat again. After midday prayer we performed ablutions; some the greater, others the less, in preparation for the "Wukuf," or Standing. From noon onwards the hum and murmur of the multitude increased, and people were seen swarming about in all directions.

A second discharge of cannon (about P.M. 3.15) announced the approach of El Asr, the afternoon prayer, and almost immediately we heard the Naubat, or band preceding the Sherif's procession as he wended his way towards the mountain. Fortunately my tent was pitched close to the road, so that without trouble I had a perfect view of the scene. First swept a cloud of mace-bearers, who, as usual on such occasions, cleared the path with scant ceremony. They were followed by the horsemen of the desert, wielding long and tufted spears. Immediately behind them came the Sherif's led horses, upon which I fixed a curious eye. All were highly bred, and one, a brown Nejdi with black points, struck me as the perfection of an Arab. They were small, and all were apparently of the northern race. Of their old crimson-velvet caparisons the less said the better; no little Indian Nawab would show aught so shabby on state occasions.

After the chargers paraded a band of black slaves on foot, bearing huge matchlocks; and immediately preceded by three green and two red flags, came the Sherif, riding in front of his family and courtiers. The prince, habited in a simple white Ihram, and bare-headed, mounted a mule; the only sign of his rank was a large green and gold-embroidered umbrella, held over him by a slave. The rear was brought up by another troop of Bedawin on horses and camels. Behind this procession were the tents, whose doors and walls were scarcely visible for the crowd; and the picturesque back-ground was the granite hill covered, wherever standing-room was to be found, with white-robed pilgrims shouting "Labbayk" and waving the skirts of their glistening garments violently over their heads.

Slowly and solemnly the procession advanced towards the hill. Exactly at the hour El Asr the two Mahmals had taken their station side by side on a platform in the lower slope. That of Damascus could be distinguished as the narrower and the more ornamented of the pair. The Sherif placed himself with his standard-bearers and retinue a little above the Mahmals, within hearing of the preacher. The pilgrims crowded up to the foot of the mountain; the loud "Labbayk" of the Bedawin and Wahhabis fell to a solemn silence, and the waving of white robes ceased—a sign that the preacher had begun the Khutbat el Wakfah, or Sermon of the Standing (upon Arafat). From my tent I could distinguish the form of the old man upon his camel, but the distance was too great for ear to reach.

But how came I to be at the tent?

A short confession will explain. They will shrive me who believe in inspired Spenser's lines—

> "And every spirit as it is more pure,
> And hath in it the more of heavenly light,
> So it the fairer body doth procure
> To habit in."

The evil came of a "fairer body." I had prepared en cachette a slip of paper, and had hid in my Ihram a pencil destined to put down the heads of this rarely heard discourse. But unhappily that red cashmere shawl was upon my shoulders. Close to us sat a party of fair Meccans, apparently belonging to the higher classes, and one of these I had already several times remarked. She was a tall girl, about eighteen years old, with regular features, a skin somewhat citrine-coloured, but soft and clear, symmetrical eyebrows, the most beautiful eyes, and a figure all grace. There was no head thrown back, no straightened neck, no flat shoulders, nor toes turned out—in fact, no "elegant" barbarisms—the shape was what the Arabs love, soft, bending, and relaxed, as a woman's figure ought to be. Unhappily she wore, instead of the usual veil, a "Yashmak" of transparent muslin, bound round the face; and the chaperone, mother, or duenna, by whose side she stood, was apparently a very unsuspicious or complaisant old person. Flirtilla fixed a glance of admiration upon my cashmere. I directed a reply with interest at her eyes. She then, by the usual coquettish gesture, threw back an inch or two of head-veil, disclosing broad bands of jetty hair, crowning a lovely oval. My palpable admiration of the new charm was rewarded by a partial removal of the Yashmak; when a dimpled mouth and a rounded chin stood out from the envious muslin. Seeing that my companions were safely employed, I ventured upon the dangerous ground of raising hand to forehead. She smiled almost imperceptibly, and turned away. The pilgrim was in ecstasy.

The sermon was then half over. I resolved to stay upon the plain and see what Flirtilla would do. Grâce to the cashmere, we came to a good understanding. The next page will record my disappointment — that evening the pilgrim resumed his soiled cotton cloth, and testily returned the red shawl to the boy Mohammed.

The sermon always lasts till near sunset, or about three hours. At first it was spoken amid profound silence. Then loud, scattered "Amins" (Amens) and volleys of "Labbayk" exploded at uncertain intervals. At last the breeze brought to our ears a purgatorial chorus of cries, sobs, and shrieks. Even my party thought proper to be affected: old Ali rubbed his eyes, which in no case unconnected with dollars could by any amount of straining be made to shed even a crocodile's tear; and the boy Mohammed wisely hid his face in the skirt of his Rida. Presently the people, exhausted by emotion, began to descend the hill in small parties; and those below struck their tents and commenced loading their camels, although at least an hour's sermon remained. On this occasion, however, all hurry to be foremost, as the "race from Arafat" is enjoyed by none but the Bedawin.

Although we worked with a will, our animals were not ready to move before sunset, when the preacher gave the signal of "Israf," or permission to depart. The pilgrims,

> "swaying to and fro,
> Like waves of a great sea, that in mid shock
> Confound each other, white with foam and fear,"

rushed down the hill with a "Labbayk" sounding like a blast, and took the road to Muna. Then I saw the scene which has given to the part of the ceremonies the name of El Daf'a min Arafat,—the "Hurry from Arafat." Every man urged his beast with might and main: it was sunset; the plain bristled with tent-pegs, litters were crushed, pedestrians were trampled, camels were overthrown: single combats with sticks and other weapons took place; here a woman, there a child, and there an animal were lost—briefly, it was a chaotic confusion.

To my disgust, old Ali insisted upon bestowing his company upon me. He gave over his newly found mule to the boy Mohammed, bidding him take care of the beast, and mounted with me in the Shugduf. I had persuaded Shaykh Mas'ud, with a dollar, to keep close in rear of the pretty Meccan; and I wanted to sketch the Holy Hill.

The senior began to give orders about the camel—I, counter orders. The camel was halted. I urged it on: old Ali directed it to be stopped. Meanwhile the charming face that smiled at me from the litter grew dimmer and dimmer; the more I stormed, the less I was listened to—a string of camels crossed our path—I lost sight of the beauty.

Then we began to advance. Again, my determination to sketch seemed likely to fail before the Zem Zemi's little snake's eye. After a few minutes' angry search for expedients, one suggested itself. "Effendi!" said old Ali, "sit quiet; there is danger here." I tossed about like one suffering from evil conscience or the colic. "Effendi!" shrieked the senior, "what art thou doing? Thou wilt be the death of us." "Wallah!" I replied, with a violent plunge, "it is all thy fault! There! (another plunge)—put thy beard out of the other opening, and Allah will make it easy to us." In the ecstasy of fear my tormentor turned his face, as he was bidden, towards the camel's head. A second halt ensued, when I looked out of the aperture in rear, and made a rough drawing of the Mountain of Mercy.

At the Akhshabayn, double lines of camels, bristling with litters, clashed with a shock more noisy than the meeting of torrents. It was already dark: no man knew what he was doing. The guns roared their brazen notes, re-echoed far and wide by the harsh voices of the stony hills. A shower of rockets bursting in the air threw into still greater confusion the timorous mob of women and children. At the same time martial music rose from the masses of Nizam, and the stouter-hearted pilgrims were not sparing of their Labbayk, and "Eed kum Mubarak"—"May your Festival be happy!"

After the Pass of the Two Rugged Hills, the road

widened, and old Ali, who, during the bumping, had been in a silent convulsion of terror, recovered speech and spirits. This change he evidenced by beginning to be troublesome once more. Again I resolved to be his equal. Exclaiming, "My eyes are yellow with hunger!" I seized a pot full of savoury meat which the old man had previously stored for supper, and, without further preamble, began to eat it greedily, at the same time ready to shout with laughter at the mumbling and grumbling sounds that proceeded from the darkness of the litter.

We were at least three hours on the road before reaching Muzdalifah, and being fatigued, we resolved to pass the night there. The Mosque was brilliantly illuminated, but my hungry companions apparently thought more of supper and sleep than devotion. Whilst the tent was raised, the Indians prepared our food, boiled our coffee, filled our pipes, and spread our rugs. Before sleeping, each man collected for himself seven "Jamrah"—bits of granite the size of a small bean. Then, weary with emotion and exertion, all lay down except the boy Mohammed, who preceded us to find encamping ground at Muna. Old Ali, in lending his mule, made the most stringent arrangements with the youth about the exact place and the exact hour of meeting—an act of simplicity at which I could not but smile. The night was by no means peaceful or silent. Lines of camels passed us every ten minutes, and the shouting of travellers continued till near dawn. Pilgrims ought to have nighted at the Mosque, but, as in Burckhardt's time, so in mine, baggage was considered to be in danger thereabouts, and consequently most of the devotees spent the sermon-hours in brooding over their boxes.

CHAPTER V.

The Ceremonies of the Yaum Nahr, or the Third Day.

AT dawn, on the Eed el Kurban (10th Zu'l Hijjah, Wednesday, 14th Sept.) a gun warned us to lose no time; we arose hurriedly, and started up the Batn Muhassir to Muna. By this means we lost at Muzdalifah the "Salat el Eed," or "Festival Prayers," the great solemnity of the Moslem year, performed by all the community at day-break. My companion was so anxious to reach Meccah, that he would not hear of devotions.

About 8 A.M. we entered the village, and looked for the boy Mohammed in vain. Old Ali was dreadfully perplexed: a host of high-born Turkish pilgrims were, he said, expecting him; his mule was missing — could never appear — he must be late — should probably never reach Meccah — what *would* become of him?

I began by administering admonition to the mind diseased; but signally failing in a cure, I amused myself with contemplating the world from my Shugduf, leaving the office of directing it to the old Zem Zemi. Now he stopped, then he pressed forward; here he thought he saw Mohammed, there he discovered our tent; at one time he would "nakh" the camel to await, in patience, his supreme hour; at another, half mad with nervousness, he would urge the excellent Mas'ud to hopeless inquiries. Finally, by good fortune, we found one of the boy Mohammed's cousins, who led us to an enclosure called Hosh el Uzam, in the southern portion of the Muna Basin, at the base of Mount Sabir. There we pitched the tent, refreshed ourselves, and awaited the truant's return. Old Ali, failing to disturb my equanimity, attempted, as those who consort with philosophers often will do, to quarrel with me. But, finding no material wherewith to build a dispute in such fragments as "Ah"—"Hem!"— "Wallah!" he hinted desperate intentions against the boy Mohammed. When, however, the youth appeared, with even more jauntiness of mien than usual, Ali bin Ya Sin lost heart, brushed by him, mounted his mule, and, doubtless cursing us "under the tongue," rode away, frowning viciously, with his heels playing upon the beast's ribs.

Mohammed had been delayed, he said, by the difficulty of finding asses. We were now to mount for "the Throwing," as a preliminary to which, we washed "with seven waters" the seven pebbles brought from Muzdalifah, and bound them in our Ihrams. Our first destination was the entrance to the western end of the long line which composes the Muna village. We found a swarming crowd in the narrow road opposite the "Jamrat el Akabah," or, as it is vulgarly called, the Shaytan el Kabir—the "Great Devil."

These names distinguish it from another pillar, the "Wusta," or "Central Place" (of stoning), built in the middle of Muna, and a third at the eastern end, "El Aula," or the "First Place."

The "Shaytan el Kabir" is a dwarf buttress of rude masonry, about eight feet high by two and a half broad, placed against a rough wall of stones, at the Meccan entrance to Muna. As the ceremony of "Ramy," or Lapidation, must be performed on the first day by all pilgrims between sunrise and sunset, and as the fiend was malicious enough to appear in a rugged Pass,* the crowd makes the place dangerous. On one side of the road, which is not forty feet broad, stood a row of shops belonging principally to barbers. On the other side is the rugged wall of the pillar, with a chevaux de frise of Bedawin and naked boys.

The narrow space was crowded with pilgrims, all struggling like drowning men to approach as near as possible to the Devil; it would have been easy to run over the heads of the mass. Amongst them were horsemen with rearing chargers. Bedawin on wild camels, and grandees on mules and asses, with outrunners, were breaking a way by assault and battery. I had read Ali Bey's self-felicitations upon escaping this place with "only two wounds in the left leg,"

* I borrow this phrase from Ali Bey, who, however, speaks more like an ignorant Catalonian than a learned Abbaside, when he calls the pillar "La Maison du Diable," and facetiously asserts that "le diable a eu la malice de placer sa maison dans un lieu fort étroit qui n'a peut-être pas 34 pieds de large."

and I had duly provided myself with a hidden dagger. The precaution was not useless. Scarcely had my donkey entered the crowd than he was overthrown by a dromedary, and I found myself under the stamping and roaring beast's stomach. Avoiding being trampled upon by a judicious use of the knife, I lost no time in escaping from a place so ignobly dangerous. Some Moslem travellers assert, in proof of the sanctity of the spot, that no Moslem is ever killed here: Meccans assured me that accidents are by no means rare.

Presently the boy Mohammed fought his way out of the crowd with a bleeding nose. We both sat down upon a bench before a barber's booth, and, schooled by adversity, awaited with patience an opportunity. Finding an opening, we approached within about five cubits of the place, and holding each stone between the thumb and the forefinger of the right hand, we cast it at the pillar, exclaiming, "In the Name of Allah, and Allah is Almighty! (I do this) in Hatred of the Fiend and to his Shame." After which came the Tahlil and the "Sana," or praise to Allah.

The seven stones being duly thrown, we retired, and entering the barber's booth, took our places upon one of the earthen benches around it. This was the time to remove the Ihram or pilgrim's garb, and to return to Ihlal, the normal state of El Islam. The barber shaved our heads, and, after trimming our beards and cutting our nails, made us repeat these words: "I purpose loosening my Ihram according to the Practice of the Prophet, Whom may Allah bless and preserve! O Allah, make unto me in every Hair, a Light, a Purity, and a generous Reward! In the Name of Allah, and Allah is Almighty!"

At the conclusion of his labour the barber politely addressed to us a "Naiman"—Pleasure to you! To which we as ceremoniously replied, "Allah give thee pleasure!" We had no clothes with us, but we could use our cloths to cover our heads and slippers to defend our feet from the fiery sun; and we now could safely twirl our mustachios and stroke our beards—placid enjoyments of which we had been deprived by the Laws of Pilgrimage. After resting about an hour in the booth, which, though crowded with sitting customers, was delightfully cool compared with the burning glare of the road, we mounted our asses, and at eleven A.M. we started Meccah-wards.

This return from Muna to Meccah is called El Nafr, or the Flight: we did not fail to keep our asses at speed, with a few halts to refresh ourselves with gugglets of water. There was nothing remarkable in the scene: our ride in was a repetition of our ride out. In about half an hour we entered the city, passing through that classical locality called "Batn Kuraysh," which was crowded with people, and then we repaired to the boy Mohammed's house for the purpose of bathing and preparing to visit the Ka'abah.

Shortly after our arrival, the youth returned home

in a state of excitement, exclaiming "Rise, Effendi! dress, and follow me!" The Ka'abah, though open, would for a time be empty, so that we should escape the crowd. My pilgrim's garb, which had not been removed, was made to look neat and somewhat Indian, and we sallied forth together without loss of time.

A crowd had gathered round the Ka'abah, and I had no wish to stand bareheaded and barefooted in the midday September sun. At the cry of "Open a path for the Haji who would enter the House," the gazers made way. Two stout Meccans, who stood below the door, raised me in their arms, whilst a third drew me from above into the building. At the entrance I was accosted by several officials, dark-looking Meccans, of whom the blackest and plainest was a youth of the Beni Shaybah family, the true-blue blood of El Hejaz. He held in his hand the huge silvergilt padlock of the Ka'abah, and presently taking his seat upon a kind of wooden press in the left corner of the hall, he officially inquired my name, nation, and other particulars. The replies were satisfactory, and the boy Mohammed was authoritatively ordered to conduct me round the building, and to recite the prayers. I will not deny that, looking at the windowless walls, the officials at the door, and the crowd of excited fanatics below—

"And the place death, considering who I was"—

my feelings were of the trapped-rat description,

acknowledged by the immortal nephew of his uncle Perez. This did not, however, prevent my carefully observing the scene during our long prayers, and making a rough plan with a pencil upon my white Ihram.

Nothing is more simple than the interior of this celebrated building. The pavement, which is level with the ground, is composed of slabs of fine and various coloured marbles, mostly however white, disposed chequer-wise. The walls, as far as they can be seen, are of the same material, but the pieces are irregularly shaped, and many of them are engraved with long inscriptions in the Suls and other modern characters. The upper part of the walls, together with the ceiling, at which it is considered disrespectful to look, are covered with handsome red damask, flowered over with gold, and tucked up about six feet high, so as to be removed from pilgrims' hands. The flat roof is upheld by three cross-beams, whose shapes appear under the arras; they rest upon the eastern and western walls, and are supported in the centre by three columns about twenty inches in diameter, covered with carved and ornamented aloe wood.

At the Iraki corner there is a dwarf door, called Bab el Taubah (of Repentance). It leads into a narrow passage and to the staircase by which the servants ascend to the roof: it is never opened except for working purposes. The "Aswad" or "As'ad" corner is occupied by a flat-topped and quadrant-shaped press or safe in which at times is placed the key of the Ka'abah. Both door and safe are of aloe wood. Between the columns and about nine feet from the ground ran bars of a metal which I could not distinguish, and hanging to them were many lamps said to be of gold.

Although there were in the Ka'abah but a few attendants engaged in preparing it for the entrance of pilgrims, the windowless stone walls and the choked-up door made it worse than the Piombi of Venice; perspiration trickled in large drops, and I thought with horror what it must be when filled with a mass of furiously jostling and crushing fanatics. Our devotions consisted of a two-bow prayer, followed by long supplications at the Shami (west) corner, the Iraki (north) angle, the Yemani (south), and, lastly, opposite the southern third of the back wall. These concluded, I returned to the door, where payment is made. The boy Mohammed told me that the total expense would be seven dollars. At the same time he had been indulging aloud in his favorite rhodomontade, boasting of my greatness, and had declared me to be an Indian pilgrim, a race still supposed at Meccah to be made of gold. When seven dollars were tendered they were rejected with instance. Expecting something of the kind, I had been careful to bring no more than eight. Being pulled and interpellated by half a dozen attendants, my course was to look stupid, and to pretend ignorance of the language. Presently the Shaybah youth bethought him of a contrivance. Drawing forth from the press the key of the Ka'abah he partly bared it of its green-silk gold-lettered étui, and rubbed a golden knob quatrefoil-shaped upon my eyes, in order to brighten them. I submitted to the operation with a good grace, and added a dollar—my last—to the former offering. The Sherif received it with a hopeless glance, and, to my satisfaction, would not put forth his hand to be kissed. Then the attendants began to demand vails. I replied by opening my empty pouch. When let down from the door by the two brawny Meccans I was expected to pay them, and accordingly appointed to meet them at the boy Mohammed's house; an arrangement to which they grumblingly assented. When delivered from these troubles, I was congratulated by my sharp companion thus: "Wallah, Effendi! thou hast escaped well! some men have left their skins behind."

All pilgrims do not enter the Ka'abah; and many refuse to do so for religious reasons. Umar Effendi, for instance, who never missed a pilgrimage, had never seen the interior. Those who tread the hallowed floor are bound, among many other things, never again to walk barefooted, to take up fire with the fingers, or to tell lies. Most really conscientious men cannot afford the luxuries of slippers, tongs, and truth. So thought Thomas, when offered the apple which would give him the tongue that cannot lie.

> "'My tongue is mine ain,' true Thomas said.
> 'A gudely gift ye wad gie to me!
> I neither dought to buy nor sell
> At fair or tryst, where I may be,
> I dought neither speak to prince or peer,
> Nor ask of grace from fair ladye!'"

Amongst the Hindus I have met with men who have proceeded upon a pilgrimage to Dwarka, and yet who would not receive the brand of the god, because lying would then be forbidden to them. A confidential servant of a friend in Bombay naïvely declared that he had not been marked, as the act would have ruined him. There is a sad truth in what he said: Lying to the Oriental is meat and drink, and the roof that shelters him.

The Ka'abah had been dressed in her new attire when we entered. The covering, however, instead of being secured at the bottom to the metal rings in the basement, was tucked up by ropes from the roof and depended over each face in two long tongues. It was of a brilliant black, and the Hizam—the zone or golden band running round the upper portion of the building —as well as the Burka' (face-veil), were of dazzling brightness.

The origin of this custom must be sought in the ancient practice of typifying the church visible by a virgin or bride. The poet Abd el Rahim el Bura'i, in one of his Gnostic effusions, has embodied the idea:—

وعروس مكة بالكرامات تتجلى

And Meccah's bride (*i.e.* the Ka'abah) appeareth decked with (miraculous) signs.

This idea doubtless led to the face-veil, the covering, and the guardianship of eunuchs.

The Meccan temple was first dressed as a mark of honour by Tobba the Himyarite when he Judaized. If we accept this fact, which is vouched for by oriental history, we are led to the conclusion that the children of Israel settled at Meccah had connected the temple with their own faith, and, as a corollary, that the prophet of El Islam introduced their apocryphal traditions into his creed. The pagan Arabs did not remove the coverings: the old and torn Kiswah was covered with a new cloth, and the weight threatened to crush the building. From the time of Kusay, the Ka'abah was veiled by subscription, till Abu Rabi'at el Mughayrah bin Abdillah, who, having acquired great wealth by commerce, offered to provide the Kiswah on alternate years, and thereby gained the name of El Adil. The Prophet preferred a covering of fine Yemen cloth, and directed the expense to be defrayed by the Bayt el Mal, or public treasury. Omar chose Egyptian linen, ordering the Kiswah to be renewed every year, and the old covering to be distributed among the pilgrims. In the reign of Osman, the Ka'abah was twice clothed, in winter and summer. For the former season, it received a Kamis, or Tobe (shirt) of brocade, with an Izar, or veil; for the latter a suit of fine linen. Muawiyah at first supplied linen and brocade; he afterwards exchanged the former for striped Yemen stuff, and ordered Shaybah bin Usman to strip the Ka'abah, and to perfume the walls with Khaluk. Shaybah divided the old Kiswah among the pilgrims, and Abdullah bin Abbas did not object to this distribution. The Caliph Ma'amun (9th century) ordered the dress to be changed three times a year. In his day it was red brocade on the 10th Muharram;

fine linen on the 1st Rajab; and white brocade on the 1st Shawwal. At last he was informed that the veil applied on the 10th of Muharran was too closely followed by the red brocade in the next month, and that it required renewing on the 1st of Shawwal. This he ordered to be done. El Mutawakkil (9th century), when informed that the dress was spoiled by pilgrims, at first ordered two to be given, and the brocade shirt to be let down as far as the pavement: at last he sent a new veil every two months. During the Caliphat of the Abassides this investiture came to signify sovereignty in El Hejaz, which passed alternately from Baghdad to Egypt and Yemen. In El Idrisi's time (12th cent. A.D.) the Kiswah was composed of black silk and renewed every year by the Caliph of Baghdad. Ibn Jubayr writes that it was green and gold. The Kiswah remained with Egypt when Sultan Kalaun (13th cent. A.D.), conveyed the rents of two villages, "Baysus" and "Sindbus," to the expense of providing an outer black, and an inner red curtain for the Ka'abah, with hangings for the Prophet's tomb at El Medinah. When the Holy Land fell under the power of the Osmanli, Sultan Selim ordered the Kiswah to be black, and his son, Sultan Sulayman the Magnificent (16th cent. A.D.), devoted considerable sums to the purpose. The Kiswah was afterwards renewed at the accession of each Sultan. And the Wahhabi, during the first year of their conquest, covered the Ka'abah with a red Kiswah of the same stuff as the fine Arabian Aba or cloak, and made at El Hasa.

The Kiswah is now worked at a cotton manufactory called El Khurunfish, of the Tumn Bab el Sha'ariyah, Cairo. It is made by a hereditary family, called the Bayt el Sadi, and, as the specimen in my possession proves, it is a coarse tissue of silk and cotton mixed. The Kiswah is composed of eight pieces—two for each face of the Ka'abah—the seams being concealed by the Hizam, a broad band, which at a distance looks like gold; it is lined with white calico, and is supplied with cotton ropes. Anciently it is said all the Koran was interwoven into it. Now, it is inscribed, "Verily, the First of Houses founded for Mankind (to worship in) is that at Bekkah; blessed and a Direction to all Creatures;" together with seven chapters, namely, the Cave, Mariam, the Family of Amran, Repentance, T. H. with Y. S. and Tabarak. The character is that called Tumar, the largest style of Eastern caligraphy, legible from a considerable distance. The Hizam is a band about two feet broad, and surrounding the Ka'abah at two-thirds of its height. It is divided into four pieces, which are sewn together. On the first and second is inscribed the "Throne verselet," and on the third and fourth the titles of the reigning Sultan. These inscriptions are, like the Burka, or door curtain, gold worked into red silk, by the Bayt el Sadi. When the Kiswah is ready at Khurunfish, it is carried in procession to the Mosque El Hasanayn, where it is lined, sewn, and prepared for the journey.

After quitting the Ka'abah, I returned home exhausted, and washed with henna and warm water to mitigate the pain of the sun-scalds upon my arms, shoulders, and breast. The house was empty, all the Turkish pilgrims being still at Muna, and the "Kabirah"—the old lady—received me with peculiar attention. I was ushered into an upper room, whose teak wainscotings, covered with Cufic and other inscriptions, large carpets, and ample Diwans still showed a ragged splendor. The family had "seen better days," the Sherif Ghalib having confiscated three of its houses; but it is still proud, and cannot merge the past into the present. In the "drawing-room," which the Turkish colonel occupied when at Meccah, the Kabirah supplied me with a pipe, coffee, cold water, and breakfast. I won her heart by praising the graceless boy Mohammed; like all mothers, she dearly loved the scamp of the family. When he entered, and saw his maternal parent standing near me, with only the end of her veil drawn over her mouth, he began to scold her with divers insinuations. "Soon thou wilt sit amongst the men in the hall!" he exclaimed. "O, my son," rejoined the Kabirah, "fear Allah, thy mother is in years!"—and truly she was so, being at least fifty. "A-a-h!" sneered the youth, who had formed, as boys of the world must do, or appear to do, a very low estimate of the sex. The old lady understood the drift of the exclamation, and departed with a half laughing "May Allah disappoint thee!" She soon, however, returned, bringing me water for ablution; and having heard that I had not yet sacrificed a sheep at

Muna, enjoined me to perform without delay that important rite.

After resuming our laical toilette, and dressing gaily for the Great Festival, we mounted our asses about the cool of the afternoon, and, returning to Muna, we found the tent full of visitors. Ali ibn Ya Sin, the Zem Zemi, had sent me an amphora of holy water, and the carrier was awaiting the customary dollar. With him were several Meccans, one of whom spoke excellent Persian. We sat down, and chatted together for an hour; and I afterwards learned from the boy Mohammed, that all had pronounced me to be an "Ajami." After their departure we debated about the victim, which is only a Sunnat, or Practice of the Prophet. It is generally sacrificed immediately after the first lapidation, and we had already been guilty of delay. Under these circumstances, and considering the meagre condition of my purse, I would not buy a sheep, but contented myself with watching my neighbours. They gave themselves great trouble, especially a large party of Indians pitched near us, to buy the victim cheap; but the Bedawin were not less acute, and he was happy who paid less than a dollar and a quarter. Some preferred contributing to buy a lean ox. None but the Sherif and the principal dignitaries slaughtered camels. The pilgrims dragged their victims to a smooth rock near the Akabah, above which stands a small open pavilion, whose sides, red with fresh blood, showed that the prince and his attendants had been busy at sacrifice. Others stood before their tents, and, directing the victim's face towards the Ka'abah, cut its throat, ejaculating, "Bismillah! Allahu Akbar!"* The boy Mohammed sneeringly directed my attention to the Indians, who, being a mild race, had hired an Arab butcher to do the deed of blood; and he aroused all Shaykh Nur's ire by his taunting comments upon the chicken-heartedness of the men of Hind. It is considered a meritorious act to give away the victim without eating any portion of its flesh. Parties of Takruri might be seen, sitting vulture-like, contemplating the sheep and goats; and no sooner was the signal given, than they fell upon the bodies, and cut them up without removing them. The surface of the valley soon came to resemble the dirtiest slaughter-house, and my prescient soul drew bad auguries for the future.

We had spent a sultry afternoon in the basin of Muna, which is not unlike a volcanic crater, an Aden closed up at the sea-side. Towards night the occasional puffs of Simum ceased, and through the air of deadly stillness a mass of purple nimbus, bisected by a thin grey line of mist-cloud, rolled down upon us from the Taif hills. When darkness gave the signal, most of the pilgrims pressed towards the square in front of the Muna Mosque, to enjoy the pyrotechnics and the discharge of cannon. But during the spectacle came on a windy storm, whose lightnings, flashing their fire

---

* It is strange that the accurate Burckhardt should make Moslems say, when slaughtering or sacrificing, "In the name of the most Merciful God!" As Mr. Lane justly observes, the attribute of mercy is omitted on these occasions.

from pole to pole, paled the rockets, and whose thunderings, re-echoed by the rocky hills, dumbed the puny artillery of man. We were disappointed in our hopes of rain. A few huge drops pattered upon the plain and sank into its thirsty entrails; all the rest was thunder and lightning, dust-clouds and whirlwind.

CHAPTER VI.

The Three Days of Drying Flesh.

ALL was dull after the excitement of the Great Festival. The heat of the succeeding night rendered every effort to sleep abortive; and as our little camp required a guard in a place so celebrated for plunderers, I spent the great part of the time sitting in the clear pure moonlight.

After midnight we again repaired to the Devils, and, beginning with the Aula, or first pillar, at the eastern extremity of Muna, threw at each 7 stones (making a total of 21), with the ceremonies before described.

On Thursday we arose before dawn, and prepared with a light breakfast for the fatigues of a climbing walk. After half an hour spent in hopping from boulder to boulder, we arrived at a place situated on the lower declivity of Jebel Sabir, the northern wall of the Muna basin. Here is the Majarr el Kabsh, "the Dragging-place of the Ram;" a small, whitewashed square, divided into two compartments. The first is entered by a few ragged steps in the S.E. angle, which lead to an enclosure 30 feet by 15. In the N.E. corner is a block of granite, in which a huge gash, several inches broad, some feet deep, and completely splitting the stone in knife-shape, notes the spot where Ibrahim's blade fell when the archangel Gabriel forbade him to slay Ismail his son. The second compartment contains a diminutive hypogeum. In this cave the patriarch sacrificed the victim, which gives the place a name. We descended by a flight of steps, and under the stifling ledge of rock found mats and praying-rugs, which, at this early hour, were not overcrowded. We followed the example of the patriarchs, and prayed a two-bow prayer in each of the enclosures. After distributing the usual gratification, we left the place, and proceeded to mount the hill, in hope of seeing some of the apes said still to haunt the heights. These animals are supposed by the Meccans to have been Jews, thus transformed for having broken the Sabbath by hunting. They abound in the elevated regions about Arafat and Taif, where they are caught by mixing the juice of the Asclepias and narcotics with dates and other sweet bait. The Hejazi ape is a hideous cynocephalus, with small eyes placed close together, and almost hidden by a disproportionate snout; a greenish-brown coat, long arms, and a stern of lively pink, like fresh meat. They are docile, and are said to be fond of spirituous liquors, and to display an inordinate affection for women. El Mas'udi tells about them a variety of anecdotes. According to him, their principal use in Hind and Chin was to protect kings from poison, by eating suspected dishes. The Bedawin have many tales concerning them. It is universally believed that they catch and kill kites, by exposing the pink portion of their persons and concealing the rest; the bird pounces upon what appears to be raw meat, and presently finds himself viciously plucked alive. Throughout Arabia an old story is told of them. A merchant was once plundered during his absence by a troop of these apes; they tore open his bales, and, charmed with the scarlet hue of the Tarbushes, began applying those articles of dress to uses quite opposite to their normal purpose. The merchant was in despair, when his slave offered for a consideration to recover the goods. Placing himself in the front, like a fugleman to the ape-company, he went through a variety of manœuvres with a Tarbush, and concluded with throwing it far away. The recruits carefully imitated him, and the drill concluded with his firing a shot: the plunderers decamped and the caps were regained.

Failing to see any apes, we retired to the tent ere the sun waxed hot, in anticipation of a terrible day. Nor were we far wrong. In addition to the heat, we had swarms of flies, and the blood-stained earth began to reek with noisome vapours. Nought moved in the air except kites and vultures, speckling the deep blue sky: the denizens of earth seemed paralysed by the fire from above. I spent the time between breakfast and nightfall lying half-dressed upon a mat, moving round the tent-pole to escape the glare, and watching my numerous neighbours, male and female. The Indians were particularly kind, filling my pipe, offering cooled water, and performing similar little offices. I repaid them with a supply of provisions, which, at the Muna market-prices, these unfortunates could ill afford.

When the moon arose the boy Mohammed and I walked out into the town, performed our second lapidation, and visited the coffee-houses. The shops were closed early, but business was transacted in places of public resort till midnight. We entered the houses of numerous acquaintances, who accosted my companion, and were hospitably welcomed with pipes and coffee. The first question always was "Who is this pilgrim?" and more than once the reply, "An Afghan," elicited the language of my own country, which I could no longer speak. Of this phenomenon, however, nothing was thought: many Afghans settled in India know not a word of Pushtu, and even above the Passes many of the townspeople are imperfectly acquainted with it. The Meccans, in consequence of their extensive intercourse with strangers and habits of travelling, are admirable conversational linguists. They speak Arabic remarkably well, and with a volubility surpassing the most lively of our continental nations. Persian, Turkish, and Hindostanee are generally known; and the Mutawwifs, who devote themselves to various races of pilgrims, soon become masters of many languages.

Returning homewards, we were called to a spot by the clapping of hands and the loud sound of song. We found a crowd of Bedawin surrounding a group engaged in their favorite occupation of dancing. The performance is wild in the extreme, resembling rather the hopping of bears than the inspiration of Terpsichore. The bystanders joined in the song; an interminable recitative, as usual in the minor key, and—Orientals are admirable timists—it sounded like one voice. The refrain appeared to be—

"Lá Yayhá! Lá Yayhá!"

to which no one could assign a meaning. At other times they sang something intelligible. For instance:—

نهار العيد فى منا شفت ســيدى
غريب الدار عند كم فارحمو نى

That is to say—

"On the Great Festival-day at Muna I saw my lord.
I am a stranger among you, therefore pity me!"

This couplet may have, like the puerilities of certain modern and European poets, an abstruse and mystical meaning, to be discovered when the Arabs learn to write erudite essays upon nursery rhymes. The style of saltation, called Rufayhah, rivalled the song. The dancers raised both arms high above their heads, brandishing a dagger, pistol, or some other small weapon. They followed each other by hops, on one or both feet, sometimes indulging in the most demented leaps; whilst the bystanders clapped with their palms a more enlivening measure. This I was told is especially their war-dance. They have other forms, which my eyes were not fated to see. Amongst the Bedawin of El Hejaz, unlike the Somali and other African races, the sexes never mingle: the girls may dance together, but it would be disgraceful to perform in the company of men.

After so much excitement we retired to rest, and slept soundly.

On Friday, the 12th Zu'l Hijjah, the camels appeared, according to order, at early dawn, and they were loaded with little delay. We were anxious to enter Meccah in time for the sermon, and I for one was eager to escape the now pestilential air of Muna.

Literally, the land stank. Five or six thousand animals had been slain and cut up in this Devil's Punch-bowl. I leave the reader to imagine the rest. The evil might be avoided by building "abattoirs," or, more easily still, by digging long trenches, and by ordering all pilgrims, under pain of mulct, to sacrifice in the same place. Unhappily, the spirit of El Islam is opposed to these precautions of common sense— "Inshallah" and "Kismat" must take the place of prevention and cure. And at Meccah, the headquarters of the faith, a desolating attack of cholera is preferred to the impiety of "flying in the face of Providence," and the folly of endeavouring to avert inevitable decrees.*

Mounting our camels, and led by Mas'ud, we entered Muna by the eastern end, and from the litter threw the remaining twenty-one stones. I could now

---

* Note to Third Edition. Since this was written there have been two deadly epidemics which began, it is reported, at Muna. The victims, however, have never numbered 700,000, nor is "Each pilgrim required to sacrifice one animal at the *shrine of Mohammed*(!)" as we find in "Cholera Prospects." By Tilbury Fox M.D. (Hardwicke).

see the principal lines of shops, and, having been led to expect a grand display of merchandise, was surprised to find only mat-booths and sheds, stocked chiefly with provisions. The exit from Muna was crowded, for many, like ourselves, were flying from the revolting scene. I could not think without pity of those whom religious scruples detained another day and a half in this foul spot.

After entering Meccah we bathed, and when the noon drew nigh we repaired to the Haram for the purpose of hearing the sermon. Descending to the cloisters below the Bab el Ziyadah, I stood wonderstruck by the scene before me. The vast quadrangle was crowded with worshippers sitting in long rows, and everywhere facing the central black tower: the showy colours of their dresses were not to be surpassed by a garden of the most brilliant flowers, and such diversity of detail would probably not be seen massed together in any other building upon earth. The women, a dull and sombre-looking group, sat apart in their peculiar place. The Pasha stood on the roof of Zem Zem, surrounded by guards in Nizam uniform. Where the principal Olema stationed themselves the crowd was thicker; and in the more auspicious spots nought was to be seen but a pavement of heads and shoulders. Nothing seemed to move but a few dervishes, who, censer in hand, sidled through the rows and received the unsolicited alms of the Faithful.

Apparently in the midst, and raised above the crowd by the tall, pointed pulpit, whose gilt spire flamed in the sun, sat the preacher, an old man with snowy beard. The style of head-dress called "Taylasan" covered his turban, which was white as his robes, and a short staff supported his left hand. Presently he arose, took the staff in his right hand, pronounced a few inaudible words, and sat down again on one of the lower steps, whilst a Muezzin, at the foot of the pulpit, recited the call to sermon. Then the old man stood up and began to preach. As the majestic figure began to exert itself there was a deep silence. Presently a general "Amin" was intoned by crowd at the conclusion of some long sentence. And at last, towards the end of the sermon, every third or fourth word was followed by the simultaneous rise and fall of thousands of voices.

I have seen the religious ceremonies of many lands but never—nowhere—aught so solemn, so impressive as this.

CHAPTER VII.

Life at Meccah, and Umrah, or the Little Pilgrimage.

My few remaining days at Meccah sped pleasantly enough. Umar Effendi visited me regularly, and arranged to accompany me furtively to Cairo. I had already consulted Mohammed Shiklibha — who suddenly appeared at Muna, having dropped down from Suez to Jeddah, and reached Meccah in time for pilgrimage — about the possibility of proceeding eastward. The honest fellow's eyebrows rose till they almost touched his turban, and he exclaimed in a roaring voice, "Wallah! Effendi! thou art surely mad." Every day he brought me news of the different caravans. The Bedawin of El Hejaz were, he said, in a ferment caused by reports of the Holy War, want of money, and rumours of quarrels between the Sherif and the Pasha: already they spoke of an attack upon Jeddah. Shaykh Mas'ud, the camel-man, with whom I parted on the best of terms, seriously advised my remaining at Meccah for some months even before proceeding to Sana'a. Others gave the same counsel. Briefly I saw that my star was not then in the ascendant, and resolved to reserve myself for a more propitious conjuncture by returning to Egypt.

The Turkish colonel and I had become as friendly

as two men ignoring each other's speech could be. He had derived benefit from some prescription; but, like all his countrymen, he was pining to leave Meccah. Whilst the pilgrimage lasted, said they, no mal de pays came to trouble them; but, its excitement over, they could think of nothing but their wives and children. Long-drawn faces and continual sighs evidenced nostalgia. At last the house became a scene of preparation. Blue china-ware and basketed bottles of Zem Zem water appeared standing in solid columns, and pilgrims occupied themselves in hunting for mementos of Meccah, ground-plans, combs, balm, henna, tooth-sticks, aloe-wood, turquoises, coral, and mother-o'-pearl rosaries, shreds of Kiswat-cloth and fine Abas, or cloaks of camels'-wool. It was not safe to mount the stairs without shouting "Tarik"—Out of the way!—at every step, on peril of meeting face to face some excited fair. The lower floor was crowded with provision-vendors; and the staple article of conversation seemed to be the chance of a steamer from Jeddah to Suez.

Weary of the wrangling and chaffering of the hall below, I had persuaded my kind hostess, in spite of the surly skeleton her brother, partially to clear out a small store-room in the first floor, and to abandon it to me between the hours of ten and four. During the heat of the day clothing is unendurable at Meccah. The city is so "compacted together" by hills, that even the Simum can scarcely sweep it; the heat reverberated by the bare rocks is intense, and the normal atmosphere of an eastern town communicates a faint lassitude to the body and irritability to the mind. The houses being unusually strong and well-built, might by some art of thermantidote be rendered cool enough in the hottest weather: they are now ovens.* It was my habit to retire immediately after the late breakfast to the little room upstairs, to sprinkle it with water, and to lie down upon a mat. In the few precious moments of privacy notes were committed to paper, but one eye was ever fixed on the door. Sometimes a patient would interrupt me, but a doctor is far less popular in El Hejaz than in Egypt. The people, being more healthy, have less faith in physic: Shaykh Mas'ud and his son had never tasted in their lives aught more medicinal than green dates and camel's milk. Occasionally the black slave-girls came into the room, asking if the pilgrim wanted a pipe or a cup of

* I offer no lengthened description of the town of Meccah: Ali Bey and Burckhardt have already said all that requires saying. Although the origin of the Bayt Ullah be lost in the glooms of past time, the city is a comparatively modern place, built about A.D. 450, by Kusay and the Kuraysh. It contains between 30,000 and 45,000 inhabitants, with lodging room for at least treble that number; and the material of the houses is brick, granite, and sandstone from the neighbouring hills. The site is a winding valley, on a small plateau, halfway "below the Ghauts." Its utmost length is two miles and a half from the Ma'abidah (north) to the southern mound Jiyad; and three-quarters of a mile would be the extreme breadth between Abu Kubays eastward—upon whose western slope the most solid mass of the town clusters—and Jebel Hindi westward of the city. In the centre of this line stands the Ka'abah.

I regret being unable to offer the reader a sketch of Meccah, or of the Great Temple. The stranger who would do this should visit the city out of the pilgrimage season, and hire a room looking into the quadrangle of the Haram. This addition to our knowledge is the more required, as our popular sketches (generally taken from D'Ohsson) are utterly incorrect. The Ka'abah is always a recognisable building: but the "View of Meccah" known to Europe is not more like Meccah than like Cairo or Bombay.

coffee: they generally retired in a state of delight, attempting vainly to conceal with a corner of tattered veil a grand display of ivory consequent upon some small and innocent facetiousness.

The most frequent of my visitors was Abdullah, the Kabirah's eldest son. This melancholy Jacques had joined our caravan at El Hamra, on the Yambu' road, accompanied us to El Medinah, lived there, and journeyed to Meccah with the Syrian pilgrimage; yet he had not once come to visit me or to see his brother, the boy Mohammed. When gently reproached for this omission he declared it to be his way—that he never called upon strangers until sent for. He was a perfect Saudawi (melancholist) in mind, manners, and personal appearance, and this class of humanity in the East is almost as uncomfortable to the household as the idiot of Europe. I was frequently obliged to share my meals with him, as his mother—though most filially and reverentially entreated—would not supply him with breakfast two hours after the proper time, or with a dinner served up forty minutes before the rest of the household. Often, too, I had to curb, by polite deprecation, the impetuosity of the old Kabirah's fiery tongue.

Thus Abdullah and I became friends, after a fashion. He purchased several little articles required, and never failed to pass hours in my closet, giving me much information about the country, deploring the laxity of Meccan morals, and lamenting that in these evil days his countrymen had forfeited their name at Cairo and Constantinople. His curiosity about the English in India was great, and I satisfied it by praising, as a Moslem would, their "politiké," their even-handed justice, and their good star. Then he would inquire into the truth of a fable extensively known on the shores of the Mediterranean and the Red Sea. The English, it is said, sent a mission to Mohammed, inquiring into his doctrines, and begging that the heroic Khalid bin Walid might be sent to proselytise them. Unfortunately, the envoys arrived too late—the Prophet's soul had winged its way to Paradise. An abstract of the Moslem scheme was, however, sent to the "Ingreez," who declined, as the Founder of the New Faith was no more, to abandon their own religion", but the refusal was accompanied with expressions of regard. For this reason many Moslems in Barbary and other countries hold the English to be, of all "People of the Books," the best inclined towards them.

As regards the Prophet's tradition concerning the fall of his birthplace "and the thin-calved from the Habash (Abyssinians) shall destroy the Ka'abah," I was informed that towards the end of time a host will pass over from Africa in such multitudes that a stone shall be conveyed from hand to hand between Jeddah and Meccah. This latter condition might easily be accomplished by 40,000 men, the distance being only 44 miles, but the citizens consider it to express a countless horde. Some pious Moslems have hoped that in Abdullah bin Zubayr's re-erection of the

Ka'abah the prophecy was fulfilled: the popular belief, however, remains, that the fatal event is still in the womb of time. In a previous part of these volumes I have alluded to similar evil presentiments which haunt the mind of El Islam; and the Christian, zealous for the propagation of his faith, may see in them an earnest of its still wider diffusion in future ages.

Late in the afternoon I used to rise, perform ablution, and either visit the Haram, or wander about the bazars till sunset. After this it was necessary to return home and prepare for supper—dinner it would be called in the West. The meal concluded, I generally sat for a time outside the street-door in great dignity, upon a broken-backed black-wood chair, traditionally said to have been left in the house by one of the princes of Delhi, smoking a Shishah, and drinking sundry cups of strong green tea with a slice of lime, a fair substitute for milk. At this hour the seat was as in a theatre, but the words of the actors were of a nature somewhat too Fescennine for a respectable public. After nightfall we either returned to the Haram or retired to rest. Our common dormitory was the flat roof of the house; under each cot stood a water-gugglet; and all slept, as must be done in the torrid lands, *on* and not *in* bed.

I sojourned at Meccah but a short time, and, as usual with travellers; did not see the best specimens of the population. The citizens appeared to me more civilised and more vicious than those of El Medinah. They often leave—

"Home, where small experience grows,"

and—"qui multum peregrinatur, rarò sanctificatur"— become a worldly-wise, God-forgetting, and Mammonish sort of folk. "Tuf w' asa'a, w' a'amil el Saba'"—"Circumambulate and run (*i. e.* between Safa and Marwah) and do the seven (deadly sins)"—is a satire popularly levelled against them. Hence, too, the proverb "El Harám f' il Haramayn"—"Harm (dwelleth) in the two Holy (Cities);" and no wonder, since plenary indulgence is so easily secured. The pilgrim is forbidden, or rather dissuaded, from abiding at Meccah after the rites, and wisely. Great emotions must be followed by a reaction. And he who stands struck by the first aspect of Allah's house, after a few months, the marvel waxing stale, sweeps past it with indifference or something worse.

There is, however, little at Meccah to offend the eye. As among certain nations further west, a layer of ashes overspreads the fire: the mine is concealed by a green turf fair to look upon. It is only when wandering by starlight through the northern outskirts of the town that citizens may be seen with light complexions and delicate limbs, coarse turbans and Egyptian woollen robes, speaking disguise and the purpose of disguise. No one within the memory of man has suffered the penalty of immorality. Spirituous liquors are no longer sold, as in Burckhardt's day, in shops and some Arnaut officers assured me that they found considerable difficulty in smuggling flasks of "raki" from Jeddah.

The Meccan is a darker man than the Medinite. The people explain this by the heat of the climate. I rather believe it to be caused by the number of female slaves that find their way into the market. Gallas, Sawahilis, a few Somal, and Abyssinians are embarked at Suakin, Zayla, Tajurrah, and Berberah, carried in thousands to Jeddah, and the Holy City has the pick of every batch. Thence the stream sets northwards, a small current towards El Medinah, and the main line to Egypt and Turkey. Most Meccans have black concubines, and, as has been said, the appearance of the Sherif is almost that of a negro. I did not see one handsome man in the Holy City, although some of the women appeared to me beautiful. In most families male children, when forty days old, are taken to the Ka'abah, prayed over, and carried home, where the barber draws with a razor three parallel gashes down the fleshy portion of each cheek, from the exterior angles of the eyes almost to the corners of the mouth. These "Mashali," as they are called, may be of modern date: the citizens declare that the custom was unknown to their ancestors. I am tempted to assign to it a high antiquity, and cannot but attribute a pagan origin to a custom still prevailing, despite all the interdictions of the Olema. In point of figure the Meccan is somewhat coarse and lymphatic. The ludicrous leanness of the outward man, as described by Ali Bey, survives only in the remnants of themselves belonging to a bygone century. The young men are rather stout and athletic, but in middle age—when man "swills and swells"—they are apt to degenerate into corpulence.

The Meccan is a covetous spendthrift. His wealth, lightly won, is lightly prized. Pay, pension, stipends, presents, and the "Ikram" here, as at El Medinah, supply the citizen with the means of idleness. With him everything is on the most expensive scale, his marriage, his religious ceremonies, and his household expenses. His house is luxuriously furnished, entertainments are frequent, and the junketings of his women make up a heavy bill at the end of the year. It is a common practice for the citizen to anticipate the pilgrimage season by falling into the hands of the usurer. If he be in luck, he catches and "skins" one or more of the richest Hajis. On the other hand, should fortune fail him, he will feel for life the effect of interest running on at the rate of at least 50 per cent., the simple and the compound forms of which are equally familiar to the wily Sarraf, or money-changer.

The most unpleasant peculiarities of the Meccans are their pride and coarseness of language. Looking upon themselves as the cream of earth's sons, they resent with extreme asperity the least slighting word concerning the Holy City and its denizens. They plume themselves upon their holy descent, their exclusion of Infidels, their strict fastings, their learned men, and their purity of language. In fact, their pride shows itself at every moment; but it is not the pride which makes a man too proud to do "dirty work." My predecessor did not remark their scurrility: he seems, on the contrary, rather to commend them for respectability in this point. If he be correct, the present generation has degenerated. The Meccans appeared to me distinguished, even in this foul-mouthed East, by the superior licentiousness of their language. Abuse was bad enough in the streets, but in the house it became intolerable. The Turkish pilgrims remarked, but they were too haughty to notice it. The boy Mohammed and one of his tall cousins at last transgressed the limits of my endurance. They had been reviling each other vilely one day at the house-door about dawn, when I administered the most open reprimand: "In my country (Afghanistan) we hold this to be the hour of prayer, the season of good thoughts, when men remember Allah; even the Kafir doth not begin the day with curses and abuse." The people around approved, and the offenders could not refrain from saying, "Thou hast spoken truth, O Effendi!" Then the bystanders began, as usual, to "improve the occasion." "See," they exclaimed, "this Sulaymani gentleman, he is not the Son of a Holy City, and yet he teacheth you — you, the children of the Prophet!—repent and fear Allah!" They replied, "Verily we do repent, and Allah is a Pardoner and the Merciful!"—were silent for an hour, and then abused each other more foully than before. Yet it is a good point in the Meccan character, that it is open to reason, it can confess itself in error, and it displays none of that doggedness of vice which distinguishes the sinner of a more stolid race. Like the people of Southern Europe, the Semite is easily managed by a jest: though grave and thoughtful, he is by no means deficient in the sly wit which we call humour, and the solemn gravity of his words contrasts amusingly with his ideas. He particularly excels in the Cervantic art, the spirit of which, says Sterne, is to clothe low subjects in sublime language. In Mohammed's life we find that he by no means disdained a joke, sometimes a little hasardé, as in the case of the Paradise-coveting old woman. The redeeming qualities of the Meccan are his courage, his bonhommie, his manly suavity of manners, his fiery sense of honour, his strong family affections, his near approach to what we call patriotism, and his general knowledge: the reproach of extreme ignorance which Burckhardt directs against the Holy City has long ago sped to the Limbo of things that were. The dark half of the picture shows pride, bigotry, irreligion, greed of gain, immorality, and prodigal ostentation.

Of the pilgrimage ceremonies I cannot speak harshly. It may be true that "the rites of the Ka'abah, emasculated of every idolatrous tendency, still hang a strange unmeaning shroud around the living theism of Islam." But what nation, either in the West or the East, has been able to cast out from its ceremonies every suspicion of its old idolatry? What are the English mistletoe, the Irish wake, the Pardon of Brittany, the Carnival and the Worship at Iserna? Better far to consider the Meccan pilgrimage rites in the light of Evil-worship turned into lessons of Good than to philosophise about their strangeness, and to blunder in asserting them to be insignificant. Even the Bedawi circumambulating the Ka'abah fortifies his wild belief by the fond thought that he treads the path of "Allah's friend." At Arafat the good Moslem worships in imitation of the "Pure of Allah (Adam);" and when hurling stones and curses at the three senseless little buttresses which commemorate the appearance of the fiend, the materialism of the action gives to its sentiment all the strength and endurance of reality. The supernatural agencies of pilgrimage are carefully and sparingly distributed. The angels who restore the stones from Muna to Muzdalifah, the heavenly host whose pinions cause the Ka'abah's veil to rise and wave, and the mysterious complement of the pilgrims' total at the Arafat sermon, all belong to the category of spiritual creatures walking earth unseen — a poetical tenet, not condemned by Christianity.

The Meccans are, it is true, to be reproached with their open Mammon-worship, at times and at places the most sacred and venerable; but this has no other effect upon the pilgrims than to excite disgust and open reprehension. Here, however, we see no such silly frauds as heavenly fire drawn from a phosphor-match; nor do two rival churches fight in the flesh with teeth and nails, requiring the contemptuous interference of an infidel power to keep decent order. Here we see no fair dames staring with their glasses "braqués" at the Head of the Church, or supporting exhausted nature with the furtive sandwich, or carrying pampered curs who, too often, will not be silent, or scrambling and squeezing to hear theatrical music, reckless of the fate of the old lady who—on such occasions there is always one—has been "thrown down and cruelly trampled upon by the crowd." If the Meccan citizens are disposed to scoff at the wild Takruri, they do it not so publicly or shamelessly as the Roman jeering with ribald jest at the fanaticism of strangers from the bogs of Ireland. Finally, at Meccah there is nothing theatrical, nothing that suggests the opera; but all is simple and impressive, filling the mind with—

"A weight of awe not easy to be borne,"

and tending, I believe, after its fashion, to good.

As regards the Meccan and Moslem belief that Abraham and his son built the Ka'abah, it may be observed that the Genesitic account of the Great Patriarch has suggested to learned men the idea of two Abrahams, one the son of Terah, another the son of Azar (fire), a Prometheus who imported civilisation and knowledge into Arabia from Harran, the sacred centre of Sabæan learning. Moslem historians all agree in representing Abraham as a star-worshipper in youth, and Eusebius calls the patriarch son of Athar; his father's name, therefore, is no Arab invention. Whether Abraham or Ishmael ever visited Meccah to build the Ka'abah is, in my humble opinion, an open question. The Jewish Scripture informs us only that the patriarch dwelt at Beersheba and Gerar, in Southern Palestine, without any allusion to the annual visit which Moslems declare he paid to their Holy City. At the same time Arab tradition speaks clearly and consistently upon the subject, and generally omits those miraculous and superstitious adjuncts which cast shadows of sore doubt upon the philosophic mind.

The amount of risk which a stranger must encounter at the pilgrimage rites is still considerable. A learned Orientalist and divine intimated his intention, in a work published but a few years ago, of visiting Meccah without disguise. He was assured that the Turkish governor would now offer no obstacle to a European traveller. I should strongly dissuade a friend from making the attempt. It is true that the Frank is no longer, as in Captain Head's day, insulted when he ventures out of the Meccan Gate of Jeddah; and that our vice-consuls and travellers are allowed, on condition that their glance do not pollute the shrine, to visit Taif and the regions lying eastward of the Holy City. Neither the Pasha nor the Sherif would, in these days, dare to enforce, in the case of an Englishman, the old law, a choice thrice offered between circumcision and death. But the first Bedawi who caught sight of the Frank's hat would not deem himself a man if he did not drive a bullet through the wearer's head. At the pilgrimage season disguise is easy, on account of the vast and varied multitudes which visit Meccah, exposing the traveller only to "stand the buffet with knaves who smell of sweat." But woe to the unfortunate who happens to be recognised in public as an Infidel — unless at least he could throw himself at once upon the protection of the government. Amidst the motley crowd of pilgrims, whose fanaticism is worked up to the highest pitch, detection would probably ensure his dismissal at once al numero de' più. Those who find danger the salt of pleasure may visit Meccah; but if asked whether the results justify the risk, I should reply in the negative. And the vice-consul at Jeddah would only do his duty in peremptorily forbidding European travellers to attempt Meccah without disguise, until the day comes when such steps can be taken in the certainty of not causing a mishap, which would not redound to our reputation, as we could not in justice revenge it.

On the 14th Z'ul Hijjah we started to perform the rite of Umrah, or Little Pilgrimage. After performing ablution, and resuming the Ihram with the usual ceremonies, I set out, accompanied by the boy Mohammed and his brother Abdullah. Mounting asses, which resembled mules in size and speed, we rode to the Haram, and prayed there. Again remounting, we issued through the Bab el Safa towards the open country N.E. of the city. The way was crowded with pilgrims, on foot as well as mounted, and their loud "Labbayk" distinguished those engaged in the Umrah rite from the many whose business was with the camp of the Damascus caravan.

About half a mile from the city we passed on the left a huge heap of stones, where my companions stood and cursed. This grim-looking cairn is popularly believed to note the place of the well where Abu Lahab laid an ambuscade for the Prophet. This wicked uncle stationed there a slave, with orders to throw headlong into the pit the first person who approached him, and privily persuaded his nephew to visit the spot at night: after a time, anxiously hoping to hear that the deed had been done, Abu Lahab incautiously drew nigh, and was precipitated by his own bravo into the place of destruction. Hence the well-known saying in Islam, "Whoso diggeth a well for his brother shall fall into it himself." We added our quota of stones, and proceeding, saw the Jeddah road spanning the plain like a white ribbon. In front of us the highway was now lined with coffee-tents, before which effeminate dancing-boys performed to admiring Syrians: a small whitewashed "Bungalow," the palace of the Emir el Hajj, lay on the left, and all around it clustered the confused encampment of his pilgrims. After cantering about three miles from the city, we reached the Alamayn, or two pillars that limit the Sanctuary; and a little beyond it, is the small settlement, popularly called El Umrah. Dismounting here, we sat down on rugs outside a coffee-tent to enjoy the beauty of the moonlit night, and an hour of "Kayf," in the sweet Desert air.

Presently the coffee-tent keeper, after receiving payment, brought us water for ablution. This preamble over, we entered the principal chapel; an unpretending building, badly lighted, spread with dirty rugs, full of pilgrims, and offensively close. Here we prayed the Isha, or night devotions, and then a two-bow prayer in honour of the Ihram, after which we distributed gratuities to the guardians, and alms to the importunate beggars. And now I perceived the object of Abdullah's companionship. The melancholy man assured me that he had ridden out for love of me, and in order to perform as Wakil (substitute) a vicarious pilgrimage for my parents. Vainly I assured him that they had been strict in the exercises of their faith. He would take no denial, and I perceived that love of me meant love of my dollars. With a surly assent, he was at last permitted to act for the "pious pilgrims Yusuf (Joseph) bin Ahmed and Fatimah bint Yunus,"—my progenitors. It was impossible to prevent smiling at contrasts, as Abdullah, gravely raising his hands, and directing his face to the Ka'abah, intoned, "I do vow this Ihram of Umrah in the Name of Yusuf Son of Ahmed, and Fatimah Daughter of Yunus; then render it attainable to them, and accept it of them! Bismillah! Allahu Akbar!"

Remounting, we galloped towards Meccah, shouting "Labbayk," and halting at every half mile to smoke and drink coffee. In a short time we entered the city, and repairing to the Haram by the Safa Gate, performed the Tawaf, or circumambulation of Umrah. After this dull round and necessary repose we left the temple by the same exit, and mounting once more, turned towards El Safa, which stands about 100 yards S.E. of the Mosque, and as little deserves its name of "Mountain" as do those that undulate the face of modern Rome. The Safa end is closed by a mean-looking building, composed of three round arches, with a dwarf flight of steps leading up to them out of a narrow road. Without dismounting, we wheeled our donkeys round, "left shoulders forward"—no easy task in the crowd—and, vainly striving to sight the Ka'abah through the Bab el Safa, we performed the Niyat, or intention of the rite El Sa'i (the Running). After Tahlil Takbir, and Talbiyat, we raised our hands in the supplicatory position, and twice repeated, "There is no god but Allah, Alone, without Partner; His is the Kingdom, unto Him be Praise; He giveth Life and Death, He is alive and perisheth not; in His Hand is Good, and He over all Things is Omnipotent."

Then, with the donkey-boys leading our animals and a stout fellow preceding us with lantern and a quarter-staff to keep off the running Bedawin, camel-men, and riders of asses, we descended Safa, and walked slowly down the street El Masa'a, towards Marwah. During our descent we recited aloud, "O Allah, cause me to act according to the Sunnat of Thy Prophet, and to die in His Faith, and defend me from Errors and Disobedience by Thy Mercy, O most Merciful of the Merciful!" Arrived at what is called the Batn el Wady (Belly of the Vale), a place now denoted by the Milayn el Akhzarayn (the two green pillars), one fixed in the eastern course of the Haram, the other in a house on the right side, we began the running by urging on our beasts. Here the prayer was, "O Lord, pardon and pity, and pass over what Thou knowest, for Thou art the most Dear and the most Generous! Save us from Hell-fire safely, and cause us safely to enter Paradise! O Lord, give us Happiness here and Happiness hereafter, and spare us the Torture of the Flames!"

At the end of this supplication we had passed the Batn, or lowest ground, whose farther limits were marked by two other pillars.* Again we began to ascend, repeating, as we went, "Verily, Safa and Marwah are two of the Monuments of Allah. Whoso, therefore, pilgrimeth to the Temple of Meccah or performeth Umrah, it shall be no Crime in him (to run between them both). And as for him who voluntarily doeth a good Deed, verily Allah is Grateful and Omniscient!"**

At length we reached Marwah, a little rise like Safa in the lower slope of Abu Kubays. The houses cluster in amphitheatre shape high above it, and from the Masa'a street, a short flight of steps leads

---

* Here once stood "Asaf" and "Nailah," two idols, some say, a man and a woman metamorphosed for stupration in the temple.
** Koran, chap. 2.

to a platform, bounded on three sides like a tennis court, by tall walls without arches. The thoroughfare, seen from above, has a bowstring curve: it is between 800 and 900 feet long, with big houses on both sides, and small lanes branching off from it. At the foot of the platform we brought "right shoulders forward," so as to face the Ka'abah, and raising hands to ears, thrice exclaimed, "Allahu Akbar." This concluded the first course, and, of these, seven compose the ceremony El Sa'i, or the running.

There was a startling contrast with the origin of this ceremony—

> "When the poor outcast on the cheerless wild,
> Arabia's parent clasped her fainting child"—

as the Turkish infantry marched, in European dress, with sloped arms, down the Masa'a to relieve guard. By the side of the half-naked, running Bedawin, they looked as if Epochs, disconnected by long centuries, had met. A laxity, too, there was in the frequent appearance of dogs upon this holy and most memorial ground, which said little in favor of the religious strictness of the administration.*

Our Sa'i ended at Mount Marwah. There we dismounted, and sat outside a barber's shop, on the right-hand of the street. He operated upon our heads, causing us to repeat, "O Allah, this my Forelock is in Thy Hand, then grant me for every Hair a Light on

---

* The ceremony of running between Safa and Marwah is supposed to represent Hagar seeking water for her son. Usually pilgrims perform this rite on the morning of visiting the Ka'abah.

the Resurrection-day, O Most Merciful of the Mercifull!" This, and the paying for it, constituted the fourth portion of the Umrah, or Little Pilgrimage.

Throwing the skirts of our garments over our heads, to show that our "Ihram" was now exchanged for the normal state, "Ihlal," we cantered to the Haram, prayed there a two-bow prayer, and returned home not a little fatigued.

CHAPTER VIII.

Places of Pious Visitation at Meccah.

THE explorer has little work at the Holy City. With exceptions of Jebel Nur and Jebel Saur, all the places of pious visitation lie inside or close outside the city. It is well worth the while to ascend Abu Kubays; not so much to inspect the Makan el Hajar and the Shakk el Kamar,* as to obtain an excellent bird's-eye view of the Haram and the parts adjacent.

The boy Mohammed had applied himself sedulously to commerce after his return home; and had actually been seen by Shaykh Nur sitting in a shop and selling small curiosities. With my plenary consent I was made over to Abdullah, his brother. On the morning of the 15th Zu'l Hijjah (19th Sept.) he hired two asses, and accompanied me as guide to the holy places.

Mounting our animals, we followed the road be-

---

* The tradition of these places is related by every historian. The former is the repository of the Black Stone during the Deluge. The latter, "splitting of the moon," is the spot where the Prophet stood when, to convert the idolatrous Kuraysh, he caused half the orb of night to rise from behind Abu Kubays, and the other from Jebel Kayka'an, on the western horizon. This silly legend appears unknown to Mohammed's day.

fore described to the Jannat el Ma'ala, the sacred cemetery of Meccah. A rough wall, with a poor gateway, encloses a patch of barren and grim-looking ground, at the foot of the chain which bounds the city's western suburb and below El Akabah, the gap through which Khalid bin Walid entered Meccah with the triumphant Prophet.* Inside stand a few ignoble whitewashed domes: all are of modern construction, for here, as at El Bakia, further north, the Wahhabis indulged their levelling propensities. The rest of the ground shows some small enclosures belonging to particular houses—equivalent to our family vaults—and the ruins of humble tombs, lying in confusion, whilst a few parched aloes spring from between the bricks and stones.

This cemetery is celebrated in local history: here the body of Abdullah bin Zubayr was exposed by order of Hajjaj bin Yusuf; and the number of saints buried in it has been so numerous, that even in the twelfth century many had fallen into oblivion. It is visited by the citizens on Fridays, and by women on Thursdays, to prevent that meeting of sexes which in the East is so detrimental to public decorum. I shall be sparing in my description of the Ma'ala ceremonies, as the prayers, prostrations, and supplications are almost identical with those performed at El Baki'a.

After a long supplication, pronounced standing at

* This is the local tradition : it does not agree with authentic history.

the doorway, we entered, and sauntered about the burial-ground. On the left of the road stood an enclosure, which, according to Abdullah, belonged to his family. The door and stone slabs, being valuable to the poor, had been removed, and the graves of his forefathers appeared to have been invaded by the jackal. He sighed, recited a Fatihah with tears in his eyes, and hurried me away from the spot.

The first dome which we visited covered the remains of Abd el Rahman, the son of Abubekr, one of the Worthies of El Islam, equally respected by Sunni and Shiah. The tomb was a simple catafalque, covered with the usual cloth. After performing our devotions at this grave, and distributing a few piastres to guardians and beggars, we crossed the main path, and found ourselves at the door of the cupola, beneath which sleeps the venerable Khadijah, Mohammed's first wife. The tomb was covered with a green cloth, and the walls of the little building were decorated with written specimens of religious poetry. A little beyond it, we were shown into another dome, the resting-place of Sitt Aminah, the Prophet's mother. Burckhardt chronicles its ill usage by the fanatic Wahhabis: it has now been rebuilt in that frugal style which characterises the architecture of El Hejaz. An exceedingly garrulous old woman came to the door, invited us in, and superintended our devotions; at the end of which she sprinkled rosewater upon my face. When asked for a cool draught she handed me a metal saucer, whose contents smelt strongly of mastic, earnestly directing me to drink it in a sitting posture. This tomb she informed us is the property of a single woman, who visits it every evening, receives the contributions of the Faithful, prays, sweeps the pavement, and dusts the furniture. We left five piastres for this respectable maiden, and gratified the officious crone with another shilling. She repaid us by signalling to some score of beggars that a rich pilgrim had entered the Ma'ala, and their importunities fairly drove me out of the hallowed walls.

Leaving the Jannat el Ma'ala, we returned towards the town, and halted on the left side of the road, at a mean building called the Masjid el Jinn (of the Genii). Here was revealed the seventy-second chapter of the Koran, called after the name of the mysterious fire-drakes who paid fealty to the Prophet. Descending a flight of steps—for this mosque, like all ancient localities at Meccah, is as much below as above ground—we entered a small apartment containing water-pots for drinking and all the appurtenances of ablution. In it is shown the Mauza' el Khatt (place of the writing), where Mohammed wrote a letter to Abu Mas'ud after the homage of the Genii. A second and interior flight of stone steps led to another diminutive oratory where the Prophet used to pray and receive the archangel Gabriel. Having performed a pair of bows, which caused the perspiration to burst forth as if in a Russian bath, I paid a few piastres, and issued from the building with much satisfaction.

We had some difficulty in urging our donkeys through the crowded street, called the Zukak el Hajar. Presently we arrived at the Bayt el Naby, the Prophet's old house, in which he lived with the Sitt Khadijah. Here, says Burckhardt, the Lady Fatimah first saw the light; and here, according to Ibn Jubayr, Hasan and Husayn were born. Dismounting at the entrance we descended a deep flight of steps, and found ourselves in a spacious hall, vaulted, and of better appearance than most of the sacred edifices at Meccah. In the centre, and well railed round, stood a closet of rich green and gold stuffs, in shape not unlike an umbrella-tent. A surly porter guarded the closed door, which some respectable people vainly attempted to open by honeyed words: a whisper from Abdullah solved the difficulty. I was directed to lie at full length upon my stomach, and to kiss a black-looking stone—said to be the lower half of the Lady Fatimah's quern—fixed at the bottom of a basin of the same material. Thence we repaired to a corner, and recited a two-bow at the place where the Prophet used to pray the Sunnat and the Nafilah or supererogatory devotions.

Again remounting, we proceeded at a leisurely pace homewards, and on the way we passed through the principal slave-market. It is a large street roofed with matting, and full of coffee-houses. The merchandise sat in rows, parallel with the walls. The prettiest girls occupied the highest benches, below them were the plainer sort, and lowest of all the boys. They were all gaily dressed in pink and other light-coloured muslins, with transparent veils over their heads; and, whether from the effect of such unusual splendor, or from the reaction succeeding to their terrible land-journey and sea-voyage, they appeared perfectly happy, laughing loudly, talking unknown tongues, and quizzing purchasers, even during the delicate operation of purchasing. There were some pretty Gallas, douce-looking Abyssinians, and Africans of various degrees of hideousness, from the half-Arab Somal to the baboon-like Sawahili. The highest price of which I could hear was 60*l.*

. Passing through the large bazaar, called the Suk el Layl, I saw the palace of Mohammed bin Aun, quondam Prince of Meccah. It has a certain look of rude magnificence, the effect of huge hanging balconies scattered in profusion over lofty walls, *claire-voies* of brickwork, and courses of various-coloured stone. The owner is highly popular among the Bedawin, and feared by the citizens on account of his fierce looks, courage, and treachery. They described him to me as "vir bonus, bene strangulando peritus;" but Mr. Cole, who knew him personally, gave him a high character for generosity and freedom from fanaticism. He seems to have some idea of the state which should "hedge in" a ruler. His palaces at Meccah, and that now turned into a Wakalah at Jeddah, are the only places in the country that can be called princely. He is now a state prisoner at Constantinople, and the Bedawin pray for his return in vain.*

The other places of pious visitation at Meccah are briefly these:—

1. Natak el Naby, a small oratory in the Zukak el Hajar. It derives its name from the following circumstance. As the Prophet was knocking at the door of Abubekr's shop, a stone gave him God-speed, and told him that the master was not at home. This wonderful mineral is of a reddish-black colour, about a foot in dimension, and fixed in the wall somewhat higher than a man's head. There are servants attached to it, and the street sides are spread, as usual, with the napkins of importunate beggars.

2. Maulid el Naby, or the Prophet's birthplace.

---

* This prince was first invested with the Sherifat by Mohammed Ali of Egypt in A.D. 1827, when Yahya, after stabbing his nephew in the Ka'abah, fled to the Benû Harb Bedawin. He was supported by Ahmed Pasha of Meccah, with a large army; but after the battle of Tarabah, in which Ibrahim Pasha was worsted by the Bedawin, Mohammed bin Aun, accused of acting as Sylla, was sent in honourable bondage to Cairo. He again returned to Meccah, where the rapacity of his eldest son Abdullah, who would rob pilgrims, caused fresh misfortunes. In A.D. 1851, when Abd el Muttalib was appointed Sherif, the Pasha was ordered to send Bin Aun to Stamboul: no easy task. The Turk succeeded by a manœuvre. Mohammed's two sons, happening to be at Jeddah, were invited to inspect a man-of-war, and were there made prisoners. Upon this the father yielded himself up; although, it is said, the flashing of the Bedawi's sabre during his embarkation made the Turks rejoice that they had won the day by state-craft. The wild men of El Hejaz still sing songs in honour of this Sherif.

Note to Second Edition. Early in 1856, when the Sherif Abd el Muttalib was deposed, Mohammed bin Aun was sent from Constantinople to quiet the insurrection caused by the new slave laws in El Hejaz. In a short space of time he completely succeeded.

This is a little chapel in the Suk el Layl, not far from Mohammed bin Aun's palace. It is below the present level of the ground, and in the centre is a kind of tent, concealing, it is said, a hole in the floor upon which Aminah sat to be delivered.

3. In the quarter "Sha'ab Ali," near the Maulid el Naby, is the birthplace of Ali, another oratory below the ground. Here, as in the former place, a "Maulid" and a Ziyarah are held on the anniversary of the Lion's birth.

4. Near Khadijah's house and the Natak el Naby is a place called El Muttaka, from a stone against which the Prophet leaned when worn out with fatigue. It is much visited by devotees; and some declare that, on one occasion, when the Father of Lies appeared to the Prophet in the form of an elderly man and tempted him to sin by asserting that the mosque-prayers were over, this stone, disclosing the fraud, caused the Fiend to flee.

5. Maulid Hamzah, a little building at the old Bab Umrah, near the Shabayki cemetery. Here was the Bazan, or channel down which the Ayn Hunayn ran into the Birkat Majid. Many authorities doubt that Hamzah was born at this place.

The reader must now be as tired of "Pious Visitations" as I was.

Before leaving Meccah I was urgently invited to dine by old Ali bin Ya Sin, the Zem Zemi; a proof that he entertained inordinate expectations, excited, it appeared, by the boy Mohammed, for the simple purpose of exalting his own dignity. One day we were hurriedly summoned about 3 P.M. to the senior's house, a large building in the Zukak el Hajar. We found it full of pilgrims', amongst whom we had no trouble to recognise our fellow-travellers the quarrelsome old Arnaut and his impudent slave-boy. Ali met us upon the staircase and conducted us into an upper room, where we sat upon Divans and with pipes and coffee prepared for dinner. Presently the semicircle arose to receive a eunuch, who lodged somewhere in the house. He was a person of importance, being the guardian of some dames of high degree at Cairo or Constantinople: the first place and the best pipe were unhesitatingly offered to and accepted by him. He sat down with dignity, answered diplomatically certain mysterious questions about the ladies, and then applied his blubber lips to a handsome mouthpiece of lemon-coloured amber. It was a fair lesson of humility for a man to find himself ranked beneath this tall-shouldered, spindle-shanked, beardless bit of neutrality, and as such I took it duly to heart.

The dinner was served up in a "Sini," a plated copper tray about six feet in circumference, and handsomely ornamented with arabesques and inscriptions. Under this stood the usual Kursi, or stool, composed of mother-o'-pearl facets set in sandal wood; and upon it a well-tinned and clean-looking service of the same material as the Sini. We began with a variety of stews; stews with spinach, stews with Bamiyah (hibiscus), and rich vegetable stews. These being removed, we dipped hands in "Biryani," a meat pillaw, abounding in clarified butter; "Kimah," finely chopped meat; "Warak Mahshi," vine leaves filled with chopped and spiced mutton, and folded into small triangles; "Kabab," or bits of rôti spitted in mouthfuls upon a splinter of wood; together with a "Salatah" of the crispest cucumber, and various dishes of water-melon cut up into squares. Bread was represented by the eastern scone; but it was of superior flavour and far better than the ill-famed Chapati of India. Our drink was water perfumed with mastic. After the meat came a "Kunafah," fine vermicelli sweetened with honey and sprinkled with powdered white sugar; several stews of apples and quinces; "Muhallibah," a thin jelly made of rice, flour, milk, starch, and a little perfume; together with squares of Rahah,[*] a comfiture highly prized in these regions, because it comes from Constantinople. Fruits were then placed upon the table; plates full of pomegranate grains and dates of the finest flavour. The dinner concluded with a pillaw of boiled rice and butter; for the easier discussion of which we were provided with carved wooden spoons.

[*] Familiar for "Rahat el Hulkum"—the Pleasure of the Throat—a name which has sorely puzzled our tourists, and which has finally degenerated into "Ratlicoom." The sweetmeat would be pleasant did it not smell so strongly of the perruquier's shop. Rosewater tempts to many culinary sins in the East; and Europeans cannot dissociate it from the idea of a lotion. However, if a guest is to be honoured, rosewater must often take the place of the pure element, even in tea.

Arabs ignore the delightful French art of prolonging a dinner. After washing your hands, you sit down, throw an embroidered napkin over your knees, and with a "Bismillah," by way of grace, plunge your hand into the attractive dish, changing ad libitum, occasionally sucking your finger-tips as boys do lollipops, and varying that diversion by cramming a chosen morsel into a friend's mouth. When your hunger is satisfied you do not wait for your companions; you exclaim "Al Hamd!" edge away from the tray, wash your hands and mouth with soap, display signs of repletion otherwise you will be pressed to eat more, seize your pipe, sip your coffee, and take your "Kayf."

Nor is it customary, in these lands, to sit together after dinner—the evening prayer cuts short the séance. Before we arose to take leave of Ali bin Ya Sin a boy ran into the room, and displayed those infantine civilities which in the East are equivalent to begging for a present. I slipped a dollar into his hand; at the sight of which he, veritable little Meccan, could not contain his joy. "The Riyal!" he exclaimed; "the Riyal! look, grandpa', the good Effendi has given me a Riyal!" The old gentleman's eyes twinkled with emotion: he saw how easily the money had slipped from my fingers, and he fondly hoped that he had not seen the last piece. "Verily thou art a good young man!" he ejaculated, adding fervently, as prayers cost nothing, "May Allah further all thy desires." A gentle patting of the back evidenced high approval.

I never saw old Ali after that evening, but entrusted to the boy Mohammed what was considered a just equivalent for his services.

CHAPTER IX.

To Jeddah.

A GENERAL plunge into worldly pursuits and pleasures announced the end of the pilgrimage ceremonies. All the devotees were now "whitewashed"— the book of their sins was a tabula rasa: too many of them lost no time in making a new departure "down south," and in opening a fresh account.

The faith must not bear the blame of the irregularities. They may be equally observed in the Calvinist, after a Sunday of prayer, sinning through Monday with a zest, and the Romanist falling back with new fervour upon the causes of his confession and penance, as in the Moslem who washes his soul clean by running and circumambulation. And, in fairness, it must be observed, that as amongst Christians, so in the Moslem persuasion, there are many notable exceptions to this rule of extremes. Several of my friends and acquaintances date their reformation from their first sight of the Ka'abah.

The Moslem's "Holy Week" over, nothing detained me at Meccah. For reasons before stated, I resolved upon returning to Cairo, resting there for awhile, and starting a second time for the interior, viâ Muwaylah.

The Meccans are as fond of little presents as are nuns: the Kabirah took an affectionate leave of me, begged me to be careful of her boy, who was to accompany me to Jeddah, and laid friendly but firm hands upon a brass pestle and mortar, upon which she had long cast the eye of concupiscence.

Having hired two camels for thirty-five piastres, and paid half the sum in advance, I sent on my heavy boxes with Shaykh, now Haji Nur, to Jeddah. Umar Effendi was to wait at Meccah till his father had started, in command of the dromedary caravan, when he would privily take ass, join me at the port, and return to his beloved Cairo. I bade a long farewell to all my friends, embraced the Turkish pilgrims, and mounting our donkeys, the boy Mohammed and I left the house. Abdullah the Melancholy followed us on foot through the city, and took leave of me, though without embracing, at the Shabayki quarter.

Issuing into the open plain, I felt a thrill of pleasure —such joy as only the captive delivered from his dungeon can experience. The sunbeams warmed me into renewed life and vigour, the air of the Desert was a perfume, and the homely face of Nature was as the smile of a dear old friend. I contemplated the Syrian caravan, lying on the right of our road, without any of the sadness usually suggested by a parting look.

It is not my intention minutely to describe the line down which we travelled that night: the pages of Burckhardt give full information about the country. Leaving Meccah, we fell into the direct road running south of Wady Fatimah, and traversed for about an hour a flat surrounded by hills. Then we entered a valley by a flight of rough stone steps, dangerously slippery and zigzag, intended to facilitate the descent for camels and laden beasts. About midnight we passed into a hill-girt Wady, here covered with deep sands, there hard with gravelly clay; and, finally, about dawn, we sighted the maritime plain of Jeddah.

Shortly after leaving the city our party was joined by other travellers, and towards evening we found ourselves in force, the effect of an order that pilgrims must not proceed singly upon this road. Coffee-houses and places of refreshment abounding, we halted every five miles to refresh ourselves and the donkeys. At sunset we prayed near a Turkish guard-house, where one of the soldiers kindly supplied me with water for ablution.

Before nightfall I was accosted, in Turkish, by a one-eyed old fellow, who—

"With faded brow,
Entrenched with many a frown, and conic beard"—

and habited in unclean garments, was bestriding a donkey jaded as himself. When I shook my head, he addressed me in Persian. The same manœuvre made him try Arabic: still he obtained no answer. He then grumbled out good Hindostanee. That also failing, he tried successively Pushtu, Armenian, English, French, and Italian. At last I could "keep a stiff lip" no longer—at every change of dialect his emphasis beginning with "Then who the d—— are you?" became more emphatic. I turned upon him in Persian, and found that he had been a pilot, a courier, and a servant to eastern tourists, and that he had visited England, France, and Italy, the Cape, India, Central Asia, and China. We then chatted in English, which Haji Akif spoke well, but with all manner of courier's phrases; Haji Abdullah so badly, that he was counselled a course of study. It was not a little curious to hear such phrases as "Come 'p, Neddy," and "'Cré nom d'un baudet," almost within earshot of the tomb of Ishmael, the birthplace of Mohammed, and the Sanctuary of El Islam.

At about 8 P.M. we passed the Alamayn, which define the Sanctuary in this direction. They stand about nine miles from Meccah, and near them are a coffee-house and a little oratory, popularly known as the Sabil Agha Almas. On the road, as night advanced, we met long strings of camels, some carrying litters, others huge beams, and others bales of coffee, grain, and merchandise. Sleep began to weigh heavy upon my companions' eyelids, and the boy Mohammed hung over the flank of his donkey in a most ludicrous position.

About midnight we reached a mass of huts, called El·Haddah. Ali Bey places it eight leagues from Jeddah. At "the Boundary," which is considered to be the half-way halting place, Pilgrims must assume the religious garb, and Infidels travelling to Taif are taken off the Meccan road into one leading northwards to Arafat. The settlement is a collection of huts and hovels, built with sticks and reeds, supporting brushwood and burned and blackened palm leaves. It is maintained for supplying pilgrims with coffee and water. Travellers speak with horror of its heat during the day; Ali Bey, who visited it twice, compares it to a furnace. Here the country slopes gradually towards the sea, the hills draw off, and every object denotes departure from the Meccan plateau. At El Haddah we dismounted for an hour's halt. A coffee-house supplied us with mats, water-pipes, and other necessaries; we then produced a basket of provisions, the parting gift of the kind Kabirah, and, this late supper concluded, we lay down to doze.

After half an hour's halt had expired, and the donkeys were saddled, I shook up with difficulty the boy Mohammed, and induced him to mount. He was, to use his own expression, "dead from sleep;" and we had scarcely advanced an hour when, arriving at another little coffee-house, he threw himself upon the ground, and declared it impossible to proceed.

This caused some confusion. The donkey-boy was a pert little Bedawi, offensively republican in manner. He had several times addressed me impudently, ordering me not to flog his animal, nor to hammer its sides with my heels. On these occasions he received a contemptuous snub, which had the effect of silencing him. But now, thinking we were in his power, he swore that he would lead away the beasts, and leave us behind to be robbed and murdered. A pinch of the wind-pipe, and a spin over the ground, altered his plans at the outset of execution. He gnawed his hand with impotent rage, and went away, threatening us with the governor of Jeddah next morning.

Then an Egyptian of the party took up the thread of remonstrance; and, aided by the old linguist, who said, in English, "by G——! you must budge, you'll catch it here!" he assumed a brisk and energetic style, exclaiming, "Yallah! rise and mount, thou art only losing our time; thou dost not intend to sleep in the Desert!" I replied, "O my Uncle, do not exceed in speech!"—"Fuzul" (excess) in Arabic is equivalent to telling a man in English not to be impertinent—rolled over on the other side heavily, as doth Encelades, and pretended to snore, whilst the cowed Egyptian urged the others to make us move. The question was thus settled by the boy Mohammed, who had been aroused by the dispute: "Do you know," he whispered, in awful accents, "what *that* person is?" and he pointed at me. "Why, no," replied the others. "Well," said the youth, "the other day the Utaybah showed us death in the Zaribah Pass, and what do you think he did?" "Wallah! what do we know!" exclaimed the Egyptian, "What *did* he do?" "He called for — his dinner;" replied the youth, with a slow and sarcastic emphasis. That trait was enough. The others mounted and left us quietly to sleep.

I have been diffuse in relating this little adventure, which is characteristic, showing what bravado can do in Arabia. It also suggests a lesson, which every traveller in these regions should take well to heart. The people are always ready to terrify him with frightful stories, which are the merest phantoms of cowardice. The reason why the Egyptian displayed so much philanthropy was that, had one of the party been lost, the survivors might have fallen into trouble. But in this place, we were, I believe — despite the declarations of our companions that it was infested with Turpins and Fra Diavoli — as safe as if in Meccah. Every night, during the pilgrimage season, a troop of about fifty horsemen patrols the roads; we were all armed to the teeth, and our party looked too formidable to be "cruelly beaten by a single footpad."

Our nap concluded, we remounted and resumed the weary way down a sandy valley, in which the poor donkeys sank fetlock-deep. At dawn we found our companions halted, and praying at the Kahwat Turki, another little coffee-house. Here an exchange of what is popularly called "chaff" took place. "Well," cried the Egyptian, "what have ye gained by halting? We have been quiet here, praying and smoking for the last hour!" "Go, eat thy buried beans!" we replied; "What does an Egyptian boor know of manliness?" The surly donkey-boy was worked up into a paroxysm of passion by such small jokes as telling him to convey our salams to the Governor of Jeddah, and by calling the asses after the name of his tribe. He replied by "foul, unmannered, scurril taunts," which only drew forth fresh derision, and the coffee-house keeper laughed consumedly, having probably seldom entertained such "funny gentlemen."

Shortly after leaving the Kahwat Turki we crossed the westernmost ridge-spur that sinks into the Jeddah Plain. This view would for some time be my last of—

"Infamous hills, and sandy, perilous wilds;"

and I contemplated it with the pleasure of one escaping from it. Before us lay the usual iron flat of these regions, whitish with salt, and tawny with stones and gravel; but relieved and beautified by the distant white walls, whose canopy was the lovely blue sea. Not a tree, not a patch of verdure was in sight; nothing distracted our attention from the sheet of turquoises in the distance. Merrily the little donkeys hobbled on, in spite of their fatigue. Soon we distinguished the features of the town, the minarets, the fortifications—so celebrated since their honeycombed guns beat off in 1817 the thousands of Abdullah bin Sa'ud, the Wahhabi—and a small dome outside the walls.

The sun began to glow fiercely, and we were not sorry when, at about 8 A.M., after passing through the mass of hovels and coffee-houses, cemeteries and sand hills, which forms the eastern approach to Jeddah, we entered the fortified Bab Makkah. Allowing eleven hours for our actual march—we halted about three—those wonderful donkeys had accomplished between forty-four and forty-six miles, generally of deep sand, in one night. And they passed the archway of Jeddah almost as nimbly as when they left Meccah.

Shaykh Nur had been ordered to take rooms for me in a vast pile of madrepore, unfossilized coral, a recent formation, once the palace of Mohammed bin Aun, and now converted into a Wakalah. Instead of so doing, Indian-like, he had made a gipsy encampment in the square opening upon the harbour. After administering the requisite correction, I found a room that would suit me. In less than an hour it was swept, sprinkled with water, spread with mats, and made as comfortable as its capability admitted. At Jeddah I felt once more at home. The sight of the sea acted as a tonic. The Maharattas were not far wrong when they kept their English captives out of reach of the ocean, declaring that we are an amphibious race, to whom the wave is a home.

After a day's repose at the Caravanserai, the camel-man and donkey-boy clamouring for money, and I not having more than tenpence of borrowed coin, it was necessary to cash at the British vice-consulate a draft given to me by the Royal Geographical Society. With some trouble I saw Mr. Cole, who, suffering from fever, was declared to be "not at home." His dragoman did by no means admire my looks; in fact, the general voice of the household was against me. After some fruitless messages, I sent up an imploring scrawl to Mr. Cole, who decided upon admitting the importunate Afghan.

An exclamation of astonishment and a hospitable welcome followed my self-introduction as an officer of the Indian army. Amongst other things, the vice-consul informed me that, in divers discussions with the Turks about the possibility of an Englishman finding his way en cachette to Meccah, he had asserted that his compatriots could do everything, even pilgrim to the Holy City. The Moslems politely assented to the first, but denied the second part of the proposition. Mr. Cole promised himself a laugh at the Turks' beards; but, since my departure, he wrote to me that the subject made the owners look so serious, that he did not like recurring to it.

Truly gratifying to the pride of an Englishman was our high official position assumed and maintained at Jeddah. Mr. Cole had never, like his colleague at Cairo, lowered himself in the estimation of the proud race with which he has to deal, by private or mercantile transactions with the authorities. He has steadily withstood the wrath of the Meccan Sherif, and taught him to respect the British name. The Abbé Hamilton ascribed the attentions of the Prince to "the infinite respect which the Arabs entertain for Mr. Cole's straightforward way of doing business—it was a delicate flattery addressed to him." And the writer was right: honesty of purpose is never thrown away amongst these people. The general contrast between our consular proceedings at Cairo and Jeddah is another proof of the advisability of selecting Indian officials to fill offices of trust at Oriental courts. They have lived amongst Easterns, they must know one Asiatic language, with many Asiatic customs, and, chief merit of all, they have learned to assume the tone of command, without which, whatever may be thought of it in England, it is impossible to take the lead in the East. The "home-bred" diplomate is not only unconscious of the thousand traps everywhere laid for him, he even plays into the hands of his crafty antagonists by a ceremonious politeness; which they interpret—taking ample care that the interpretation should spread—to be the effect of fear or fraud.

Jeddah has been often described by modern pens. Burckhardt (in A.D. 1814) devoted 100 pages of his two volumes to the unhappy capital of the Tehamet el Hejaz, the lowlands of the mountain region. Later still, MM. Mari and Chedufau wrote upon the subject, and two other French travellers, MM. Galinier and Ferret, published tables of the commerce in its present state, quoting as authority the celebrated Arabicist M. Fresnel. These have been translated by the author of "Life in Abyssinia." Abdulkerim, writing in 1742, informs us that the French had a factory at Jeddah; and in 1760, when Bruce revisited the port, he found the East India Company in possession of a post, whence they dispersed their merchandise over the adjoining regions. But though the English were at an early epoch of their appearance in the East received here with especial favour, I failed to procure a single ancient document.

Jeddah, when I visited it, was in a state of commotion, owing to the perpetual passage of pilgrims, and provisions were for the same reason scarce and dear. The two large Wakalahs, of which the place boasts, were crowded with travellers, and many were reduced to encamping upon the squares. Another subject of confusion was the state of the soldiery. The Nizam, or Regulars, had not been paid for seven months, and the Arnauts could scarcely sum up what was owing to them. Easterns are wonderfully amenable to discipline; a European army, under the circumstances, would probably have helped itself. But the Pasha knew that there is a limit to man's endurance, and he was anxiously casting about for some contrivance that would replenish the empty pouches of his troops. The worried dignitary must have sighed for those beaux jours when privily firing the town and allowing the soldiers to plunder, was the Oriental style of settling arrears of pay.

Jeddah displays all the licence of a seaport and garrison town. Fair Corinthians establish themselves even within earshot of the Karakun, or guard-post; a symptom of excessive laxity in the authorities, for it is the duty of the watch to visit all such irregularities with a bastinado preparatory to confinement. My guardians and attendants at the Wakalah used to fetch Raki in a clear glass bottle, without even the decency of a cloth, and the messenger twice returned from these errands decidedly drunk. More extraordinary still, the people seemed to take no notice of the scandal.

The little "Dwarka" had been sent by the Bombay Steam Navigation Company to convey pilgrims from El Hejaz to India. I was still hesitating about my next voyage, not wishing to coast the Red Sea at this season without a companion, when one morning Umar Effendi appeared at the door, weary, and dragging after him an ass more weary than himself. We supplied him with a pipe and a cup of hot tea, and, as he was fearful of pursuit, we showed him a dark hole full of grass under which he might sleep concealed.

The student's fears were realised; his father appeared early the next morning, and having ascertained from the porter that the fugitive was in the house, politely called upon me. Whilst he plied all manner of questions, his black slave furtively stared at everything in and about the room. But we had found time to cover the runaway with grass, and the old gentleman departed, after a fruitless search. There was, however, a grim smile about his mouth, which boded no good.

That evening returning home from the Hammam I found the house in an uproar. The boy Mohammed, who had been miserably mauled, was furious with rage, and Shaykh Nur was equally unmanageable, by reason of his fear. In my absence the father had returned with a posse comitatus of friends and relatives. They questioned the youth, who delivered himself of many circumstantial and emphatic mis-statements. Then they proceeded to open the boxes; upon which the boy Mohammed cast himself sprawling, with a vow to die rather than to endure such a disgrace. This procured for him some scattered slaps, which presently became a storm of blows, when a prying little boy discovered Umar Effendi's leg in the hiding-place. The student was led away unresisting, but mildly swearing that he would allow no opportunity of escape to pass. I examined the boy Mohammed, and was pleased to find that he was not seriously hurt. To pacify his mind, I offered to sally out with him, and to rescue Umar Effendi by main force. This, which would only have brought us all into a brunt with quarter-staves, and similar servile weapons, was declined, as had been foreseen. But the youth recovered complacency, and a few well-merited encomiums upon his "pluck" restored him to high spirits.

The reader must not fancy such escapade to be a serious thing in Arabia. The father did not punish his son; he merely bargained with him to return home for a few days before starting to Egypt. This the young man did, and shortly afterwards I met him unexpectedly in the streets of Cairo.

Deprived of my companion, I resolved to waste no time in the Red Sea, but to return to Egypt with the utmost expedition. The boy Mohammed having laid in a large store of grain, purchased with my money, having secured all my disposable articles, and having hinted that, after my return to India, a present of twenty dollars would find him at Meccah, asked leave, and departed with a coolness for which I could not account. Some days afterwards Shaykh Nur explained the cause. I had taken the youth with me on board the steamer, where a bad suspicion crossed his mind.

"Now, I understand," said the boy Mohammed to his fellow-servant, "your master is a Sahib from India; he hath laughed at our beards." He parted as coolly from Shaykh Nur. These worthy youths had been drinking together, when Mohammed, having learned at Stambul the fashionable practice of "Bad-masti," or "liquor-vice," dug his "fives" into Nur's eye. Nur erroneously considering such exercise likely to induce blindness, complained to me; but my sympathy was all with the other side. I asked the Hindi why he had not returned the compliment, and the Meccan once more overwhelmed the "Miyan" with taunt and jibe.

It is not easy to pass the time at Jeddah. In the square opposite us was an unhappy idiot, who afforded us a melancholy spectacle. He delighted to wander about in a primitive state of toilette, as all such wretches do; but the people of Jeddah, far too civilised to retain Moslem respect for madness, forced him, despite shrieks and struggles, into a shirt, and when he tore it off they beat him. At other times the open space before us was diversified by the arrival and the departure of pilgrims, but it was a mere réchauffé of the feast, and had lost all power to please. Whilst the boy Mohammed remained he used to pass the time in wrangling with some Indians, who were living next door to us, men, women, and children, in a promiscuous way. After his departure I used to spend my days at the vice-consulate; the proceeding was not perhaps of the safest, but the temptation of meeting a fellow-countryman, and of chatting "shop" about the service, was too great to be resisted. I met there the principal merchants of Jeddah; Khwajah Sower, a Greek; M. Anton, a Christian from Baghdad, and others.* And I was introduced to Khalid Bey, brother of Abdullàh bin Saud, *the* Wahhabi. This noble Arab once held the official position of Mukayyid el Jawabat, or Secretary, at Cairo, where he was brought up by Mohammed Ali. He is brave, frank, and unprejudiced, fond of Europeans, and a lover of pleasure. Should it be his fate to become chief of the tribe, a journey to Central Arabia, will offer no difficulties to our travellers.

I now proceed to the last of my visitations. Outside the town of Jeddah lies no less a personage than Sittna Hawwa, the Mother of mankind. The boy Mohammed and I, mounting asses one evening, issued through the Meccan gate, and turned towards the north-east over a sandy plain. After half an hour's ride, amongst dirty huts and tattered coffee-hovels, we reached the enceinte, and found the door closed. Presently a man came running with might from the town; he was followed by two others; and it struck me at the time that they applied the key with peculiar empressement, and made inordinately low congées as we entered the enclosure of whitewashed walls.

* Many fell victims to the "Jeddah Massacre" in June 30, 1858. I must refer the reader to "Lake Regions of Central Africa" (Appendix, vol. II.) for an account of this event, for the proposals which I made to ward it off, and for the miserable folly of the "Bombay Government" who rewarded me by an official reprimand and with bad offices whose effects still endure (1874).

The "Mother" is supposed to lie, like a Moslemah, fronting the Ka'abah, with her feet northwards, her head southwards, and her right cheek propped by her right hand. Whitewashed, and conspicuous to the voyager and traveller from afar, is a diminutive dome with an opening to the west; it is furnished as such places usually are in El Hejaz. Under it and in the centre is a square stone, planted upright and fancifully carved, to represent the omphalic region of the human frame. This, as well as the dome, is called El Surrah, or the navel. The cicerone directed me to kiss this manner of hieroglyph, which I did, thinking the while that, under the circumstances, the salutation was quite uncalled for. Having prayed here, and at the head, where a few young trees grow, we walked along the side of the two parallel dwarf walls which define the outlines of the body: they are about six paces apart, and between them, upon Eve's neck, are two tombs, occupied, I was told, by Usman Pasha and his son, who repaired the Mother's sepulchre. I could not help remarking to the boy Mohammed, that if our first parent measured 120 paces from head to waist, and 80 from waist to heel, she must have presented much the appearance of a duck. To this the youth replied, flippantly, that he thanked his stars the Mother was under ground, otherwise that men would lose their senses with fright.

Ibn Jubayr (twelfth century) mentions only an old dome "built upon the place where Eve stopped on the way to Meccah." Yet El Idrisi (A.D. 1154) declares Eve's grave to be at Jeddah. Abdelkarim (1742) compares it to a parterre, with a little dome in the centre, and the extremities ending in barriers of palisades; the circumference was 190 of his steps. In Rooke's Travels we are told that the tomb is 20 feet long. Ali Bey, who twice visited Jeddah, makes no allusion to it; we may therefore conclude that it had been destroyed by the Wahhabis. Burckhardt, who, I need scarcely say, has been carefully copied by our popular authors, was informed that 'it was a "rude structure of stone, about four feet in length, two or three feet in height, and as many in breadth;" thus resembling the tomb of Noah, seen in the valley of El Buka'a in Syria. Bruce writes: "Two days' journey east from this place (Meccah or Jeddah?) Eve's grave, of *green sods*, about 50 yards in length, is shown to this day;" but the great traveller probably never issued from the town-gates. And Sir W. Harris, who could not have visited the holy place, repeats, in 1840, that "Eve's grave of *green sod* is still shown on the barren shore of the Red Sea." The present structure is clearly modern; anciently, I was told at Jeddah, the sepulchre consisted of a stone at the head, a second at the feet, and the navel-dome.

The idol of Jeddah, in the days of Arab litholatry, was called "Sakhrah Tawilah," the Long Stone. May not this stone of Eve be the Moslemized revival of the old litholatry? It is to be observed that the Arabs, if the tombs be admitted as evidence, are inconsistent in their dimensions of the patriarchal stature. The sepulchre of Adam at the Masjid el Khayf is, like that of Eve, gigantic. That of Noah at El Buka'a measures 104 feet 10' by 8 feet 8'. Job's tomb near Hulah (seven parasangs from Kerbela) is small. The grave of Moses (south-east of the Red Sea), which is known by the bitumen cups there sold to pilgrims, is about 13 feet long; and Aaron's sepulchre in the Sinaitic peninsula is of moderate dimensions.

On leaving the graveyard I offered the guardian a dollar, which he received with a remonstrance, that a man of my dignity should give so paltry a fee. Nor was he at all contented with the assurance that nothing more could be expected from an Afghan Dervish, however pious. Next day the boy Mohammed explained the man's empressement and disappointment—I had been mistaken for the Pasha of El Medinah.

* * * * * *

For a time my peregrinations ended. Worn out with fatigue, and the fatal fiery heat, I embarked (Sept. 26) on board the "Dwarka," experienced the greatest kindness from the commander and chief officer (Messrs. Wolley and Taylor), and, wondering the while how the Turkish pilgrims who crowded the vessel did not take the trouble to throw me overboard, in due time I arrived at Suez.

And here, reader, we part. Bear with me while I conclude, in the words of a brother traveller, long gone, but not forgotten—Fa-hian—this Personal Narrative of my Journey to El Hejaz: "I have been exposed to perils, and I have escaped from them; I have traversed the sea, and have not succumbed under the severest fatigues; and my heart is moved with emotions of gratitude, that I have been permitted to effect the objects I had in view."*

* The curious reader will find details concerning Patriarchal and Prophetical tombs in "Unexplored Syria," L. 33—35.

REMARKS ON THE MAP.

BY

A. SPRENGER.

REMARKS ON THE MAP.
BY
A. SPRENGER.

In the map to the former edition* of the Pilgrimage, Captain Burton's route from Madîna to Meccah is wrongly laid down, owing to a typographical error of the text; it bears vol. II. p. 150, last line (corresponding to vol. II. p. 294 of this edition): "From Wady Laymun to Meccah S.E. 45°;" whereas the road runs S.W. 45° or, as Hamdâny expresses himself in the commentary on the Qaçyda Rod., "Between West and South; and therefore the setting sun shines at the evening prayer (your face being turned towards Meccah) on your right temple." The account of the *eastern* route from Madîna to Meccah by so experienced a traveller as Captain Burton is an important contribution to our geographical knowledge of Arabia. It leads over the lower terrace of Nejd, the country which Muslim writers consider as the home of the genuine Arabs and the scene of Arabic chivalry. As by this mistake the results of my friend's pilgrimage, which, though pious as he unquestionably is, he did not undertake from purely religious motives,

* London, 1857.

have been in a great measure marred, I called in 1871 his attention to it. At the same time I submitted to him a sketch of a map in which his own and Burckhardt's routes are protracted, and a few notes culled from Arabic geographers, with the intention of showing how much light his investigations throw on early geography if illustrated by a corrected map; and how they fail to fulfil this object if the mistake is not cleared up. The enterprising traveller approved of both the notes and the map, and expressed it as his opinion, that it might be useful to append them to the new edition. I therefore thought proper to recast them, and to present them herewith to the reader.

At Sufayna Burton found the Baghdâd Caravan. The regular Baghdâd-Meccah Road, of which we have two itineraries, the one reproduced by Hamdâny and the other by Ibn Khordâdbeh, Qodâma and others, keeps to the left of Sufayna, and runs parallel with the Eastern Madînah-Meccah Road to within one stage of Meccah. We find only one passage in Arabic geographers from which we learn that the Baghdâdlies, as long as a thousand years ago, used under certain circumstances to take the way of Sufayna. Yâcût, vol. III. p. 403, says: "Sufayna (صفينة Çufayna), a place in the 'Âliya (Highland) within the territory of the Solaymites, lies on the road of Zobayda. The pilgrims make a roundabout, and take this road, if they suffer from want of water. The pass of Sufayna by which they have to descend is very difficult." The ridges over which the road leads are called al-Sitâr, and are described by Yâcût, vol. III. p. 38, as a range of *red* hills, flanking Sufayna, with defiles which serve as passes. Burton, vol. II. p. 268, describes them as low hills of *red* sandstone and bright porphyry. Zobayda, whose name the partly improved, partly newly opened Hajj-Road from Baghdâd to Meccah bore, was the wife of the Caliph Harun, and it appears from Burton, pp. 274 and 276, that the improvements made by this spirited woman—as the wells near Ghadîr, and the Birkat (Tank)—are now ascribed to her weak, fantastical and contemptible husband.

Burton's description of the plain covered with huge boulders and detached rocks (p. 271) puts us in mind of the Felsenmeer in the Odenwald. Yâcût, vol. III. p. 370, describes the two most gigantic of these rock-pillars, which are too far to the left of Burton's road than that he could have seen them: "Below Sufayna in a desert plain there rise two pillars so high that nobody, unless he be a bird, can mount them; the one is called ʿAmûd (column) of al-Bân, after the place al-Bân, and the other ʿAmûd of al-Safh. They are both on the right-hand side of the (regular) road from Baghdâd to Meccah, one mile from Ofayʿiya (a station on the regular road which answers to Sufayna)." Such desolate, fantastic scenery is not rare in Arabia nor close to the western coast of the Red Sea. The Fiumara, from which Burton (p. 278) emerged at 6 A.M., Sept. 9, was crossed by Burckhardt at Kholayç, and is a more important feature of the country than the two travellers were aware of. There are only five or six

Wâdies which break through the chain of mountains that runs parallel with the Red Sea, and of these, proceeding from South to North, Wâdy Nakhla (Wâdy Laymûn) is the first, and this Fiumara the second. Early geographers call it Wâdy Amaj, or after a place of some importance situated in its lower course, Wâdy Sâya. Hamdâny, p. 294, says: "Amaj and Ghorân are two Wâdies which commence in the Ḥarra (volcanic region) of the Benî Solaym and reach the sea." The descriptions of this Wâdy compiled by Yâcût, vol. III. pp. 26 and 839, are more ample. According to one it contains seventy springs; according to another it is a Wâdy which you overlook if you stand on the Sharât (the mountain now called Jebel Çobḥ). In its upper course it runs between the two Ḥâmiya, which is the name of two black volcanic regions. It contains several villages of note, and there lead roads to it from various parts of the country. In its uppermost part lies the village of Fâri‘ with date-groves, cultivated fields and gardens, producing plantains, pomegranates and grapes, and in its lower course close to Sâya, the rich and populous village Mahâya. The whole Wâdy is one of the A‘râdh (oasis-like districts) of Madîna, and is administered by a Lieutenant of the Governor of that city. Yâcût makes the remark to this description: "I do not know whether this valley is still in the same condition, or whether it has altered." Though we know much less of it than Yâcût, we may safely assert that the cultivation has vanished and the condition has altered.

REMARKS ON THE MAP. 167

At Zariba (ضريبة, Dhariba) Burton and his party put on the Ihrâm (pilgrim-garb). If the Baghdâdlies follow the regular road they perform this ceremony at Dzât-'Irq, which lies somewhat lower down than Dharîba, to the S.E. of it, and therefore the rain-water, which falls in Dharîba, flows in the shape of a torrent to Dzât-'Irq, and is thence carried off by the Northern Nakhla. Above the station of Dzât-'Irq there rise ridges called 'Irq; up these ridges the regular Baghdâd Road ascends to the high-plateau, and they are therefore considered by early geographers as the western limit of Nejd. 'Omâra *apud* Yâcût, vol. IV. p. 746, says: "All the country in which the water flows in an easterly (north-easterly) direction, beginning from Dzât-'Irq as far as Babylonia, is called Nejd; and the country which slopes westwards, from Dzât-'Irq to Tihâma (the coast), is called Ḥijâz." The remarks of Arabic geographers on the western watershed, and those of Burton, vol. II. pp. 282 and 292, illustrate and complete each other most satisfactorily. It appears from Yâcût that the Fiumara in which Burton's party was attacked by robbers takes its rise at Ghomayr close to Dzât-'Irq, that there were numerous date-groves in it, and that it falls at Bostân Ibn 'Âmir into the Nakhla, wherefore it is called the *Northern* Nakhla. The Southern Nakhla, also called simply Nakhla, a term which is sometimes reserved for the trunk formed by the junction of the Southern and Northern Nakhla from Bostân Ibn 'Âmir downwards, is on account of its history one of the most interesting spots in all Arabia; I therefore make no apology for entering on its geography. In our days it is called Wâdy Laymûn, and Burckhardt, vol. I. p. 158, says of it: "Zeyme is a half-ruined castle, at the eastern extremity of Wady Lymoun, with copious springs of running water. Wady Lymoun is a fertile valley, which extends for several hours (towards West) in the direction of Wady Faṭmé (anciently called Baṭn Marr or Marr-Tzahrân, which is in fact a continuation of Wady Nakhla). It has many date-plantations, and formerly the ground was cultivated; but this, I believe, has ceased since the Wahabi invasion: its fruit-gardens, too, have been ruined. This (he means the village Laymun, compare Burton, vol. II. p. 287) is the last stage of the Eastern-Syrian Hadj Route. To the S.E. or E.S.E. of Wady Lymoun is another fertile valley, called Wady Medyk, where some sherifs are settled, and where Sherif Ghaleb possessed landed property."* In the commentary on the Qaçyda Rod.

* Medyk is Burton's El Mazik, the spelling in Arabic being مَضْيِق, Madhyq. Burckhardt's account leads us to think that the village now called Madhyq or Wady Laymûn lies on the left bank of the Fiumara, and is identical with Bostân Ibn 'Amir, which is described by Yâcût as situated in the fork between the Northern and Southern Nakhlas, and which in ancient times had, like the village Wady Laymûn, the name of the valley of which it was the chief place, viz. Baṭn Nakhla. Burton gives no information of the position of the village, but he says: "On the *right* bank of the Fiumara stood the Meccan Sherif's state pavilion." Unless the pavilion is separated from the village by the Fiumara, there is a discrepancy between the two accounts, which leads me to suspect that "right" is an oversight for "left."

Anciently نَخْلَة was pronounced Nakhlat, and, if we suppress the guttural, as the Greeks and Romans sometimes did, Nalat. Strabo, p. 782, in his narrative of the retreat of Aelius Gallus mentions a place which he calls Malôtha, and of which he says it stood on the bank of a river—a position which few

Wády Nakhla, as far as the road to Meccah runs through it, is described as follows: From the ridges with whose declivity the western watershed begins, you descend into Wady Baubât; it is flanked on the left side by the Sarât mountains on which Ṭâyif stands, and contains Qarn-almanâzil (once the capital of the Minaeans, the great trading nation of antiquity). Three or four miles below Qarn is Masjid Ibrâhym, and here the valley assumes the name of Wady Nakhla. At no great distance from the Masjid there rise on the left hand side of the Wady two high peaks called Jebel Yasûm and Jebel Kafw. Both were the refuge of numerous monkeys, who used to invade the neighbouring vineyards. As you go down Wady Nakhla the first place of importance you meet is al-Zayma. Close to it was a garden which, during the reign of Moqtadir, belonged to the Hâshimite Prince 'Abd Allah, and was in a most flourishing condition. It produced an abundance of henna, plantains and vegetables of every description, and yielded a revenue of five thousand Dinâr-mithqâls (about £2,860) annually. A canal from Wady (the river) Nakhla feeds a fountain which jets forth in the midst of the garden, and lower down a tank. In the garden stood a fort (which in a dilapidated condition is extant to this day, and spoken of by Burckhardt). It was built of huge stones, guarded for the defence of the property by the Banû Sa'd, and tenanted by the servants and

towns in Arabia have. The context leaves no doubt that he means Baṭn Nakhla, and that Malôtha is a mistake for Najôtha.

followers of the proprietor. Below al-Zayma is Sabûha, a post-station where a relay of horses was kept for the transport of Government Despatches. To give an idea of the distances, I may mention that the post-stages were 12 Arabic miles asunder, which on this road are rather larger than an English geographical mile. The first station from Meccah was Moshâsh, the second Sabuha, and the third was at the foot of the hill Yâsûm. The author of the commentary from which I derive this information leaves Wâdy Nakhla soon after Sabûha, and turns his steps towards the holy city. He mentions "the steep rocky Pass" up which Burton toiled with difficulty, and calls it Orayk. Though he enters into many details he takes no notice of the hill-girt plain called Sôla. This name occurs however in an Arabic verse, *apud* Yâcût, vol. II. p. 968: "In summer our pasture grounds are in the country of Nakhla, within the districts of al-Zayma and Sôla."

In Wâdy Fâtima Burckhardt found a perennial rivulet, coming from the eastward, about three feet broad and two feet deep. It is certain that Wâdy Fâtima, formerly called Wâdy Marr, is a continuation of Wâdy Nakhla, and Yâcût considers in one passage Nakhla as a subdivision of Marr, and in another Marr as part of Wâdy Nakhla; but we do not know whether the rivulet which at al-Zayma seems to be of considerable size, disappears under the sand in order to come forth again in Wâdy Marr, or whether it forms an uninterrupted stream. In ancient times the regular

Baghdâd-Meccah Road did not run down from Dzât-'Irq by the Northern Nakhla which Burton followed, but it crossed this Wâdy near its northern end and struck over to the Southern Nakhla as far as Qarn al-marâzil, which for a long time was the second station from Meccah, instead of Dzât-'Irq.

THE MECCA PILGRIMAGE.

THE MECCA PILGRIMAGE.

HAVING resolved to perform the Mecca pilgrimage, I spent a few months at Cairo, and on the 22nd of May embarked in a small steamer at Suez with the "mahmil" or litter, and its military escort, conveying the "kiswah" or covering for the "kábah." On the 25th the man at the wheel informed us that we were about to pass the village of Rábikh, on the Arabian coast, and that the time had consequently arrived for changing our usual habiliments for the "ihram," or pilgrim-costume of two towels, and for taking the various interdictory vows involved in its assumption: such as not to tie knots in any portion of our dress, not to oil the body, and not to cut our nails or hair, nor to improve the tints of the latter with the coppery red of henna. Transgression of these and other ceremonial enactments is expiated either by animal sacrifice, or gifts of fruit or cereals to the poor.

After a complete ablution and assuming the ihram, we performed two prayer-flections, and recited the meritorious sentences beginning with the words "Labbaik Allah huma labbaik!" "Here I am, O God, here I am! Here I am, O Unassociated One, here I am, for unto Thee belong praise, grace, and empire, O Unassociated One!"

This prayer was repeated so often, people not unfrequently rushing up to their friends and shrieking the sacred sentence into their ears, that at last it became a signal for merriment rather than an indication of piety.

On the 26th we reached Jeddah, where the utter sterility of Arabia, with its dunes and rocky hills, becomes apparent. The town, however, viewed from the sea, is not unpicturesque. Many European vessels were at anchor off the coast, and as we entered the port, innumerable small fishing-boats darting in all directions, their sails no longer white, but emerald green from the intense lustre of the water, crowded around us on all sides, and reminded one by their dazzling colours and rapidity of motion of the shoals of porpoises so often seen on a voyage round the Cape.

On disembarking we were accosted by several "mutawwafs," or circuit-men, so termed in Arabic, because, besides serving as religious guides in general, their special duty is to lead the pilgrim in his seven obligatory circuits around the Kābah. We encamped outside the town, and, having visited the tomb of "our Mother Eve," mounted our camels for Mecca.

After a journey of twenty hours across the Desert, we passed the barriers which mark the outermost limits of the sacred city, and, ascending some giant steps, pitched our tents on a plain, or rather plateau, surrounded by barren rock, some of which, distant but a few yards, mask from view the birthplace of the Prophet. It was midnight; a few drops of rain were falling, and lightning played around us. Day after day we had watched its brightness from the sea, and many a faithful ḥāji had pointed out to his companions those fires which were Heaven's witness to the sanctity of the spot. "Al ḥamdu Lillah!" Thanks be to God! we were now at length to gaze upon the "Kiblah," to which every Mussulman has turned in prayer since the days of Muhammad, and which for long ages before the birth of Christianity was reverenced by the Patriarchs of the East. Soon after dawn arose from our midst the shout of "Labbaik! Labbajk!" and, passing between the rocks, we found ourselves in the main street of Mecca, and approached the "Gateway of Salvation," one of the thirty-nine portals of the Temple of Al-Haram.

On crossing the threshold we entered a vast unroofed quadrangle, a mighty amplification of the Palais Royal, having on each of its four sides a broad colonnade, divided into three aisles by a multitude of slender columns and rising to the height of about thirty feet. Surmounting each arch of the colonnade is a small dome: in all there are 120, and at different points arise seven minarets, dating from various epochs, and of somewhat varying altitudes and architecture. The numerous pigeons which have their home within the temple have been believed never to alight upon any portion of its roof, thus miraculously testifying to the holiness of the building. This marvel having however of late years been suspended, many discern another omen of the approach of the long predicted period when unbelievers shall desecrate the hallowed soil.

In the centre of the square area rises the far-famed Kabah, the funereal shade of which contrasts vividly with the sun-lit walls and precipices of the town. It is a cubical structure of massive stone, the upper two-thirds of which are mantled by a black cloth embroidered with silver, and the lower portion hung with white linen. At a distance of several yards it is surrounded by a balustrade provided with lamps, which are lighted in the evening, and the space thus enclosed is the circuit-ground along which, day and night, crowds of pilgrims, performing the circular ceremony of Tawāf, realize the idea of perpetual motion. We at once advanced to the black stone imbedded in an angle of the Kabah, kissed it, and exclaimed, "Bismillah wa Allahu Akbar"—"In God's name, and God is greatest." Then we commenced the usual seven rounds, three at a walking pace, and four at a brisk trot. Next followed two prayer-flections at the tomb of Abraham, after which we drank of the water of Zamzam, said to be the same which quenched the thirst of Hagar's exhausted son.

Besides the Kabah, eight minor structures adorn the quadrangle, the well of Zamzam, the library, the clock-room, the triangular staircase, and four ornamental resting-places for the orthodox sects of Hanafī, Shāfī, Malikī and Hanbalī.

We terminated our morning duties by walking and running seven times along the streets of Safa and Marwa, so named from the flight of seven steps at each of its extremities.

After a few days spent in visiting various places of interest, such as the slave market and forts, and the houses of the Prophet and the Caliphs 'Ali and Abubakr, we started on our six hours' journey to the mountain of 'Arifāt, an hour's sojourn at which, even in a state of insensibility, confers the rank of ḥaji. It is a mountain spur of about 150 feet in height, presenting an artificial appearance from the wall encircling it and the terrace on its slope, from which the imān delievers a sermon before the departure of his congregation for Mecca. His auditors were, indeed, numerous, their tents being scattered over two or three miles of the country. A great number of their inmates were fellow-subjects of ours from India. I surprised some of my Mecca friends by informing them that Queen Victoria numbers nearly 20,000,000 of Mohammedans among her subjects.

On the 5th of June, at sunset, commencing our return, we slept at the village of Muzdalifah, and there gathered and washed seven pebbles of the size of peas, to be flung at three piles of whitewashed masonry known as the Shaitans (satans) of Munā. We acquitted ourselves satisfactorily of this duty on the festival of the 6th of June, the 10th day of the Arabian month Zu'lhijah. Each of us then sacrificed a sheep, had his hair and nails cut, exchanged the iḥrām for his best apparel, and, embracing his friends, paid them the compliments of the season. The two following days the Great, the Middle, and the Little Satan were again pelted, and, bequeathing to the unfortunate inhabitants of Muna the unburied and odorous remains of nearly 100,000 animals we returned, 80,000 strong, to Mecca. A week later, having helped to insult the tumulus of stones which marks, according to popular belief, the burial-place of Abulahab, the unbeliever, who, we learn from the Koran, has descended into hell with his wife, gatherer of sticks, I was not sorry to relinquish a shade temperature of 120 degrees, and wend my way to Jeddah en route for England, after delegating to my brethren the recital of a prayer in my behalf at the Tomb of the Prophet at Medina.

In penning these lines I am anxious to encourage other Englishmen, especially those from India, to perform the pilgrimage, without being deterred by exaggerated reports concerning the perils of the enterprise. It must, however, be understood that it is absolutely indispensable to be a Mussulman (at least externally) and to have an Arabic name. Neither the Koran nor the Sultan enjoins the killing of intrusive Jews or Christians; nevertheless, two years ago, an incognito Jew, who refused to repeat the creed, was crucified by the Mecca populace, and in the event of a pilgrim again declaring himself to be an unbeliever the authorities would be almost powerless to protect his life.

An Englishman who is sufficiently conversant with

the prayers, formulas, and customs of the Mussulmans and possesses a sufficient guarantee of orthodoxy, need, however, apprehend no danger if he applies through the British Consulate at Cairo for an introduction to the Amīrul Haj, the Prince of the Caravan.

Finally, I am most anxious to recommend as Muṭawwaf at Mecca Shaikh Muḥammad 'Umr Fanāirjızādah. He is extremely courteous and obliging, and has promised me to show to other Englishmen the same politeness which I experienced from him myself.

1862	1278	الحاج عبد الواحد
A.D.	A.H.	(EL HAJ ABD EL WAHID.)

INDEX.

INDEX.

AAKAL, or fillet, of the Arabs, L. 230.

Aaron, burial-place of, on Mount Ohod, II. 57, 131.

Aba, the, or camel's hair cloak of Arab shaykhs, L. 231.

Abar, Saba, or seven wells, of Kuba, II. 133.

Abbas Effendi, deputy-governor of Alexandria, an interview with, L. 21.

Abbas, prayers for, II. 40.

Abbas, El, uncle of Mohammed the Prophet, II. 64.

Abbas, the fiery Shaykh of the Hawazim, II. 173.

Abbas, Ibn, his statement respecting the settlement of the family of Noah, II. 54.

Abbas ibn Abd el Muttalib, his tomb, II. 184.

Abbas Pasha (Viceroy of Egypt), his *enlightened* policy, L. 18. His intention to erect a magnificent mosque, 96, 97. His present to the Prophet's mosque, II. 27.

Abbasiyah, Kubbat el (Dome of Abbas), visit to the, II. 183.

Abbasiyah Palace, at Cairo, the, L. 77.

Abd el Ashhal, tribe of, El Islam preached by the Prophet to, II. 62. Converted to Mohammedanism, 63.

Abd el Hamid, the Sultan, his restoration of the mosque of El Kuba, II. 118.

Abd el Malik bin Marwan, the caliph, his additions to the House of Allah, III. 34.

Abd el Mejid, Sultan, his mahmal turned back by robbers, L 250. Imbecility of his government in Arabia, 251. His Tanzimat, 251. Sends gifts to the robbers of Arabia, 253. His war with the Czar, II. 7. His additions to the Prophet's mosque at El Medinah, 23, 78.

Abd el Muttalib bin Ghalib, sherif of Meccah, L 252. Description of him, II. 290. His cavalcade, 290, 291. His children, 290. His palace, 291. His procession to the ceremonies of the day of Arafat, III. 75, 76.

Abd el Rahim el Barai, the saint of Jahaydah, L 356.

Abd el Rahim el Bura'i, the poet, quoted, III. 92.

Abd el Rahman, meaning of the name, L 13.

Abd el Rahman, son of Abubekr, tomb of, III. 131.

Abd el Wahab, Shaykh, the chief of the Afghan College at Cairo, L 122—124. His kindness to the pilgrim, 122, 124, 135.

Abdullah bin Jaish, his burial-place, II. 137.

Abdullah bin Salam, the Jew, of El Medinah, converted to El Islam, II. 68, 69.

Abdullah bin Saud, the Wahhabi, concludes a peace with the Egyptians, II. 79.

Abdullah bin Zubayr, nephew of Ayisha, builds the ninth House of Allah, III. 33. Slain, 34.

Abdullah, Pasha of Damascus, L 256.

Abdullah, Shaykh, the assumed name of the author, L 13. Meaning of the name, 13.

Abdullah, Sahib, Shaykh, the Indian physician of El Medinah, II. 150.

Abdullah, Shaykh, (the pilgrim's namesake) introduced, II. 269. His acquirements, 270. His success

INDEX. 187

with the Syrians in the Desert, 273. Acts as director of the pilgrim's consciences, 273, 280. His accident on camel back, 286, 287.

Abdullah, son of the Sherif of Meccah, II. 290.

Abdullah the Saudawi, or melancholist, III. 111. Performs a wakil for the pilgrim's parents, 124. His farewell of the pilgrim, 142.

Abraham, I. 205. Mosque at Meccah connected with, II. 21. Stone on which he stood, preserved at Meccah, III. 20. History of it, 20, n. Legend respecting his having learnt the rites of pilgrimage, 30, 31. The Moslem idea of the existence of two Abrahams, 120.

Abrahat el Ashram, destruction of the host of, II. 93. n.

Abrar, or call to prayer, I. 85.

Absinthe, the, of the Desert, I. 148.

Abu Abbas el Andalusi, the Wali of Alexandria, tomb of, I. 11.

Abu Ali, the fiery Shaykh of the Hawazim, II. 173.

Abu Ayyub, the Ansari, his reception of Mohammed after the Flight, II. 62, 66, 68.

Abubekr, the caliph, his window at El Medinah, II. 30, 33, 34. The benediction bestowed on, 34. His tomb, 37. Elected caliph, 51. His dwelling near the mosque, 68. His mosque at El Medinah, 104.

Abu Deraj (Father of Steps), the mountain of, I. 150.

Abu Hurayrah, his account of the building of the Prophet's mosque, II. 71.

Abu Jubaylah, his destruction of the power of the Jews in El Medinah, II. 60.

Abu Kubays, the hill, the burial-place of Adam, III. 39, 51.

Abu Lahab, his ambuscade laid for the Prophet, site of, III. 123.

Abulfeda, his limits of El Hejaz, II. 86.

Abu Said el Khazari, tomb of, at El Baki'a, II. 180.

Abu Zulaymah, Shaykh, the Red Sea Saint, L. 191, 192.

Abyssinian slaves in Egypt, L. 61. Style of courtship of, 62, 63. Abyssinian slave girls, their value, II. 156. Abyssinian mead, 271.

Acacia, quantities of, II. 211, 215.

Acacia-barren, terrors of an, II. 212.

Academia, the, of El Medinah, II. 50.

Adam. Legend of Adam and Eve at Mount Arafat, III. 67, 68. His place of prayer at Arafat, 73.

Adas (lentils). *See* Lentils.

Adultery, how punished at El Medinah, II. 168.

Ælius, Gallus, expedition of, referred to, L. 180.

Aërolite worship, III. 8. n.

Afghans, the, a chivalrous race, L. 41.

Africans, their susceptibility to religious frenzy, III. 55.

Aghas, or eunuchs of the tomb of the Prophet, II. 42.

Ague, prevalence of, in the East, L. 12.

Ahali, or burghers of El Medinah, II. 152.

Ahl el Kisa, or the "people of the garment," II. 39.

Ahmed Pasha, of El Hejaz, L. 249.

Ahmed, son of the sherif of Meccah, II. 290.

Ahzab, the Masjid el, II. 189, 190.

Ahzab, El, the battle of, II. 190.

Aimmat, the Shaykh el, of the Prophet's mosque, II. 83.

Ajami, meaning of the term, L. 10.

Ajwah, the date so called, II. 110.

Akabah, the ill-omened, L. 195, 206.

Akd el Nikah, or Ziwaj (Arab marriage), the, at El Medinah, II. 167.

Akhshabayn, El (the "two

INDEX. 189

rugged hills"), near Arafat, III. 62. Confusion of the return of the pilgrims at, 80.

Akhawal, El, the Black Mail among the Bedawin so called, II. 255.

Akif, Haji, accosts the pilgrim, III. 144.

Akik, the Wady el, I. 272.

Aksa, the Masjid El, at Jerusalem, II. 21.

Akhawat, the relationship among the Bedawin so called, II. 255.

Alamayn (the "Two Signs"), near Arafat, II. 87; III. 62. Visit to the, 123.

Albanians, or Arnaouts, their desperate manners and customs, I. 126. The man-shooting amusements, 126. A drinking bout with one, 129. One killed by a sunstroke, 258. Parade of irregular horse, 259. Their singular appearance, 259. Fight between them and the hill Arabs, 261, 266. A quarrelsome one in the caravan, II. 277.

Alexandria, I. 7. A city of misnomers, 9. Shopping in, 10. Venerable localities in, 11. The Foreign Office of, 22. The Transit Office of, 26.

Alhamdulillah, meaning of the ejaculation, I. 8.

Ali, the fourth caliph. His spouse, Lady Fatimah, II. 39 et seq. Column of, in the Prophet's mosque, 48. Remains with the Prophet, 64. Joins Mohammed at Kuba, 66. His dwelling near the mosque, 68. His mosque at El Medinah, 104. Called the "Musalla el Eed," 104. His birthplace at Meccah, III. 136.

Ali, the Masjid, at El Kuba, II. 122. At El Medinah, 51.

Ali Agha, an Albanian captain of irregulars or Yuzbashi, I. 124, 125. His personal appearance, 124, 125. Origin of the pilgrim's acquaintance with him, 125. Manners and customs of his countrymen, 126. His call and invitation, 127. A drinking bout with him, 128, 129.

Ali ibn Ya Sin, the Zemzemi, II. 264. A type of the Arab old man, 264. His accident on camel-back, 287. His appearance at the ceremonies of the day of Arafat, III. 74. Insists upon bestowing his company on the pilgrim, 79. His irritation, 83, 84. His invitation to the pilgrim to dinner, 136. Description of the meal, 137, 138.

Ali el Urays, a descendant of the Prophet, his tomb, II. 203.

Ali Murad, owner of the pilgrimship, I. 180, 184—186.

Aliki tribe of Arabs, I. 138.

Alms (Sadaka), given to the Prophet's mosque, II. 26.

Amalik, the tribe. *See* Aulad Sam bin Nuh.

Amalikah tribes, their mixture with the Himyaritic, II. 222.

Amalikah, their foundation of the fifth house of Allah, III. 31.

Ambari gate of El Medinah, II. 2, 4, 104.

American Indians, North, compared with the Bedawin, II. 261, 262.

Amin, El (the Honest), origin of the surname of the Prophet, III. 33.

Aminah, Sitt (mother of the Prophet), III. 131.

Amlak bin Arfakhshad bin Sam bin Nuh, II. 54.

Amlak (property in land) of the Beni Hosayn, II. 148.

Amm Jemal, the Medinite, I. 325.

Amr, tribe of, saved from the deluge of Irem, II. 59. Their abodes at El Medinah, 66.

Amr bin Amin Ma-el-Sama, his stratagem, II. 59. Saved from the Yemenian deluge, 59. The forefather of Mohammed, 59.

Amr el Kays, poet and warrior, his death from ulcer, II. 97.

Amusements of the Cairenes, I. 108. Of the Arabs, 70, 71.

Anatolia, pilgrims from, I. 183.

Angels, (place of the Malaikah), at El Medinah, II. 38. Prayer at the, 38.

Anizah, the Beni (a Jewish tribe), their temperament, II. 221.

Ansar, the, Arab tribe of, II. 58.

Ansar (or Auxiliaries), of El Medinah, II. 65, 67. Assist Mohammed in building the first Mosque, 71. One of the, sells his house to the Prophet, 72.

Antar, songs of, Warburton's opinion of the, II. 238.

Antimony (Kohl), used as a remedy in small-pox, II. 94.

Anzah (iron-shod javelin), of Mohammed, II. 117.

Apes, the, of El Hejaz, III. 101. Stories told of them, 102.

"Arabesque," origin of, I. 93.

Arabesques, the vulgar, of the riwaks at El Medinah and of the tombs at Cairo, II. 46, 47.

Arabia, horses of, I. 3. The Ruba el Khali, 4. Abounds in fiumaras, 4. Possesses no river worthy of the name, 4. The three distinct races of, 4. Remnants of heathenry in, 4. Destruction of the idols of the Arab pantheon, 89. Arabia closed against trade with Christians as early as the 7th century, 105. n. The "Mountains of Paradise" with which it abounds, 217. The "dry storm" of, 239. A caravan in, 241, 242. The watercourses (Misyal) of, 243, 246. Journey through a country fantastic in its desolation, 244. Excellent water found in the deserts of, 247. Depopulation of villages and districts in, 247. Bands of robbers in, 249, 250. Imbecility of the Turkish government in, 251, 252. Wells of the Indians in Arabia, 267. Moslem account of the first settlements in, II. 54, 55. One of the nurseries of

mankind, 55. Causes of the continual emigrations from, 55. Said to have been governed by the Benú Israel, from the destruction of the Amalik, 57. The Flood of Irem, 59. Diseases of, 93 *et seq.* Description of an Arabian Desert, 271. A night journey in, 272, 273.
Arab el Aribah, the, II. 221.
Arab el Mustaajamah, the, II. 222.
Arab el Mustaaribah, the, or half-caste Arab, II. 222.
Arabs. (*See* also Bedawin.) Good feelings of Arabs easily worked upon, 249. Douceurs given by the Turkish government to the Arab Shaykhs of El Hejaz, 258. Fight between the troops and Arabs, 261, 266. The world divided by Arabs into two great bodies, viz. themselves and the "Ajam," 273. II. Their affectionate greetings, II. 4. Their fondness for coffee, 15. Bad behaviour and bad language of their children, 8, 9. An Arab breakfast, 14. Tenets of the Wahhabis, 22. Capitulation of the Benú Kurayzah to the Prophet, 48. Early Moslem history of some of the tribes, 59 *et seq.* Dwellings of the Arabs in the time of Mohammed, 68. The seasons divided by them into three, 92. Diseases of the Arabs of El Hejaz, 93 *et seq.* Arabs not the skilful physicians that they were, 98. Portrait of the former race of Arabs, 116. The Arzah, or war dance, 128. Arab superstitions, 137. Difference between the town and country Arab, 157, 158. Their marriages, 165 *et seq.* Their funerals, 168. Their difficulty of bearing thirst, 213. The races of El Hejaz, 220 *et seq.* Arab jealousy of being overlooked, III. 28. II.
Arabic. Its facilities for rhyming, II. 33. II. Traditions respecting its origin, 54. Suited to poetry

241—243. The song of Maysunah, III. 70. The beautiful Tumar character, 95.

Arafat, the Masjid, at El Kuba, II. 121. Tall Arafat, 121.

Arafat, Mount (anciently Jebel Ilal, now Jebel el Rahmah), description of, III. 66. Derivation of the word Arafat, 67. n. The camp arrangements at, 68. Superstitious rite on behalf of women at, 69. The ceremonies of the Day of Arafat, 72 et seq. The sermon, 76. The Hurry from Arafat, 78. The approach to the Arafat plain, 62.

Arbun (earnest money), II. 195.

Arches, pointed, simple tastes of the Arabs in, II. 105. The climate inimical to the endurance of the buildings, 105.

Arimi, tribe of Arabs so called, I. 138.

Aris, El (a bridegroom), II. 167.

Arkam bin Arkam, last king of the Amalik, II. 56.

Armenian marriage, an, I. 116.

Arms prohibited being carried in Egypt, I. 17, 18. Arms of Arabs, 232, 241; II. 246, 247. Those worn by Oriental travellers, I. 232, 233. Should always be kept bright, 233. Arms of Arnaout irregular horse, 259.

Army, amount of the Turkish, of El Hejaz, II. 102.

Arnaouts. *See* Albanians.

Arsh, or throne, of God, III. 29.

Arusah, El (a bride), II. 167.

Arzah, or Arab war-dance, the, II. 128.

Asad bin Zararah, his conversion by the Prophet, II. 63.

Asclepias gigantea (ashr), its luxuriance in the deserts of Arabia, II. 278.

Ashab, or Companions of the Prophet, II. 34. n.

Graves of the, at El Baki'a, 176.

Ashab, the relationship among the Bedawin so called, II. 255.

Ashgar, Ali Pasha, the Emir el Hajj, II. 215.

Ashr (Asclepias gigantea), which see.

Ashwat, or seven courses, round the Ka'abah, III. 46.

Askar, the Masjid el, II. 191.

Assayd, the Jewish priest of El Medinah, II. 61.

"Asses turning their backs upon Allah's mercy," II. 58.

Asses, the of El Medinah, II. 161.

Astronomy, among the Bedawin, II. 249.

Atakah, Jebel (Mountain of Deliverance), I. 187.

Atfeh, I. 30.

Aukaf, or bequests left to the Prophet's mosque, II. 84. Those given to the Benú Husayn, 148. The Nazir el Aukaf at Constantinople, 153. *See* Wakf.

Aulad Sam bin Nuh (or Amalikah, Amalik) inspired with a knowledge of the Arabic tongue, II. 54. Settles at El Medinah, 54. Supplanted by the Jews, 58.

Aus, Arab tribe of the, II. 58. 60. Their wars with the Khazraj, 60. Converted by Mohammed, 62. Their plot against Mohammed, 69. Their mixture with the Amalikah, 222.

Austrians, despised in Egypt, I. 104.

Awali, the, or plains about Kuba, II. 89.

Awam, the, or nobile vulgus of El Medinah, II. 84.

Ayat, or Koranic verse, II. 64.

Ayisha, accedes to the wishes of Osman and Hasan to be buried near the Prophet, II. 37, 38. Her pillar in the mosque of the Prophet, 47. Her chamber, or the Hujrah, 73.

Ayn el Birkat, the, I. 223.

Ayn el Zarka (azure spring),

the, of El Medinah, L 90.

Ayr, Jebel, its distance from El Medinah, II. 87. Cursed by the Prophet, 130.

Ayyas bin Ma'az, converted by the Prophet, II. 62.

Ayyub, Abu, the Ansari, II. 117. The Bait Ayyub, his descendants, 117.

Ayyub, well of, at El Medinah, II. 71.

Azan, the, or summons to prayer, L 75; II. 73.

Azhar, El, mosque, the, at Cairo, L 95, 97 et seq. Foundation of, 98, 99. Immense numbers of students at, 99. Course of study pursued in, 100. The principal of the Afghan College, Shaykh Abd el Wahhab ibn, Yunus el Sulaymani, 122—124.

Azrael, the angel of death, II. 18, 75.

Bab el Nasr, the gate of Cairo so called, L 138.

Bab el Nisa, the, at El Medinah, II. 44.

Bab el Rammah (Gate of Pity), at El Medinah, II. 44, 45.

Bab el Salam, anciently called the Bab el Atakah, II. 45.

Bab Jibrail (Gate of the Archangel Gabriel), II. 45.

Bab Mejidi (Gate of the Sultan Abd el Mejidi), at El Medinah, II. 44.

Babel or Babylon, settled by the family of Noah, II. 54.

Badanjan (egg-plant), II. 113.

Bad-masti, or liquor-vice, III. 155.

Baghdad. Quarrel between the Baghdad and Damascus caravans, II. 268.

Baghlah (corrupted to Buggalow), the, I. 171.

Bakhshish. In the deserts of Arabia, L 240, 241; II. 115. The odious sound for ever present in Egypt, II. 115.

Baki'a, El, cemetery of, at El Medinah, II. 3. 39. Prayers for the souls of the blessed who rest in, 39, 40. Visitation of, 175. Graves of

13*

the Ashab and Sadat at, 176. Foundation of the place by the Prophet, 177. Description of a funeral at, 178. The martyrs of, 181. Tombs of the wives and daughters of the Prophet at, 182. The beggars of, 182. The Benediction of, 185.

Bamiyah, an esculent hibiscus, II. 113.

Banca tin, L 172.

Baras, the kind of leprosy so called. *See* Leprosy.

Barr, El, at Medinah, II. 4, 13.

Barsim, or Egyptian clover, II. 113.

Basalt (Hajar Jehannum, or hell-stone), II. 218.

Bashat el Askar, or commander of the forces of the caravan, II. 215.

Bashi Buzuks, irregular troops at Cairo, L 150.

Bashir Agha College, the, at El Medinah, II. 168.

Bastarah, and its trees, L 29.

Bath, the, in the Harat Zawaran of El Medinah, II. 100.

Batn Arnah, near Mount Arafat, III. 66.

Batn el Muhassir (Basin of the Troubler), at Muna, III. 60.

Battalin, the lowest order of the Eunuchs of the Tomb, II. 81.

Bawwabin, one of the orders of the Eunuchs of the Tomb, II. 81.

Bayazi schismatics, the, II. 151.

Bayt el Ansari, the, at El Medinah, II. 146. The Bayt Abu Jud, 146. The Bayt el Sha'ab, 146. The Bayt el Karrani, 146.

Bayt el Ma'amur, III. 29.

Bayt el Naby (the Prophet's old house), at Meccah, III. 133.

Bayt Ullah, or house of Allah at Meccah. *See* Ka'abah.

Bazaar, the of El Medinah, II. 99.

Bedawin (*see* also Arabs). Mode of proceeding of Bedawi robbers, L 120. Awed only by the Albanian irregulars, 127. Their habits,

136, 137. Their songs, 137, 235. Their tobacco-pipes, 137. Remarks on the modern Sinaitic or Tawarah race of Arabs, 137 *et seq.* Ethnographical peculiarities of, 138, 139. Purity of blood of the Muzaynah, 138. Improvement in the condition of the Bedawin, 140. How manageable in the Desert, 141. How treated by the city Arab, 145, 146. A Bedawi ambuscade, 149. Their dislike to bathing in cold water, 167. Their food, 204. The wreckers of the coast of the Red Sea, 197. Their bad character at Marsa Damghah, 207. The camel Bedawin of Arabia, 225. The Hazimi tribe "out," 226. Description of a Shaykh fully equipped for travelling, 230, 231. Dress of the poorer class, 232. Their suspicions of persons sketching, 233. Bedawi woman leading sheep and goats, 239. Character of the tribe of Beni-Harb, 240. Their pride, 241. Their ingenuity in distinguishing between localities the most similar, 243. Quarrel with them, 248, 249. The Sumaydah and Mahamid, sub-families of the Hamidah, 249. The Beni Amr, 249. Their defeat of Tussun Bey in 1811, 256. Fight between them and the Albanian troops, 261, 266. Their attack on the caravan, 266. Shape of their graves, 267. Their contempt for mules and asses, II. 20. Their appearance in the Damascus caravan, 125. The Benú Husayn at El Medinah, 148. Almost all the Bedawin of El Medinah of the Shafe'i school, 151. Their idea of the degradation of labour, 155. Furious fight between the Hawazim and the Hawamid, 172, 173. Practice of entrusting children to their care that they may be hardened by the discipline of the Desert, 232. The Sobh tribe inveterate plunderers, 202. Their difficulty of bearing thirst, 213. Account of the Bedawin of El Hejaz, 220 *et seq.* The three races, 220. The indigens, or autochthones, 221. The Ishmaelites, 221, 222. Mixture of the Himyaritic and Amalikah tribes, 222. Immutability of race in the Desert, 222. Portrait of the Hejazi Bedawin, 222, 223. Their features, complexion, &c., 223, 226. Their stature, 226. Their systematic intermarriage, 227. Appearance of the women, 228. Manners of the Bedawin, 228. Their true character, 229. How Arab society is bound together, 229, 230. Fitful and uncertain valour of the Bedawin, 230. Causes of their bravery, 231, 232. The two things which tend to soften their ferocity, 232. Tenderness and pathos of their old poets, 235, 236. Heroism of the women, 237. Bedawi platonic affection, and their chivalry, 237, 238. Dakhl, or protection, among them, 241. Their poetic feeling, 241, 242. Effect of Arab poetry in the Desert, 242. Brigandage honourable among the Bedawin, 244. The price of blood among them, 245. Intensity of their passions, 245. Their sports, 246. Their weapons, 246—248. Their sword-play, 248, 249. Their music and musical instruments, 249. Their surgery, 250. Their religion, 252. Their ceremonies, 252, 253. Circumcision, 252. Marriage, 252. Funeral rites, 253. Methods of living on terms of friendship with them, 254, 255. Their bond of salt, 254. Their government, 255. The threefold kind of relationship among the tribes: the Ashab, the Kiman, and the Akhawat, 256. Their dress, 257, 258. Their food, 260. Smoking, 260, 261. The Bedawin compared with the North

American Indians, 261, 262. Superiority of the former, 262. Ferocity of the Utaybah Bedawin, 276. Their visit to the House of Allah, III. 47. Their appearance in the Damascus caravan on the Arafat plain, 61. Their cleanliness compared with the dirt of the city Arabs, 69. Their fondness for the song of Maysunah, 70. Their wild dances and songs, 103, 104. A pert donkey-boy, 146. (*See* also Arabs.)

Bedr, El, the scene of the Prophet's principal military exploits, L 220, 253.

Beef, considered unwholesome by the Arabs, II. 161.

Beggars in the Prophet's mosque, II. 26. Female beggars near the tomb of the Lady Fatimah, 40, 43. At the tomb of the Prophet, 43. Strong muster of, at El Baki'a, 182.

Bekkah, or Place of Crowding, Meccah so called, III. 95.

Belal, the Prophet's muezzin, II. 46.

Belal, his mosque at El Manakhah, II. 104.

Beni-Harb, the Arab tribe, L 240. Their pride, 241. Sub-families and families of the, 249. Their defeat of Tussun Bey and his 8000 Turks, 256.

Beni Israel, Dr. Wilson's observations on the, L 140.

Beni-Kalb, the, L 240.

Bequests (Aukaf) left to the Prophet's mosque, II. 84.

Berberis, characteristics of the, L 63, 64.

Beybars, El Zahir, Sultan of Egypt, his contribution to the mosque of the Prophet, II. 77.

Bilious complaints common in Arabia, II. 94.

Bir Abbas, in El Hejaz, L 256. Description of it, 257.

Bir el Aris, the, in the garden of Kuba, II. 122. Called also the Bir el Taflat (of Saliva), 123.

Bir el Hindi, the halting-place, L. 267.
Bir Sa'id (Said's well), L. 243.
Birds, the, of the palm-groves of El Medinah, II. 108. Carrion birds on the road between El Medinah and Meccah, 205. The Rakham and Ukab, 205. Vicinage of the kite and crow to the dwellings of man, 216.
Birkah, El, the village so called, L. 29.
Birkat, El (the Tank), description of, II. 276.
Birni, El, the date so called, II. 110. The grape so termed, 114.
Bizr el Kutn (cotton seed), used as a remedy in dysentery, II. 96.
Black mail levied by the Bedawin, II. 256.
Black Stone (Hajar el Aswad), the famous, of the Ka'abah, III. 30, 46, 48. Traditions respecting the, 8. n. Its position, 9. Its appearance, 9. Ceremonies on visiting it, 43, 46.
Blesan, or Balsam of Meccah, used in the cure of wounds, II. 97. See Gilead, balm of.
Blood-revenge, the, L. 231.
Blood-feud, proper use of the, L. 252. Its importance in Arab society, II. 230. The price of blood, 245.
Books, Moslem, those read in schools in Egypt, I. 100, 101. Works on Moslem divinity, 101 et seq. Abundance of books at El Medinah, II. 168.
Borneo, pilgrims from, to Meccah, L. 172.
Botany of the Arabian desert, II. 278.
Bravado, its effect in Arabia, III. 146.
Bread in Arabia, L. 238.
Breakfast, an Arab, II. 14.
Brigandage, held in honour among the Bedawin, II. 244.
Buas, battle of, between the Aus and Khazraj tribes, II. 60.
Bughaz, or defile, the, where Tussun Bey was defeated, L. 256.

INDEX.

Bukht el Nasr (Nebuchadnezzar), invasion of, II. 57.
Bulak, the suburb of, L 30.
Buraydat el Aslami, escorts Mohammed to El Medinah, II. 65.
Burckhardt, error in his Map of Arabia, L 245. Extracts from his descriptions of the Bait Ullah, III. 1 et seq.
Burma, or renegade, derivation of the word, L 23.
Burnoos, the, L 182.
Burton, Lieut., what induced him to make a pilgrimage, L L His principal objects, 3. Embarks at Southampton, 5. His Oriental "impedimenta," 5. His eventless voyage, 6. Trafalgar, 7. Gibraltar ("Gib"), 7. Malta, 7. Lands at Alexandria, 7. Successfully disguises himself 7, 8. Supposed by the servant to be an Ajami, 10. Secures the assistance of a Shaykh, 13. Visits El Nahl and the venerable localities of Alexandria, I L His qualifications as a fakir, magician, and doctor, 12. Assumes the character of a wandering Dervish as being the safest disguise, 13. Adopts the name of Shaykh Abdullah, 13. Elevated to the position of a Murshid, 14. Leaves Alexandria, 16. His adventures in search of a passport, 18, 19. Reasons for assuming the disguise, 23. His wardrobe and outfit, 24. Leaves Alexandria, 28. Voyage up the Nile, 29. Arrives at Bulak, 30. Lodges with Miyan Khudabakhsh Namdar, 36. Life in the wakaleh of Egypt, 42 et seq. Makes the acquaintance of Haji Wali, 45. Becomes an Afghan, 45, 46. Interposes for Haji Wali, 50. Engages a Berberi as a servant, 64. Takes a Shaykh, or teacher, Shaykh Mohammed el Attar, 66, 67. The Ramazan, 73. Visits the "Consul-General" at Cairo, 83. Pleasant acquaintances at Cairo, 115. Account of the pilgrim's companion,

Mohammed el Basyuni, 116. Lays in stores for the journey, 118. The letter of credit, 119. Meets with difficulties respecting the passport, 120. Interview with the Persian consul, 121, 122. Obtains a passport through the intervention of the Chief of the Afghan college, 122. An adventure with an Albanian captain of irregulars, 124 et seq. Departure from Cairo found necessary, 133. A display of respectability, 134. Shaykh Nassar, the Bedawi, 134, 135. Departs from Cairo, 135, 136. The Desert, 137 et seq. The midnight halt, 147. Resumes the march, 148. Rests among a party of Maghrabi pilgrims, 149. Adventure on entering Suez, 151, 152. An uncomfortable night, 152. Interview with the governor of Suez, 153. Description of the pilgrim's fellow-travellers at Suez, 154 et seq. Advantages of making a loan, 158, 159. Suspicion awakened by a sextant, 161. Passports a source of trouble, 162, 163. Kindness of Mr. West, 163. Preparations for the voyage from Suez, 165. Society at the George Inn, 166. The pilgrim-ship, the "Golden Wire," 178 et seq. A battle with the Maghrabis, 184 and 185. Leaves Suez, 187. Course of the vessel, 187, 188. Halts near the Hammum Bluffs, 189. The "Golden Wire" aground, 192. Re-embarks, 193. Reaches Tur, 195. Visits Moses' Hot Baths, 195. Leaves Tur, 200. Effects of a thirty-six hours' sail, 203. Makes Dhamghah anchorage, 207. Enters Wijh Harbour, 209. Sails for Jebel Hasan, 212. Nearly wrecked, 214. Makes Jebel Hasan, 215. Wounds his foot, 216. The halt at Yambu', 220. Bargains for camels, 225. An evening party at Yambu', 227, 228.

Personates an Arab, 228. His Hamail or pocket Koran, 233. Departs from Yambu', 235. The Desert, 236. The halting ground, 237. Resumes the march, 239. Alarm of "Harami" or thieves, 242. Reaches Bir Sa'id, 243. Encamps at El Hamra, 245. Visits the village, 246. A comfortless day there, 248. Attempt of the Bedawin to levy black mail, 254. Encamps at Bir Abbas, 256. A forced halt, 263. Prepares to mount and march, 265. Scene in the Shuab el Hajj, 265. Arrives at Shuhada, 267. The favourite halting place, Bir el Hindi, 267. Reaches Suwaykah, 268. Has a final dispute with Sa'ad the Demon, 269. Disappearance of the camelmen, 270. First view of the city of El Medinah, 272. Poetical exclamations and enthusiasm of the pilgrims, 272, 273. Stays at the house of Shaykh Hamid, II. 4. The visitors and children there, 7-10. The style of living at El Medinah, 11-20. View from the Majlis' windows, 13. Visits the Prophet's tomb, 20-53. Expensiveness of the visit, 43. Reasons for doubting that the Prophet's remains are deposited in the Hujrah, 52. Visits the mosque of Kuba, 107. Sums spent in sight-seeing, 121. Takes "Kayf" at El Kuba, 122. Arrival of the "Damascus pilgrimage" at El Medinah, 128. The visitation of Ohod, 128. Attends at the Haram in the evening, 142. Visits the Cemetery of El Baki'a, 176. Prepares to leave El Medinah, 194. Adieus, 197. The last night at El Medinah, 200. The next dangers, 200, 201. The march from El Medinah, 202-204. The first halt, 206, 207. A gloomy pass, 207. Journey from El Suwayrkijah to Meccah, 263 *et seq.* A small feast, 266. A night journey, 272. An attack of the Utaybah, 284. The pilgrim sights Meccah, 291. His first visit to the House of Allah, III. 38. His uncomfortable lodging, 49, 50. Returns to the Ka'abah, 51. Ceremonies of the day of Arafat, 72 *et seq.*; and of the day of Victims, 83. Accident at the Great Devil, 85. Revisits the Ka'abah, 87. The sacrifices at Muna, 97, 98. The sermon at the Haram, 107. Life at Meccah, and the Little Pilgrimage, 108. Description of a dinner at Meccah, 137, 138. Leaves Meccah, 142. Events on the road, 142 *et seq.* Enters Jeddah, 148. End of the pilgrim's peregrinations, 159.

Business, style of doing, in the East, I. 27.

Butter clarified ("Samn" in Arabia, the Indian "ghi") used in the East, I. 174. 238. Fondness of Orientals for, II. 155, 156.

Buzaat, Bir el, at Kuba, II. 123.

Cagliostro, Count (Giuseppe Balsamo), the impostor, II. 169.

Cairo, its celebrated latticed windows, I. 36. Medical practitioners in, 59. Expenses of a bachelor in, 66. A Cairo druggist described, 67. The Abbasiyeh palace, 77. Scene from the Mosque of Mohammed Ali by moonlight, 82, 83. A stroll in the city at night, 86. Immense number of mosques at, 93. The corporations, or secret societies, of, 106. Description of the festival following the Ramazan, 107. The "New Year Calls" at Cairo, 109. The pressgang in, 110. The inhabitants panic-stricken at the rumours of a conspiracy, 111. Scenes before the police magistrate, 112. Gardens in the mosques of, II. 49, 50. The magician of 95, 96 *n.*

INDEX.

Cambay, Gulf of, L. 206.
Camel-grass of the Desert, L. 244.
Camels, observations on riding, L. 135, 136. The "nakh," 144. The Shaykh or agent of (the Mukharrij), 226. Loading camels in Arabia, 230. Mounting a camel, 234. Travelling in Indian file, 236. Camel-travelling compared with dromedary travelling, 274. The she-camel which guided Mohammed, II. 65, 66, 70. Cathartic qualities of camels' milk. The huge white Syrian dromedary, 127. The Dalul, 127. The camels of El Medinah, 160. Camel hiring at El Medinah, 195. The camel's surefootedness, 211. A night-journey with, in the Desert, 272, 273.
Canal, the proposed, between Pelusium and Suez, L. 105.
Capparis, the wild, in Arabia, II. 215.
Caramania, pilgrims from, L. 183.

Caravan, a, L. 141. The escort, 141. The Tayyarah, or flying caravan, II. 193. The Rakb, or dromedary caravan, 193. Principal officers of the caravan to Meccah, 215.
Caravanserai, the, of Egypt. See Wakaleh.
Castor-plant, the, II. 113.
Cattle, breeding of, among the Bedawin, II. 249.
Cautery, the actual, used in cases of dysentery, II. 96. And of ulcers, 97.
Cavalry, Albanian irregular, L. 259. English cavalry tactics defective, 261. Ancient and modern cavalry, 261. The Chasseurs de Vincennes, 261.
Cave, the, of Mount Ohod, II. 131.
Cemetery of El Baki'a. See Baki'a.
Cemetery of Meccah, (Jannat el Ma'ala), visit to the, III. 130.
Cephren, pyramid of, L. 30.

Cereals, the, of the Medinah plain II. 113.
Chaldæans, the, in Arabia, II. 221.
Chasseurs de Vincennes, L 261.
Chaunting the Koran, L 101.
Cheops, pyramid of, L 30.
Children of the Arabs, II. 8. 9. Their bad behaviour and bad language, 8, 9. Causes of this, 9. Custom of entrusting children to Bedawin, II. 232.
Chivalry, Arab, II. 238. Songs of Antar, 238. Chivalry of the Caliph El Mutasim, 239.
Cholera Morbus in El Hejaz. *See* Rih el Asfar.
Christians, colony of, on the shores of the Red Sea, L 194.
Circumambulation. *See* Tawwaf.
Circumcision, ceremony of, among the Bedawin, II. 252. The two kinds, Taharah and Salkh, 252.
Cleopatra's Baths, L 9.

Cleopatra's Needle, L 9.
Coffee-house, description of an Eastern, L 210. The coffee-houses of El Medinah, II. 99. Coffee-drinking on the march, 100. The coffee-houses at Muna, 206. Coffee-houses on the road near Meccah, III. 143.
Cole, Mr. Charles, Vice-consul at Jeddah, his account of the population of the principal towns of Arabia, II. 102. His straightforwardness and honesty of purpose, III. 150.
Colleges (Madrasah), the two, of El Medinah, II. 168.
Colligation, system of, in battle, II. 232.
Coloquintida, its growth in the deserts of Arabia, II. 278.
Comet, apprehensions of the Madani at the appearance of one, II. 172.
Commerce, the, of Suez, L 171, 172.
Conversation, specimen of

Oriental, I. 84, 85. Coptic artists employed on the mosque of El Medinah, II. 75.

Coral Reefs of the Red Sea, I. 212, 213.

Corinthians, fair, not any at El Medinah, II. 163. Those of Jeddah, 294.

Cot, Column of the, in the Prophet's mosque, II. 48.

Cotton seed (Bizr el Kutun), used as a remedy in dysentery, II. 96.

Courtship, Abyssinian style of, I. 63.

Covetousness of the Arab, its intensity, II. 245.

Cressets (Mashals), of the East, II. 272.

Crown of Thorns, the, II. 114. n.

Curtain, the, of the Prophet's tomb, II. 35. *See* Kiswah.

Custom, strictness of, everywhere in inverse ratio to that of the lex scripta, II. 230. n.

Daggers of the Bedawin, II. 248.

Dakhl, or protection, among the Arabs, II. 241.

Dakuri, El, shrine of the saint, I. 147.

Damascus, Cathedral of, II. 74.

Damascus caravan. Rejoicing at El Medinah on the arrival of the carravan, II. 46. Description of its arrival at El Medinah, 125. The Emir el Hajj, 129. Quarrel between it and that from Baghdad, 268. Stopped in a perilous pass, 283. Grand spectacle afforded by the, on the plain of Arafat, III. 61.

Damghah, Marsa, on the Red Sea, I. 207.

Dancing of the Bedawin, its wildness, III. 103, 104.

Daniyal, El Nabi (Daniel the Prophet), tomb of, I. II.

Dar el Baida, the viceroy's palace in the Desert, I. 147.

Dara'ijah, the capital city of the Wahhabis, II. 79.

Daraj, El (the ladder), at the Ka'abah, III. 19. n.

Darb el Sharki, or Eastern road, from El Medinah to Meccah, II. 202.

Darb Sultani (the Sultan's road), I. 253.; II. 202.

Dates, the delicious, of Tur, I. 197. Those of the hypæthral Court of the Prophet's mosque, II. 49. The date-groves of Kuba, 90. The Tamr el Birni kind used as a diet in small-pox, 94. Celebrity of the dates of El Medinah, 109. Varieties of the date-tree, 109. El Shelebi date, 109. The Ajwah, 110. El Hilwah, 110. El Birni, 110. The Wahshi, 110. The Sayhani, 110. The Khuzayriyah, 110. The Jebeli, 111. The Laun, 111. The Hilayah, 111. Fondness of the Madani for dates, 111. Rutab, or wet dates, 111. Variety of ways of cooking the fruit, 111. The merry-makings at the fruit gatherings, 112. Causes of the excellence of the dates of El Medinah, 112.

Daud Pasha, his palace El Medinah, II. 103.

Daughters of the Prophet, tombs of the, II. 182.

Daurak, or earthen jars, used for cooling the holy water of Zem Zem, III. 18. n.

David, King, I. 205.

Death-wail, the, of Oriental women, I. 110.

Dervishes, wandering, I. 13. A dervish's the safest disguise, 14. The two orders of dervishes, 15.

Desert, the Great, by moonlight, I. 82. Camel riding in, 136, 137. Habits and manners of the Bedawi camel-men, 136, 137. Feeling awakened by a voyage through the Desert, 141, 142. The oases, 143. The pleasures of the Desert, 143, 144. Pleasures of smoking in the, 145. A midnight halt in the, 147. The absinthe of the, 148. Rest under the shade of the mimosa tree, 148. Perfect safety of the Suez road across the, 149. A

INDEX.

Bedawi ambuscade, 149. Charms of the Desert, 151. That near Yambu', 236. Fears of the travellers in crossing, 237. Breakfast in the, 237. Dinner in the, 238. Hot winds in the, 239. Desert valleys, 244. Effect of Arab poetry in the, II. 242. Description of an Arabian desert, 246.

Descendants of the Prophet, one of the five orders of pensioners at El Medinah, II. 84.

Devil, the Great (Shaytan el Kabir), ceremony of throwing stones at, III. 84, 86. Second visit to the, 100.

Dews in Arabia, I. 238.

Dickson, Dr. Samuel, his discovery of the chronothermal practice of physic, I. 12.

Dinner, in the Desert, I. 238. Description of one at Meccah, III. 137, 138.

Deir, I. 180.

Discipline, Oriental, must be based on fear, I. 206.

Diseases, the, of El Hejaz, II. 93. The Rib el Asfar, or cholera morbus, 93. The Ta'un, or plague, 93. The Judari, or small-pox, 93. Inoculation, 93. Diseases divided by Orientals into hot, cold, and temperate, 93. 94. Ophthalmia, 94. Quotidian and tertian fevers (Hummah, Salis), 94. Low fevers (Hummah), 94. Jaundice and bilious complaints, 94. Dysenteries, 96. Popular medical treatment, 96. The Filaria Medinensis (Farantit) 96. Vena in the legs, 96. Hydrophobia, 96. Leprosy (Baras), 97. Ulcers, 97.

Divinity, study of, in Egypt, I. 100. The Sharh, 100. Books read by students in, 101.

Divorces, frequency of, among the Bedawin, II. 253.

Doctors. *See* Medicine.

Dogs, pugnacity of those of El Medinah, II. 17, 18. Superstitions respecting them, 18.

Donkeys despised by the Bedawin, II. 20.

Mecca and Medina III.

14

Dress, Oriental; Dress of the Maghrabis, L. 148. The face-veil of Moslem ladies, 224. That of Arab Shaykhs, 230. Description of an Arab Shaykh fully equipped for travelling, 230. The Kamis, or cotton shirt, 231. The Aba, or camel's hair cloak, 231. Dress of the poorer classes of Arabs, 232. The belt for carrying arms, 232. Dress of the Beni-Harb, 240. Costume of the Skaykhs of the Harbis, 259. Dress of a Medinite Shaykh, II. 5, 6. Dress of the Benú Husayn, 149. Costume of the Madani, 158, 159. Dress of the Bedawin, 257, 258. The ceremony of El Ihram (or assuming the pilgrim dress) on approaching Meccah, 278. Costume of the regions lying west of the Red Sea, 279. The style of dress called Taylasan, III. 107.

Drinking bout with an Albanian, L. 129.

Drinking water, Oriental method of, L. 6.

Drinks, intoxicating, not known to the Bedawin, II. 260.

Dromedaries, sums charged for the hire of, L. 134. Those of El Medinah, II. 160.

Dromedary-travelling compared with camel-travelling, L. 274.

Drusian mysteries, foundation of, L. 95.

Dry storms of Arabia, L. 239.

Dust storms, II. 269.

Dye used for the beard, II. 158.

Dysentery, frequent occurrence of, in the fruit season in Arabia, II. 96. Popular treatment of, 96.

Dwellings of the Arabs in the time of Mohammed, II. 68.

Earnest money (Arbun), II. 195.

Edden, El, the dress in the baths at Cairo, so called, II. 279.

Education, Moslem, L. 99,

100 et seq. Remarks on Dr. Bowring's strictures on 102, 103.

Egypt, curiosity of its police, I. 2. Alexandria. (*See* Alexandria.) Egypt's first steps in civilisation, 17. Inconveniences of the passport system of, 18, 19. Officials of, 19, 20. Her progress during the last half-century, 29. The Nile, 30. The Barrage bridge, 30. The Wakalehs or inns of, 42. The worst part of the day in, 76. Subjects taught in Egyptian schools, 99, 100 et seq. Theology in Egypt, 101. State of learning not purely religious, 101 et seq. Bigotry of the Egyptians, 103. Their feelings at the prospect of the present Russian war, 104, 109, 110. Their views respecting various nations of foreigners, 104. Their longings for European rule, 105. Their hatred of a timid tyranny, 105. The proposed ship canal and railway in, 105. Importance of, to the rulers of India, 105. Press-gangs in, 110. Employment of Albanian irregulars in, 126. Seasons of severe drought, 173. Diseases of the country, 173, 174. Food of the Suezians, 174. Reason of the superiority of Egyptian soldiers in the field, 177.

Embracing, Oriental mode of, II. 3.

Emir el Hajj, the, of the Damascus caravan, II. 129.

English, how regarded in Egypt, I. 104. Fable in Arabia respecting their desire to become Moslems, III. 112.

Epithets, Arab, applied to the Syrians, II. 273.

Era, the Moslem, commencement of, II. 66.

Esma Sultanah, sister of Sultan Mahmud, II. 80.

Etiquette in El Hejaz, II. 129. n.

Eunuchs of the Prophets' tomb, II. 30. n., 42, 45, 49, 52, 80. Shaykhs of the

14*

Eunuchs, 80. The three orders of Eunuchs of the Tomb, 81. The curious and exceptional character of the eunuch, 81. His personal appearance, 81. Value of eunuch slaves at El Medinah, I. 156. Eunuchs of the mosque at Meccah, III. 28. Respect paid to a eunuch at Meccah, 137. *See* Aghas.

Euphorbiæ, in Arabia, II. 215.

Eve's tomb, near Jeddah, III. 156. Traditions respecting it, 157. 158.

Ezbekiyeh, the, of Cairo, I. 79.

Ezion-Geber, I. 180.

Fadak, town of, founded by the Jews, II. 58.

Fahd, Shaykh, the robber chief, I. 249, 250.

Fa-hian quoted, III. 159, 160.

Falconry, among the Arabs, II. 246.

Fara'inah (Pharaohs), the, origin of, according to the Moslem writers, II. 54.

Faraj Yusuf, the merchant of Jeddah, I. 48.

Farantit. *See* Filaria Medinensis.

Farrash (tent-pitchers, &c.), II. 214.

Farrashin, or free servants of the mosque, II. 82.

"Farsh el Hajar," the, of the mosque of the Prophet, II. 44.

Faruk (the Separator), a title of the Caliph Omar, II. 34.

Fasts, Moslems', I. 75.

Fath, the Masjid el (of Victory), II. 190.

Fatihah, the, I. 186. 192. Repeated at the tomb of the Prophet, II. 33.

Fatimah, the Lady, gate of, II. 29. Prayer repeated at her tomb, 39. Epithets applied to her, 39. Her garden in the mosque of the Prophet, 49. Three places lay claim to be her burial-place, 51. Mosque of, at Kuba, 120.

Fattumah, the name, I. 168.

Fatur (breakfast), I. 78.

Fayruz, the murderer of Omar, II. 143.

Fazikh, the Masjid el (of date-liquor), II. 188.
"Fealty of the Steep, the First," II. 62, 63. "The Second Fealty of the Steep," 63. "Great Fealty of the Steep," 64.
Festivals, the, following the Ramazan, L. 107, 108. Scene of jollity at the cemetery outside the Bab el Nasr, 107, 108.
Feuds between the Desert and City Arabs, II. 162.
Fevers, quotidian and tertian (Hummah Salis), in Arabia, II. 94. Remedies for, 94.
Fijl (radishes), II. 114.
Fikh (holy law), study of, in schools, L. 100.
Filaria Medinensis (Farantit), not now common at El Medinah, II. 96.
Finati, Giovanni, L. 255. n.; II. 37.
Fiumaras, the, of Arabia, L. 4. The fiumara "El Sayh," II. 108. That of Mount Ohod, 134.
Flight, the, of Mohammed, II. 64.

Flowers of Arabia, L. 243, 244. Of India, 244. Of Persia, 244.
Food of the Bedawin, II. 259, 260. Their endurance of hunger, 259. Method of cooking locusts, 260. Their favorite food on journeys, 260.
Forskal, his description of the Red Sea, L. 213.
Forster, Rev. C., strictures on his attack on Gibbon, II. 220. n.
Fortress of El Medinah, II. 102, 103.
Forts of the East, a specimen of, L. 149.
Fountain, the public (Sabil), of El Medinah, II. 99.
French, their popularity in Egypt, L. 104. Causes of this, 105.
Friday Sermon, the, of the Prophet, II. 47.
Fruit-trees, the, of El Medinah, II. 114.
Fugitives, pillar of, in the mosque of the Prophet, II. 48.
Fukaha, the, or poor divines,

of the mosque of the Prophet, II. 84.
Funerals, Arab, II. 167, 168. Description of a burial at El Baki'a, 178. Funeral ceremonies of the Bedawin, 253.

Gabriel the Archangel. *See* Jibrail.
Gabriel's place (Makan Jibrail), in the mosque of the Prophet, II. 49.
Gabriel, the Archangel, his communications to the Prophet, II. 70, 71, 73.
Galla slave girls, their value, II. 156.
Gallantry of Orientals, I. 204. Ungallantry of some "Overlands," 204.
Gambling unknown amongst the Bedawin, II. 249.
Gara tribe of Arabs, I. 138. Low development of the indigens of, II. 221.
Garden of our Lady Fatimah in the mosque of the Prophet, II. 49. Date trees of the, 49. Venerable palms of, 49. Gardens not uncommon in mosques, 49.

Garlic and onions, use of, in the East, I. 32, 33.
Gates, the, of El Medinah, II. 98.
Geesh, Lord of, I. 7.
Geographical Society of London, Royal; its zeal for discovery, I. I.
Geology of the neighbourhood of El Medinah, II. 3. Of the road between El Medinah and Meccah, 218.
George Inn, the, at Suez, I. 166. Society at the, 167.
Ghabbah, El, or the watershed of El Medinah, II. 89.
Ghadir, El, description of the plain of, II. 274. The three wells of the Caliph Harun at, 274.
Ghalib, sherif of Meccah, purchases the treasures of the Prophet's tomb from Sa'ad the Wahhabi, II. 79.
Ghaliyah, her heroism, II. 237.
Ghazi (twenty-two piastres), paid to the free servants of the Mosque, II. 82.
Ghi, the, of India, II. 156.
Ghoury, El, the Sultan, his

INDEX.

additions to the Ka'abah, III. 14.
Ghul (Devil), how expelled from persons suffering from hydrophobia, II. 97.
Ghul, the hill near Meccah, II. 288.
Giaffar Bey (governor of Suez), I. 140, 153. Account of him, 153.
Giants (Jababirah), the, who fought against Israel, II. 54.
Gibbon, Edmund, his derivation of the name Saracens, II. 220. n. The Rev. C. Forster's attack on him, 220. n.
Gilead, balm of, grows as a weed in El Hejaz, II. 289.
Goat, milk of the, II. 161. Flesh of the, 161.
"Golden Wire," the pilgrim-ship, I. 179. Its wretched state, 180, 181. Ali Murad, the owner, 180. The passengers, 181—184. Riot on board, 183, 184. Halt near the Hamman Bluffs, 189. Runs aground, 192.
Grammar, how taught in Egyptian schools, I. 100.

Granites (Suwan), the, of the plains of Arabia, II. 218.
Grapes of El Medinah, II. 114. The Sheriff grape, 114. The Hejazi, 114. The Sawadi, or black grape, 114. The Raziki, or small white grape, 114.
Gratitude, no Eastern word for, I. 53.
Graves, shape of the, of the Bedawin, I. 267. At Mount Ohod, II. 138. Musannam, or raised graves, 138. Musattah, or level graves, 138. The graves of the saints at El Baki'a, 175.
Greek Emperor, the, his presents to the mosque of El Medinah, II. 75.
Greeks, the, hated in Egypt, I. 104. Those settled on the Red Sea, 194. Those in El Medinah, II. 8.
Guebres, the, their claim to the Ka'abah as a sacred place, III. 9. n.
Guest-dish, the, II. 155.
"Gugglets," for cooling water, II. 108.
Gunpowder play (La'ab el

Barut) of the Arabs, II. 229.
Guns sounding the order of the march, II. 214. Guns of the Bedawin, 246.
Gypsum, tufaceous, in the Desert, II. 274.

Habash (Abyssinia), I. 170.
Haddah, El, the settlement so called, III. 145.
Hadis (the traditions of the Prophet), study of, in schools, I. 100; II. 21.
Hæmorrhoids, frequency of, in El Hejaz, II. 96. Treatment of, 96.
Hagar, her tomb at Meccah, III. 12. n.
Hajar el Akhzar, or green stone, of the Ka'abah, III. 12. n.
Hajar el Aswad (Black Stone), the famous, of the Ka'abah. (See Black Stone.)
Hajar Shumaysi (yellow sandstone) of Meccah, III. 2. n.
Haji Wali, I. 45. His advice to the pilgrim, 45—47. His lawsuit, 48, 49. His visit to the "Consul General" at Cairo, 83, 84. Accompanies the author in paying visits, 109. Introduces the pilgrim to the Persian consul, 120. His horror at a drinking bout, 130, 131. Takes leave of the pilgrim, 135.
Hajj (pilgrimage), difference between the, and the Ziyarat, II. 21.
Hajj bin Akhtah, plots against Mohammed, II. 69.
Hajj el Shami (the Damascus pilgrimage), II. 125.
Hajjaj bin Yusuf, general of Abd el Malik, ordered to rebuild the house of Allah, III. 34.
Hakim, El b'amr Illah, his attempt to steal the bodies of the Prophet and his two companions, II. 76.
Hakim, El, the Sultan of Egypt, I. 95.
Halimah, the Lady, the Bedawi wet-nurse of the Prophet, II. 180.
Hamail, the, or pocket Koran, of pilgrims, I. 233.
Hamid el Samman, Shaykh, description of, I. 158, 193.

Lands at Yambu', 220. Vaunts the strong walls of Yambu', 235. Leaves Yambu', 236. His fear of the Bedawin, 253. His determination to push through a nest of robbers, 264. Takes his place in the caravan, 265. Arrives at El Medinah, 274. His toilet after the journey, II. 5. His hospitality, 5, 6. Improvement in his manners, 6. Behaviour of his children, 8, 9. His politeness, 9, 10. Description of his abode, 11—13. His household, 13 *et seq.* Accompanies the pilgrim to the Prophet's tomb, 20. Introduces the pilgrim to the Prophet's window, 35. Accompanies him to the mosque of Kuba, 107. To Mount Ohod, 128 *et seq.* And to the cemetery of El Baki'a, 175 *et seq.* Procures a faithful camel-man for the journey to Meccah, 195. His debt forgiven, 200.

Hamidah, the principal family of the Beni-Harb, I. 249. Their attack on the caravan, 266, 267.

Hammam, or the hot bath, the, I. 70.

Hammam Bluffs (Hammam Far'aun), I. 189.

Hamra, El, I. 242. Derivation of its name, 245. Called also El Wasitah, 245. Encampment at, 246. Description of the village of, 247. The fortress of, 247, 248. The third station from El Medinah in the Darb Sultani, 253.

Hamzah, friend of Mohammed, prayer in honour of, II. 40. Sent forward by the Prophet to El Medinah, 64. Mosque of, 134, 135. The place where he was slain, 142.

Hanafi school. Mufti of the, at El Medinah, II. 82. Holds the first rank at El Medinah, 151. Their station for prayer at the Ka'abah, III. 15. Their importance in Meccah, 16. n. Their practice of nighting at Muzdalifah, 81.

Hanbali school, the, II. 82.

Station of the, for prayer at the Ka'abah, III. 15.

"Hanien," the word, L. 81.

Haram (or Sanctuary), the Prophet's, at Medinah, II. 11, 22. The Shaykh el, or principal officer of the mosque, 80. The Mudir el, or chief treasurer of the Tomb of the Prophet, 81. The Hudud el Haram, 87.

Haramayn, or sanctuaries, the, two of El Islam, L. 225. n.; II. 21.

"Harami," or thieves, in the Desert, L. 242.

Harb, the Beni, the present ruling tribe in the Holy Land, L. 249. Its divisions and subdivisions, 249.

Harb, the, of El Hejaz, L. 259.

Harem, the, of a Medinite, II. 12. Arrangements of the, 233. Its resemblance to a European home, 234.

Harrah, the, or ridges of rock, L. 243; II. 2. El Harratayn, L. 272.

Harrah, the, or ridge, as represented in our popular works, II. The second Harrah, 133.

Harun, the Kubbat (or Aaron's tomb), on Mount Ohod, II. 131.

Harun, Bir (well of Harun), II. 214.

Harun el Reshid, his three wells at El Ghadir, II. 274.

Hasan, grandson of Mohammed, prayers for, II. 39. His descendants at El Medinah, 148. n. His tomb, 183, 184.

Hasan el Marabit, Shaykh, tomb of, on the shore of the Red Sea, L. 212.

Hasan the Imam, requests to be buried near the Prophet, II. 37, 38.

Hasan, Sultan, mosque of, at Cairo, L. 95.

Hasan, Jebel (Mount Hasan), L. 215.

Hasanayn mosque, the, at Cairo, L. 95.

Hashish, smoking the, L. 45.

Haswah, or gravelled place, II. 23.

Hatchadur Nury, Mr., his

friendship with the author, L. 115.

Hatim, the generous Arab chieftain, L. 159.

Hatim, El (the broken), of the Ka'abah, III. 13.

Hawamid Arabs, their fight with the Hawazim, II. 173.

Hawazim Arabs, their furious fight with the Hawamid, II. 172. Their Shaykhs, Abbas and Abu Ali, 173.

"Haykal! ya, ibn Haykal!" (O Haykal! sons of Haykal!), the exclamation explained, L. 30.

Hazirah (or presence), the, II. 30.

Hazrat Ali, apparition of, III. 63.

Heat, the reflected, at Yambu', L. 227. The hot wind of the Desert, 239, 257. The hour at which the sun is most dangerous, 268. Terrible heat in El Hejaz, III. 102. Unbearable in Meccah, 110.

Heathenry, remnants of, in Arabia, I. 4.

Hejaz, El, dangers and difficulties of, L. 2. Antiquity and nobility of the Muzaynah tribe in, 138. Land route to, in Suez, 150. Description of the shugduf or litter of, 228. Abounds in ruins, 247. Sa'ad the robber chief of, 249. Shaykh Fahd, the robber, 249. Wretched state of the government in, 250. The charter of Gulkhaneh, 251. The Darb Sultani, 253. Heat in El Hejaz, 258. Douceurs given by the Turks to the Arab shaykhs of, 258. Fight between the Arabs and soldiers in, 261. Peopled by the soldiers of the children of Israel, II. 56, 57. Limits of, 86. Meaning of the name, 86. Rainy season in, 91, 92. Diseases of, 93, 94. Number of the Turkish forces in, 102. Account of the Bedawin of, 220 *et seq.* (*See* Bedawin.) Observations on the watershed of, 292, 293. Purity of the water throughout, III. 74. Healthiness of the people of, 110.

Hejazi, the, grape so called, II. 114.
Hemp-drinkers, Egyptian, III. 68, 71.
Herklot's, Dr., reference to his work "Qanoon-i-Islam," II. 95. n. Quoted, III. 11. n.
"Herse," in military tactics, I. 260.
Hijriyah, El, halt at, II. 214.
Hilayah, the date so called, II. 111.
Hilwah, El, the date so called, II. 110.
Himyaritic tribes, their mixture with the Amalikah, II. 222.
Hindi, Jebel, at Meccah, II. 292.
Hindus, their square temples similar in form to the mosque, III. 7. n. Their litholatry, 8. n. The Ka'abah claimed as a sacred place by them, 9. n.
Hogg, Sir James, I. I.
Honorarium (Ikram), given to the Madani who travel, II. 152. *See* Ikram.
Horses, Arabian, I. 3. The celebrated, of Nijd, III. 75. Horses of the Arnaout Irregulars, II. 259. The, of El Medinah, 17, 160.
Hosh, El, or the central area of a dwelling-house, II. 23. 106.
Hosh ibn Sa'ad, at Medinah, the residence of the Benú Husayn, II. 148.
Hospitality in the East, I. 38.
House hire in Egypt, I. 44, 66. Houses of the Arabs at the time of Mohammed, II. 68. Those of El Medinah, 101. Those of Meccah, III. 49, 50.
Hudud el Haram (or limits of the sanctuary), II. 87.
Hufrah (holes dug for water in the sand), II. 205.
Hufrah, El (the digging), of the Ka'abah, III. 11. n.
Hujjaj, or pilgrims, II. 41.
Hujrah, the, or Chamber of Ayisha, description of, II. 28. Referred to, 38. Surrounded by the Caliph Omar with a mud wall, 73. Enclosed within the Mosque by El Walid, 76. Spared from destruction by lightning, 78.

INDEX.   221

Hukama (or Rationalists), of El Islam, III. 41.
Hurayah, Abu, his account of the Benú Israel in Arabia, II. 57.
Husayn, the Benú, become guardians of the Prophet's tomb, II. 77, 148. Head-quarters of the, at Suwayr-kiyah, 148. Their numbers and power at one period, 149. Their heretical tenets, 149. Their personal appearance, 149.
Husayn bin Numayr, his siege of Meccah, III. 33.
Hydrophobia, rarity of, in El Hejaz, II. 96. Popular superstitions respecting, 97. Treatment of, 97.
"Hypocrites," conspiracy of the, II. 69.

Iambia, the, of Ptolemy, I. 220.
Ibn Asm, or Ibn Rumi, his death, II. 237. His sister Kurdi Usman, 237.
Ibn Dhaber Berkouk, King of Egypt, rebuilds the mosque at Meccah, III. 4.
Ibn Zubayr, chief of Meccah, rebuilds the Ka'abah, III. 7.
Ibrahim, the Makam, at the Ka'abah, III. 15. n., 19, 36.
Ibrahim, infant son of the Prophet, his burial-place, II. 177, 181.
Ibrahim Pasha, his ships on the Red Sea, I. 164.
Ichthyophagi, the modern, of the Red Sea, I. 216.
Ihlal, the pilgrim dress so called, III. 86.
Ihram, El (assuming the pilgrim garb), the ceremony so called, II. 278. Change from Ihram to Ihlal, III. 86.
Ijabah, the Masjid el (the Mosque of Granting), II. 189.
Ikram (honorarium), given to the Madani who travel, I. 225; II. 152. The four kinds of, 152.
Ilal, Jebel (Mount of Wrestling in Prayer). See Arafat, Mount.
Imams, the, of the Prophet's mosque, II. 83, 84. Place where they pray, 50.

Imlik, great-great-grandson of Noah, the ancestor of the Amalikah, III. 31.
India, style of doing business in, I. 27. Real character of the natives of, 38—40. No European should serve an Eastern lord, 40. The natives a cowardly and slavish people, 41. Their cowardice compared with the bravery of the North American Indians, 41. Luxuriance of the plains of India, 244. Indian pilgrims protected by their poverty, 258. Their sinful method of visiting the Prophet's tomb, II. 21. Dress and customs of the Indian women settled at El Medinah, 150, 151. Recklessness of poor Indian pilgrims, III. 64. Remedies proposed, 64.
Indian Ocean (Sea of Oman), the shores of, when first peopled, according to Moslem accounts, II. 54.
Inns. See Wakaleh.
Inoculation practised in El Medinah, II. 93.

"Inshallah bukra" (please God, to-morrow), II. 165.
Intermarriages, theory of the degeneracy which follows, II. 227. Dr. Howe's remarks on, 227. n.
Intonation and chaunting of the Koran taught in Moslem schools, I. 101.
Irak, El, expedition of Tobba el Asghar against, II. 60, 61.
Irem, flood of, the, II. 59.
Isa bin Maryam, spare tomb at El Medinah for him after his second coming, II. 37.
Ishah, the (or Moslem night prayer), I. 228.
Ishmael (Ismayl), his tomb at Meccah, III. 12. n., 13. The two prostration prayer over the grave of, 55.
Ishmaelites, the, of the Sinaitic peninsula, II. 222. Their distinguishing marks, 222.
Israel, Benû, rule of the, in Arabia, II. 57. See Jews.
Israelites, course of the, across the Red Sea, I. 188.

Istikharah, or divination, II. 167.
Italians, how regarded in Egypt, I. 105.
Izar, the portion of a pilgrim's dress so called, II. 279.

Ja El Sherifah, the halting-ground, II. 207.
Jababirah (giants), the, who fought against Israel, II. 54.
Jabarti, the, from the Habash, I. 170.
Jahaydah (a straggling line of villages), I. 255.
Jama Taylun, mosque, I. 94.
Jami' el Sakhrah, at Arafat, III. 72.
Jami Ghamamah at El Manakhah, II. 105.
"Jangli," an opprobrious name applied to the English rulers of India, I. 37.
Jannat el Ma'ala (the cemetery of Meccah), visit to the, III. 130.
Jauhar el Kaid, founder of the mosque of El Azhar, I. 99.

Jaundice, common in Arabia, II. 94. Popular cure for, 94.
Java, number of Moslem pilgrims from, to Meccah, I. 172; II. 246. 150
Javelin (Mirzak), description of the Arab, I. 232.
Jebeli, the, the date so called, II. 111.
Jeddah, slave trade at, I. 48. Price of perjury at, 49. Value of the exports from Suez to, 171, 172. Population of, II, 102. Considered by the Meccans to be a perfect Gibraltar, III. 150. The Wakaleh of Jeddah, 151. The British vice-consul, Mr. Cole, 151. Different descriptions of the town, 151. The fair Corinthians at, 152. How time passes at Jeddah, 155.
Jehaymah, tribe of Arabs, I. 138.
Jemal Amm, his advice to the pilgrim, I. 228. Reproved for his curiosity, I. 236.
Jenabah, low development of the indigens of, II. 221.

Jenazah, Darb el (Road of Biers), at El Medinah, II. 103. 177.
Jerid, or palm-sticks, with which the houses of the Arabs were formerly made, II. 68.
Jews, ancient settlements of, in Arabia, II. 57, 58. Take refuge from Nebuchadnezzar in Arabia, 58. Fall into idolatry, 58. Given over to the Arabs, 58. Their power in El Medinah, 60. Their conspiracy against the Prophet, 68, 69.
Jezzar Pasha, I. 356.
Jibrail, Mahbat, or places of Gabriel's Descent, II. 38.
Jibrail, Makam (Gabriel's Place), in the mosque of the Prophet, II. 49.
Jibrail, Bab el (Gabriel's Gate), II. 72.
Jinn, the Masjid el, (mosque of the Genii), at Meccah, III. 132.
Jiyad, Jebel, the two hills so called, III. 32.
Jizyat, the (or capitation tax levied on infidels), I. 228.

Job, tomb of, III. 159.
Jubbah, the, I. 16.
Judari, El (or small-pox), indigenous to the countries bordering the Red Sea, II. 93. Inoculation practised in El Medinah, 93. And in Yemen, 93. n. The disease, how treated, 94. Diet of the patient, 94.
Jum'ah, Bab el (or Friday gate), of El Medinah, II. 99. The cemetery of schismatics near, 103.
Jum'ah, the Masjid el, near El Medinah, II. 187.
Jurham, the Beni, their mixture with the Himyaritic tribes, II. 222. Their foundation of the sixth House of Allah, III. 31. Legend of their origin, 32.

Ka'ab, the Jewish priest of El Medinah, II. 61.
Ka'ab el Akhbar (or Akhbar), I. 138.
Ka'abah (or Bayt Ullah) the, II. 2L. Superstitious reverence of the Jews of El Medinah for, 61. n. Mira-

INDEX.

culously shown to Mohammed by the archangel Gabriel, 71. Extracts from Burckhardt's description of the, III. L. Its dimensions, L. Its domes and pillars, 1, 2. Periods of opening it, 6. The doors of, 6, 7. The famous Hajar el Aswad, or Black Stone, of the, 8-10. The Rukn el Yemani, 10. n. El Ma'ajan, or Place of Mixing, 11-n. The Myzab, or water-spout, 12. The mosaic pavement, 12. Tombs of Hagar and Ishmael, 12, 12. n. Limits of the Ka'abah, 14. El Mataf, or Place of Circumambulation, 14, 15, 14. n. The four Makams, or stations for prayer, 15. The Zem Zem, or the holy well, 17. El Daraj, or the Ladder, 19. n. The stone on which Abraham stood, 20. The boast that the Ka'abah is never, night or day, without devotees, 26. n. Legends of the ten Houses of Allah, 28 *et seq.* Proofs of the sanctity of the Ka'abah, 35. The pilgrim's first visit to the, 35. Legend of the Bab Beni Shaybah, 40. Ceremonies of the visit to the, 43 *et seq.* Sketch of the interior of the building, 89. Expenses of visiting, 90, 91. Reasons for all pilgrims not entering the, 91. The first covering of the, 92. Changes in the style and make of the Kiswah, or curtain, 93. Inscriptions on the Kiswah, 95.

Ka'abah, Jebel, the residence of the Beni Jurham, III. 32.

Kabirah, El (or lady of the house), III. 38. Kindness of one to the pilgrim at Meccah, 96. Her affectionate farewell of the pilgrim, 142.

Kadiriyah, an order of Dervishes, L 13.

Kafr ei Zayyat, L 30.

Kaid Bey, the Mamluk sultan of Egypt, rebuilds the mosque of the Prophet, II. 52. 78. Establishes

"Wakf" for the tomb of the Prophet, 79.
Kairom and its potteries, I. 29.
Kalkashandi, El, his testimony respecting the tomb of the Prophet, II. 36.
Kamis, the cotton shirt, of Arab Shaykhs, I. 231.
Kanat (spears), of the Bedawin, II. 247.
Kanisah or Christian Church, II. 75.
Kara Gyuz, the amusement so called, I. 79.
Karashi, tribe of Arabs, I. 138.
Kaswa, El, the she-camel of Mohammed the Prophet, II. 65, 66, 70, 116, 119.
Kata, or sand grouse, the (Pterocles melanogaster), I. 147.
Katibs, or writers of the tomb of the Prophet, II. 81.
Katirah race, its mixture with the Himyaritic tribes, II. 222.
Kaukab el Durri, or constellation of pearls suspended to the curtain round the Prophet's tomb, II. 35. Its apparent worthlessness, 35. Plundered by the Wahhabis, 79.
Kawwas, or police officer, of Egypt, I. 20.
Kayf, explanation of, I. 8. Enjoyment of Kayf on the brink of the well at El Kuba, II. 122.
Kazi (Cadi), or chief judge of El Medinah, II. 82. Customs of the, 230.
Khadijah (one of the Prophet's fifteen wives), her burial-place, II. 182.
Khadim (or guardian), of a mosque, II. 121. Of the tombs at El Baki'a, 180.
Khalid Bey, brother of Abdullah bin Sa'ud, his noble qualities, II.
Khaluk, a perfume so called, III. 156.
Khandak (the moat) celebrated in Arabian history, II. 108.
Khakani, the Persian poet, quoted, III. 41.
Khazraj, Arab tribe of, II. 58, 59. Their wars with the Aus, 60. Converted by

INDEX.

Mohammed, 62. Their plot against Mohammed, 69. Its mixture with the Amalikah, 222.

Khatan bin Saba, the tribe of, II. 59.

Khatib, or Moslem preacher, III. 21. The Khatibs of the mosque of the Prophet, II. 83, 84.

Khattabi, El his opinions respecting El Medinah, II. 88.

Khaybar, in Arabia, Israelite settlements at, II. 57, 58. Capture of, 71. Its distance from El Medinah, 174.

Khayf, El, I. 256. The mosque of, at Muna, III. 60.

Khaznadar, the treasurer of the Prophet's tomb, II. 81.

Khitbah, or betrothal, in Arabia, II. 167.

Khubziyah, one of the orders of the Eunuchs of the Tomb, II. 81.

Khudabaksh Namdar, Miyan, the Lahore shawl merchant, I. 36.

Khurunfish, El, the manufactory at which the Kiswah is now worked, III. 95.

Khutaba, the Shaykh el, of the Prophet's mosque, II. 83.

Khutbah, or Friday Sermon, of the Prophet, II. 47, 72.

Khutbat el Wakfah ("Sermon of the Standing" upon Arafat), III. 76.

Khuzayriyah, the date so called, II. 110.

Khwayah Yusuf, his adventures, I. 115.

Kiblatayn, the Mosque El, foundation of the, II. 186.

Kichhri, the Indian food so called, II. 206.

Kiman, the relationship among the Bedawin so called, II. 255.

"Kirsh Hajar," a stone dollar so called by the Bedawin, II. 79. n.

Kissing the hand, III. 44.

Kiswah, the (or "garment" or curtain round the Prophet's tomb), purloining bits of the, III. 56. Detailed notice of the, 94.

Kiswah, or cover of a saint's tomb, II. 137.

Knight errantry, Arab, II. 238.

Kohl (antimony), used as a remedy in small-pox, II. 94.

Koran, intonation of, taught in schools, L. 101. Exegesis of the, 102. Mode of wearing the Hamail, or pocket Koran, 135. Texts of, respecting Moses, Abraham, David, Solomon, and Mohammed, 205. The Hamail, or pocket Koran, of pilgrims, 233. The Cufic MSS. written by Osman, the fourth Caliph, II. 77.

Koraysh, tribe of Arabs, I. 138.

Kuba, El, Gardens of, II. L. Receives the Prophet, 65. Date-groves of, 90. The Kuba well, 90. II. Cool shades of Kuba, 113. Description of the village, 115. Its inhabitants, 115, 116. History of its mosque, 116, 117. Purity of the place and people of El Kuba, 120. The Mosque called Masjid el Takwa, or Mosque of Piety, 120. The mosque of Sittna Fatima, 120. That of Arafat, 121.

Kubar, or Masters of the Muezzins of El Medinah, II. 83.

Kubbat el Masra, the at Ohod, II. 141.

Kubbat el Sanaya (or Dome of the Front Teeth), at Mount Ohod, II. 130.

Kulsum bin Hadmah, gives refuge to Mohammed at Kuba, II. 66.

Kummayah, Ibn, the infidel, II. 139.

Kuraysh, legend of their foundation of the eighth House of Allah, III. 33.

Kurayzah, a tribe of the Benu Israel, II. 60.

Kurayzah, town of, founded by the Jews, II. 58. The Masjid el Kurayzah, 188. Extermination of the Jewish tribe of El Kurayzah, 188.

Kurbaj, or "cat o'nine tails," of Egypt, L. 21.

Kurdi, Usman, her heroism, II. 237.

INDEX. 229

Kusah, (scant-bearded man), II. 158.
Kusay bin Kilab, his foundation of the seventh house of Allah, III. 32.
Kuskusu, the food so called, I. 190.
Kuwwat Islam (strength of Islam), the building near El Medinah, so called, II. 191.

La'ab el Barut (gunpowder play) of the Arabs, II. 229.
Labour, price of, at El Medinah, II. 154.
Lance, the Arab. *See* Javelin.
Land-cess (Miri), not paid by the Madani, II. 151.
Lane, Mr., reference to his discovery of the frauds of the Cairo magician, II. 95. n.
Lapidation (Rajm), a punishment for adultery, II. 163. Diabolical practice of, in Arabia, III. 60.
Lapidation (Rami) ceremony of, III. 85, 86. The second day's ceremony, 103.

Larking, Mr. John, I. 7.
Latrinæ, not allowed in El Medinah, II. 88.
Laun, the date so called, II. 111.
Lawsuit, a Mohammedan, description of, I. 47.
Laymun, Wady, or El Mazik, II. 287. Its celebrity, 287.
Lebid, the poet, his description of the rainy seasons of El Hejaz, II. 92. His suspended poem, 236.
Legends of the house of Allah, III. 28 *et seq.*
Lentils (Adas), the diet during an attack of smallpox, II. 94. Their cheapness on the banks of the Nile, 94 n. Revalenta Arabica, 94 n.
Leprosy, the kind called Baras only known in El Hejaz, II. 97. Considered incurable, 97.
Levick, Henry, Esq., late vice consul at Suez, I. 163. His remarks respecting Suez, 164 *et seq.*
Lex Scripta, strictness of the, everywhere in inverse ratio to that of custom, II. 230. n.

Lift (turnips), II. 114.
Lisam, of the Arab Shaykhs, I. 231.
Litholatry, III. 8. n.
Litter (Shugduf), description of the, as used in El Hejaz, I. 228. The Mahmal, or Syrian litter, 229.
Locusts eaten as food by the Bedawin, II. 260. Method of cooking them, 260.
Lots, pillar of, in the mosque of the Prophet, II. 47.
"Lotus eaters," II. 114.
Lubabah, Abu, column of, in the Rauzah, II. 48. Story of him, 48.
Lying among Orientals, III. 92.

Ma'abidah, El, or northern suburb of Meccah, II. 291.
Ma'ajan, El (or place of mixing), at the Ka'abah, III. I.I. Its origin, II. n.
Ma'mun, El, makes additions to the mosque of the Prophet, II. 76.
Mabrak el Nakah (place of kneeling of the she dromedary), at El Kuba, II. 119.

Madani. *See* Medinah.
Madrasah (or Colleges) the two of El Medinah, II. 169.
Madshuniyah, El, the garden of, near El Medinah, II. 134.
Ma-el-Sama ("the water, or the splendour of heaven"), a matronymic of Amr bin Amin, II. 59.
Maghrabi pilgrims, I. 149, 166, 179. Their treachery, 149. Habits and manners of the Maghrabis, 182, 183. Their bad character, 179. Frays with them on board, 183-186. Their repentance of their misdeeds, 190. Their efforts to get the ship off the sand, 192. Return of their surliness, 195. Their desire to do a little fighting for the faith, 198.
Mahamid, a sub-family of the Beni-Harb, I. 249.
Mahattah Ghurab (Station of Ravens), halt at the, II. 209.
Mahjar, or stony ground, II. 213.
Mahár Marsa (Mahar anchorage), I. 215.

INDEX. 231

Mahmal, the Sultan's, turned back by robbers in Arabia, I. 250. Its appearance in the caravan, II. 208. Places of the Egyptian and Damascus Mahmals during the sermon on Arafat, III. 73, 74.

Mahmud, the late Sultan, his dream, I. 11.

Mahmudiyah Canal, the, I. 29. Barrenness of its shores, 29, 30.

Mahmudiyah College, the, at El Medinah, II. 168.

Mahr, the, or sum settled upon the bride before marriage, II. 167.

Mahrah, the indigens of, II. 221. Their low development, 221.

Majarr el Kabsh (Dragging-place of the Ram), notice of the, III. 100.

Makams. *See* Hanafi; Hanbali; Ibrahim; Maliki.

Makam Jibrail (place of Gabriel), at the Ka'abah, 49.

Makam el Ayat (place of signs), the, at the mosque of Kuba, II. 120.

Malabar, Suez trade in the pepper of, I. 172.

Malaikah (or the Angels), at El Medinah, II. 38. Prayer at the, 38.

Malbus (religious frenzy), a case of, at Meccah, III. 54.

Malik, the Imam, his followers, II. 22. His strictness respecting El Medinah, 88. Mufti of the at El Medinah, 82. Station of the sect of, for prayer at the Ka'abah, III. 120.

Malik ibn Anas, Imam, his tomb, II. 182.

Malta, I. 7. The Maltese regarded with contempt in Egypt, 104.

Mambar, the, or pulpit of the Prophet's mosque, II. 25. Origin of, 72. The, of the Mosque of Meccah, III. 21.

Manakhah, El, the suburb of El Medinah, II. 4. The Harat (Quarter) El Ambariyah, 4. Population of, 102.

Mandeville, Sir John, his opinion of the Bedawin, I. 140.

Mansur, the camel-man, L 255. Bullied by Mohammed El Basyuni, 270.
Marble, white (Rukham), of Meccah, III. 2. n.
March, the Sariyah or night march, II. 210.
Mareb, dyke of, II. 58.
Maryiah, the Coptic girl of Mohammed, her infant son Ibrahim, II. 181.
Maryam, El Sitt (the Lady Mary, I. 237, 257, 263, 264. Affection of her younger son, II. 3.
Markets, the, of El Medinah, II. 99.
Marriage, an Armenian, L 116. An Arab, II. 165-167. The Khitbah, or betrothal, 167. The Mahr, or sum settled upon the bride, 167. The marriage ceremony, 253.
Martineau, Miss, her strictures on the harem, II. 233.
Martyrs, the, of Mount Ohod, II. 40. Of El Baki'a, 40. Visitation to the, of Mount Ohod, 128.

Marwah, Ceremonies at, III. 126, 127.
Marwan, El, governor of El Medinah, II. 90.
Mashab, the, or stick for guiding camels, L 232.
Masajid, Khamsah, the, of the suburb of El Medinah, II. 104.
Mashali, the Madani children's bodies marked with, III. 115.
Mash'als (lights carried on poles), II. 272, 273.
Mashar el Haram (Place dedicated to Religious Ceremonies), at Muna, III. 60.
Mashrabit Umm Ibrahim, the Masjid, II. 189.
Mashrabiyah, or famous carved latticed window of Cairo, L 36.
Masjid. *See* Mosque.
Masjid El Jumah, the, II. 66.
Mastabah, the, of the shops in Cairo, L 68.
Mastabah, or stone bench before the mosque of El Kuba, II. 118.
Mastich-smoke, the perfume, II. 14.

INDEX. 233

Mas'ud, of the Rablah, engaged for the journey to Meccah, II. 195, 203, 209, 210, 214. Heavy charges for watering his camels, 269. His dislike of the Shamar, 275. His quarrel with an old Arnaut, 277. His skill in steering the desert craft, 284. His disgust at the dirt of the Meccans, III. 69.

Maula Ali, leader of the Maghrabis, L 182.

Maulid el Naby (or the Prophet's birth-place), III. 135.

Maulid Hamzah (or birth-place of Hamzah), at Meccah, III. 136.

Mauz'a el Khatt (place of writing), at Meccah, III. 132.

Mawali (or clients of the Arabs), II. 60.

Maysunah, the Bedawi wife of the Caliph Muawiyah, III. 70. The beautiful song of, 70. Her son Yezid, 70 n.

Mazghal (or matras), long loopholes in the walls of Medinah, II. 100.

Mazik, El. *See* Laymun, Wady.

Meccah, remnants of heathenry in, L 4. "Tawaf," or circumambulation of the House of Allah at, II. 21. Its mosque compared with that of El Medinah, 23. A model to all Moslems, L 93. The four roads leading from El Medinah to, II. 202. The sherif of, Abd el Muttalib bin Ghalib, 290. The Saniyat Kuda'a near, 291. The sherif's palace at, 291. The haunted house of the Sherif bin Aun at, 291. The Jannat el Ma'ala, or cemetery of, 291. The Afghan and Syrian quarters, 291. Extracts from Burckhardt's description of the Bayt Ullah, or Ka'abah, III. 1. *et seq.* The gates of the mosque, 22. Expenses during "season" at Meccah, 26. a. Description of a house at, 50. Resemblance of, to Bath or Florence, 53. Admirable linguistic acquirements of the Meccans, 103. Life at Meccah, 108. The city modern, 110. n. Character of the inhabitants, 113, 114. Their appearance, 115. Dangers of visiting Meccah, 121. Places of pious visitation at, 129.

Medicine, Oriental practice of, I. 11, 12. The chronothermal practice, 12. Experiences respecting the medicine-chest, 26. Asiatic and European doctors contrasted, 52, 53. A medical man's visit in the East, 54, 55. Amount of a fee, 56. Medical treatment in Asia, 57, 58. A prescription, 57, 58. Method of securing prescriptions against alteration, 59. Doctors in Cairo, 59. Inefficacy of European treatment in the East, 59. Superstitious influences of climate, 60. Description of a druggist's shop, 68.

Medinah, El, the first mosque erected at, I. 89. Men of, respected by Bedawi robbers, 226. First view of, 272. Poetical exclamations and enthusiasm of the pilgrims, 272, 273. Distance of, from the Red Sea, 274. View of, from the suburbs, at sunrise, II. 1. Scenery of the neighbourhood, 2. The Ambari gate, 2. The Takiyah erected by Mohammed Ali, 4. Fortress of, 2. Its suburb "El Manakhah," 2. "The trees of El Medinah," 3. The Bab el Misri, or Egyptian gate, 4. Coolness of the nights at, 16. Pugnacity of the horses and dogs of, 17. Account of a visit to the Prophet's tomb at, 20-35. Tents of the people of El Medinah, compared with those of the Meccans. Its mosque compared with that of Meccah, 23. Moslem account of the settlement of El Medinah, 54. Destruction of the Jewish power in, 60. El Medinah ever favourable to Mohammed, 62. The Prophet escorted to, 65. Joy on his arrival, 67. Tomb of the Prophet, 69. Various fortunes of the city, 69. Erection of the Prophet's mosque at, 70. Construction of the second mosque (or mosque of the Caliph Osman), 73. The third mosque erected by El Walid the Caliph, 74. The fourth mosque built by El Mehdi the Caliph, 76. Additions of El Ma'mun, 76. The fifth and sixth mosques built, 77. Besieged and sacked by the Wahhabis, 78, 79. The people of, almost all act as Muzawwirs, 83. Its geographical position, 87. All Muharramat, or sins, forbidden within the, 88. Causes of its prosperity, 89. Manner of providing water at, 89. Its climate, 91, 92. Diseases of, 93 *et seq*. The three divisions of, 98. The gates of, 99. The bazaar, 99. The walls, 100. The streets, 100. The Wakalehs, 100. The houses, 101. Population, 102. The fortress of, 102, 103. The suburbs of, 103. The Khamsah Masajid, 104. Inhabitants of the suburbs, 106. Celebrity of the dates of El Medinah, 109. The weights of, 111. n. The cereals, vegetables, &c., of the Medinah plain, 113, 114. The fruits of, 114. Arrival of the Damascus caravan at, 125. Account of the people of El Medinah, 146. The present ruling race at, 150. Privileges of the citizens of, 151. Trade and commerce of, 153, 154. Price of labour at, 154. Pride and indolence of the Madani, 154, 155. Dearness of provisions at, 155. The households of the Madani, 156. Their personal appearance, 157. Scarcity of animals at, 160. Manners of the Madani, 161, 162. Their character, 163, 164. Their marriages and funerals, 165—168. Abundance of books at, 168. The two Madrasah or colleges,

168. The Olema of El Medinah, 168. Learning of the Madani not varied, 169. Their language, 170. Their apprehensions at the appearance of a comet, 172. Their cemetery of El Baki'a, 175. The mosques in the neighbourhood of the city, 186—192. The four roads, leading from El Medinah to Meccah, 202.

Mehdi, El, or El Mohdy, the caliph, erects the fourth mosque of El Medinah, II. 76; III. 35.

Mejidi Riwak (or arcade of the Sultan Abd el Mejid), at El Medinah, II. 24.

Mihrab el Nabawi (or place of prayer), II. 25, 72. The Mihrab Sulaymani of the Prophet's mosque, 25.

Milk, *laban* both in Arabic and Hebrew, L. 239. Milk-seller, an opprobrious and disgraceful term, 239. The milk-balls of the Bedawin, II. 260.

Mimosa tree, compared by poetic Arabs to the false friend, L. 268.

Minarets, the five, of the mosque of the Prophet, II. 45, 46. The erection of the four, of the mosque of the Prophet, 75; III. 27. Dangers of looking out from a minaret window, 28. *n.*

Mirage, II. 215. Beasts never deceived by the, 216.

Mirayat (or magic mirrors), used for the cure of bilious complaints, II. 95. Antiquity of, 95. *n.* Those of various countries, 95. *n.* The Cairo magician, 95. *n.* Mr. Lane's discovery, 95.*n.* Sir Gardiner Wilkinson's remarks respecting, 95. *n.*

Mirba'at el Bair (or place of the beast of burden), in the mosque of the Prophet, II. 49.

Mirbad (or place where dates are dried), II. 70.

Miri (or land-cess), not paid by the Madani, II. 151.

Mirror, the Magic. *See* Mirayat.

Mirza, meaning of, L. 13.

Mirza Husayn, "Consul General," at Cairo, L. 83.
Misri, Bab el, or Egyptian gate, of El Medinah, II. 99.
Misri, pomegranates of El Medinah, II. 115.
Miyan, or "Sir," a name applied to Indian Moslems, L 227.
Moat, battle of the, II. 190.
Mohammed Abu Si Mohammed, his mandate for the destruction of the diseased population of Yemen, II. 97.
Mohammed Ali Pasha, his mosque, L. 82, 96. His wise regulations for insuring the safety of travellers across the Desert, 149. His expedition to El Hejaz, 170. His strong-handed despotism capable of purging El Hejaz of its pests, 251. The "Takiyah" erected by him at El Medinah, II. 2.
Mohammed bin Aun, (quondam prince of Meccah), his palaces, III. 136, 149. His imprisonment at Constantinople, 136.
Mohammed el Attar, Shaykh, the druggist, L. 67. Description of his shop, 68. His manners, 69. His sayings and sarcasm, 70—72. His plan for releasing the pilgrim from a difficulty, 122.
Mohammed el Bakir, the Imam, tomb of, II. 184.
Mohammed el Basyuni, account of, L. 116. Starts for Suez, 134. Meets the author in the Desert near Suez, 145. His joy at the meeting, 145. His treatment of the Bedawin, 145. His usefulness at Suez, 151. His *savoir faire*, 153. His joke, 169. Promises to conduct the devotions of the Maghrabis at Meccah, 191. Change in his conduct at Yambu', 227. His quarrel with the Bedawin, 248, 249. And with the Medinites, 262. Bears the brunt of the ill-feeling of the pilgrims, 269. Bullies the camel men, 270. Down-

cast and ashamed of himself in his rags at El Medinah, II. 6. Made smart, 11. Confounded by a Persian lady, 18, 19. Distributes the pilgrim's alms in the mosque at El Medinah, 27. Takes a pride in being profuse, 43. Accompanies the pilgrim to the mosque of El Kuba, 107. His economy at El Medinah, 121. His indecorous conduct, 139. His fondness for clarified butter, 155, 209. His adventures in search of water on the march to Meccah, 209. Mounts a camel, 269, 270. But returns tired and hungry, 276. His mother's house at Meccah, 292. His welcome home, III. 38. Becomes the host of the pilgrim, 38. His introduction of hard words into his prayers, 47. His resolution to be grand, 63. His accident at the Great Devil, 86. Conducts the pilgrim round the Ka'abah, 88. His sneers at his mother, 96. His taunts of Shaykh Nur, 98. Receives a beating at Jeddah, 153. Departs from the pilgrim with coolness, 154.

Mohammed el Busiri, the Wali of Alexandria, tomb of, I. 11.

Mohammed ibn Abdillah el Sannusi, his extensive collection of books, II. 168, 169.

Mohammed Jamal el Layl, his extensive collection of books, II. 168.

Mohammed Khalifah, keeper of the mosque of Hamzah, II. 136.

Mohammed Shafi'a, his swindlings, I. 47. His lawsuit, 47.

Mohammed Shiklibha, I. 158, 234.

Mohammed the Prophet, founds the first mosque in El Islam, I. 89. His traditionary works studied in Egypt, 101. His cloak, 138 The moon and El Burak subjected to, 205. The "Bedr," the scene of his principal military exploits,

253. His attack of Abu Sufiyan, and the infidels, II. 131, 134. Distant view of his tomb at El Medinah, II. 3. Account of a visit to his mosque at El Medinah, 20. A Hadis or traditional saying of, 21. His tomb, how regarded by the orthodox followers of El Malik and the Wahhabis, 22. El Rauzah, or the Prophet's Garden, 24. His pulpit at El Medinah, 26. The Shubak el Nabi, or Prophet's window, 30. The Prophet, how regarded as an intercessor, 32, 33. His prayers for the conversion of Omar, 34, 35. The Kiswah round his tomb, III. 93. The exact place of the tomb, II. 35. The Kaukab el Durri suspended to the Kiswah, 35. The tomb and coffin, 36. Position of the body, 37. Reasons for doubting that his remains are deposited in the mosque at El Medinah, 52. His ancestors preserved from the Yemenian deluge, 59. Doubts respecting his Ishmaelitish descent, 220. Finds favour at El Medinah, 62. Meets his new converts on the steep near Muna, 63. Receives the inspired tidings that El Medinah was his predestined asylum, 64. Escorted to El Medinah, 65. His she-camel, El Kaswa, 65, 66. His halt near the site of the present Masjid el Jumah, 66. Joy on his arrival at El Medinah, 67. His stay at the house of Abu Ayyub, 66—68. Builds dwellings for his family, 68. The conspiracy of the "Hypocrites," 69. Erects the mosque, 70. Abode of his wives, family, and principal friends, 73. Places of his death and burial, 73. Attempt to steal his body, 76. His mosque in the suburb of El Manakhah at El Medinah, 104. Foundation of the mosque of El Kuba, 116, 117. His "Kayf" on the brink of the well at El Kuba, 122. His miraculous

authority over animals, vegetables, &c., 130. Tombs of his wives, 182. And of his daughters, 182. Origin of his surname of El Amin, the Honest, III. 33. His tradition concerning the fall of his birthplace, 112. His old house (Bayt el Naby) at Meccah, 133. The birth-place of the Prophet, 135.

Mohdy, EL *See* Mehdi, EL

Money, the proper method of carrying, in the East, L 25. Value of Turkish paper money in El Hejaz, II. 102. The Sarraf, or money-changer, III. 116.

Monday, an auspicious day to El Islam, II. 66.

Monteith, General, L 1.

Moon, the crescent, II. 214.

Moplah, race, foundation of the, II. 55.

Mosaic pavement of the Ka'abah, III. 12.

Moses' Wells (Uyun Musa), the, at Suez, L 187. Visit to, 195, 196. Hot baths of, 196. His pilgrimage to Meccah, II. 57. Inters his brother Aaron on Mount Ohod, 57. His tomb, III. 159.

"Moskow," the common name of the Russians in Egypt and El Hejaz, II.' 8.

Mosque (Masjid), the origin of the, L 88, 89. Form and plan of, 89. Erection of the first, in El Islam, 89. First appearance of the cupola and niche, 90. Varied forms of places of worship, 90, 91. Byzantine combined with Arabesque, 92, 93. Use of colours, 92. Statuary and pictures forbidden in mosques, 93. The Meccan mosque a model to the world of El Islam, 93. Immense number of mosques at Cairo, 93. Europeans not excluded from, 94. The Jama Taylun, 94. That of the Sultan El Hakim, 95. The Azhar and Hasanayn mosques, 95, 97. That of Sultan Hasan, 95. Of Kaid Bey and the other Mameluke kings, 95. The modern mosques, 95, 96. That of

Sittna Zaynab, 96. Mohammed Ali's "Folly," 96. Mode of entering the sacred building, 97. Scene in the Azhar, 98. The Riwaks, 98. The collegiate mosque of Cairo, 98, 99. Those of Suez, 167. Account of a visit to the Prophet's tomb, II. 20—53. The Masjid el Nabawi, one of the two sanctuaries, 21. The Masjid el Haram at Meccah, 21. The Masjid el Aksa at Jerusalem, 21. How to visit the Prophet's, 21. Ziyarat, or visitation, 21. Points to be avoided in visiting the Prophet's, 21. Comparison between the El Medinah and Meccah mosques, 22, 23. Description of the Masjid el Nabi, 23. Its gates, 44, 45. The five minarets of the, 45, 46. The four porches of the, 46, 47. The celebrated pillars, 47. The garden of our Lady Fatimah in the hypæthral court of the, 49. Gardens not uncommon in, 49. Building of the Prophet's mosque, 70. The second, erected by Osman, 73. The Masjid erected with magnificence by the Caliph El Walid, 74. Various improvements in the, 75. The fourth mosque of El Medinah erected by the Caliph el Mehdi, 76. Additions of El Ma'mun, 76. Erection of the fifth and sixth mosques, 77. The treasures of the tomb stolen by the Wahhabis, 79. The "sacred vessels" repurchased from them, 79. The various officers of the mosque, 80, 81. The executive and menial establishment of the Prophet's mosque, 82. Revenue of the, 83, 84. Pensioners of the, 84. Description of that at El Manakhah, 104, 105. History of the, of El Kuba, 116, 117. That of Sittna Fatima at El Kuba, 120. The Masjid Arafat at El Kuba, 121. Hamzah's mosque, 134. The mosques in the neighbourhood of El Medinah, 186—192. Description of the mosque at Meccah, III. 1 *et seq.* Enumeration of the gates of the, 22, 23. The mosque El Khayf at Muna, 60. The mosque Muzdalifah, 60, 61. The Masjid el Jinn, 132.

Mother of pearl, brought from the Red Sea, L 172.

Mothers of the Moslems (the Prophet's wives), II. 73.

"Mountains of Paradise," L 217.

Mourning forbidden to Moslems, II. 160. Mourning dress of the women, 160.

Muawiyah, El, Caliph, his Bedawi wife Maysunah, III. 70. His son Yezid, 70. n.

Muballighs, the (or clerks of the mosque), II. 26. n.

Mubariz, the (or single combatant), of Arab chivalrous times, II. 18.

Mudarrisin, the (or professors), of the Prophet's mosque, II. 84.

Mudir (or chief treasurer) of the Prophet's mosque, II. 49.

Muezzin, the, L 77. The Prophet's, II. 46. The Ruasa, or chief of the, 46, 83. The muezzins of El Medinah, 83. Reasons for preferring blind men for muezzins, III. 28. n.

Muftis, the three, of El Medinah, II. 82.

Muhafiz, or Egyptian governor, L 19.

Muhajirún (or Fugitives), the, from Meccah, II. 71.

Muhallabah, the dish so called, L 78.

Muharramat (or sins), forbidden within the sanctuary of the Prophet, II. 88.

Mujawirin, or settlers in El Medinah, II. 85.

Mujrim (the Sinful), the pilgrim's friendship with him, II. 173.

Mukabbariyah, the, of the mosque, II. 26. n.

Mukaddas, Bayt el (Jerusalem), prostrations at, II. 117.

Mukhallak, El, the pillar in the mosque of the Prophet so called, II. 48.

Mukattam, Jebel, I. 150.
Mules, despised by the Bedawin, II. 20. Not to be found at El Medinah, 160.
Multazem, El, the place of prayer in the Ka'abah so called, III. 6, n., 48.
Mulukhiyah (Corchorus olitorius), a mucilaginous spinach, II. 113.
Muna, place of meeting of the new converts with the Prophet, II. 63. Sanctity of, III. 59. The pebbles thrown at the Devil at, 59. The mosque El Khayf, 60. Sacrifices at, 97. A storm at, 98, 99. Coffee-houses of, 103. Its pestilential air, 105.
Munafikun, or "Hypocrites," conspiracy of the, II. 69.
Munar Bab el Salam of the mosque of the Prophet, II. 45. Munar Bab el Rahmah, 45. The Sulaymaniyah Munar, 45. Munar Raisiyah, 46.
Murad Bey, the Mameluke, I. 96.
Murad Khan, the Sultan, his improvements in building the House of Allah, III. 35.
Murchison, Sir Roderick, I. I.
Murshid, meaning of the term, I. 13, 14.
Musab bin Umayr, missionary from the Prophet to El Medinah, II. 63.
Musahhal, village of, I. 238, 245.
"Musalla el Eed," the mosque of Ali at El Medinah so called, II. 104. The Musalla el Nabi (Prophet's place of prayer), in the mosque of El Medinah, 105, 118.
Musannam (or raised graves) of the Bedawin, II. 138.
Musattah (or level graves) of the Bedawin, II. 138.
Muscat, I. I.
Music and musical instruments of the Bedawin, I. 137; II. 249.
Muslim bin Akbah el Marai, his defeat of the Madani, II. 181.
Mustachios, clipped short by the Shafe'i school, II. 196. n.

Mustarah, the (or resting place), on Mount Ohod, II. 132.
Mustasim, El, last caliph of Bagdad, his assistance in completing the fifth mosque of the Prophet, II. 77.
Mustaslim, or chief of the writers of the tomb of the Prophet, II. 81.
Mutamid, El, the Caliph, his additions to the House of Allah, III. 35.
Mutanabbi, El, the poet, his chivalry, II. 240. Admiration of the Arabs for his works, 242.
Mutasim, El, the Caliph, his chivalry, II. 239.
Mutazid, El, the Caliph, his additions to the House of Allah, III. 35.
Muttaka, El, legend of the stone at Meccah so called, III. 136.
Muwajihat el Sharifah (or Holy Fronting), in the Prophet's mosque, II. 24.
Muzaykayh, El, a surname of Amru bin Amin, II. 59.
Muzaynah tribe of Arabs, I. 138. Its antiquity and nobility, 138. Its purely Arab blood, 139.
Muzdalifah (the Approacher), the mosque so called, III. 60.
"Muzzawir," the, almost all the Medinites act as, II. 83. Importance of the office of, 83.
Myzab (water-spout) of the Ka'abah, III. 12. Generally called Myzab el Rahmah, 12. u.
Nabawi, the Mihrab el, in the mosque of the Prophet, II. 47.
Nabi, Bir el, at Kuba, II. 50.
Nabi, the Masjid el, or the Prophet's mosque at El Medinah, built by Mohammed, description of the, II. 23, 70.
Nabi, the Shubak el (or Prophet's window), II. 30, 41.
Nabi, El, visit to, I. II.
Nafi Maula, El (Imam Nafi el Kari), son of Omar, tomb of, II. 182.
Nafr, El (the Flight), from Muna to Meccah, III. 87.
Najjar, Benú, the, II. 68.

INDEX.   245

Meaning of the name, 68. n.

Nahw (syntax), study of, in schools, I. 100.

Naib el Haram, or vice-intendant of the mosque of Meccah, III. 28.

Nakhawilah, the race of heretics so called, at El Medinah, II. 146. Their principles, 147.

Nakhil (or palm plantations), the, of El Medinah, II. 108.

"Nakhwali," the, II. 112.

Nakib (or assistant mustaslim of the tomb of the Prophet), II. 81.

Namrud (Nimrod), dispersion under him, II. 54.

Nassar, Shaykh, the Bedawi of Tur, I. 134 *et seq.* His finesse, 146.

Nâsur (or ulcer), of El Hejaz. *See* Diseases of El Hejaz; Ulcers.

Natak el Naby, the, at Meccah, origin of, III. 135.

Nazir, the, a tribe of the Benú Israel, II. 188.

Nebek, the fruit of a palm tree so called, II. 49.

Nebek (or jujube tree), the, of El Medinah, II. 114. Supposed to have been the thorn which crowned our Saviour's head, 114. n.

Nebuchadnezzar (Bukht el Nasr), invasion of, II. 57, 58.

Nejd, view of the ground of, II. 1. The Nejdi tribes of Bedawin, 22I.

Niebuhr, his remarks on the Sinaitic Arabs referred to, I. 140.

Night journey in Arabia description of a, II. 272, 275.

Nile, steam-boat of the, I. 29. The Barrage (bridge), 30. Objects seen on the banks of the, 31. The country about compared with that of Sindh, 31.

Nimrah, Masjid, the (or mosque without the minaret), III. 61, 62.

Nisa, the Bab el (or women's gate), at El Medinah, II. 24, 44.

Niyat, the, in Moslem devotions, I. 75. The, in the visitation of the mosque of

El Kuba, II. 118. At the Little Pilgrimage, III. 125.
Nizám (or Turkish infantry), I. 220.
Noachians, the, in Arabia, II. 221.
Noah, account of Ibn Abbas respecting the settlement of his family, II. 54.
Nolan, Captain, reference to his work on cavalry, I. 260.
Nur el Din, el Malik el Adil, II. 76.
Nur el Din Shahid Mahmud bin Zangi, the Sultan, II. 77.
Nur, Jebel, III. 59.
Nur, Shaykh, sensation caused by his appearance in the streets of Cairo, I. 118, 119. His defection, 151. His return, 154. His fishing tackle, 190. His dirty appearance at El Medinah, II. 6. His improved aspect, 11. Enraptured with El Medinah, 150. His preparations for leaving El Medinah, 150. His ride in the shugduf of Ali bin Ya Sin, 266. Accompanies the pilgrim to the Ka'abah, III. 51. Becomes Haji Nur, 142. His quarrel with Mohammed el Busyani, 153.

Oases, the, I. 143.
Officials, Asiatic, how to treat, I. 20. Habits and manners of, 21, 22.
Ogilvie, Mr., English consul at Jeddah, shot at for amusement by Albanian soldiers, I. 126.
Ohod, Jebel (Mount Ohod), II. 1, 13. Prayer in honour of the martyrs of, 40. Grave of Aaron on, 57. Its distance from El Medinah, 87. Winter on, 91. Visitation of the martyrs of, 128. The Prophet's declaration concerning it, 130. Causes of its present reputation, 131. The Mustarah or resting place of, 132. The fiumara of, 133. Its distance from El Medinah, 134. Its appalling look, 134.
Olema, one of the five orders of pensioners of the Prophet's mosque, II. 84.

INDEX.

Omar, the Caliph, his window in the Prophet's mosque, II. 30, 34. Benediction bestowed on him, 34, 35. His tomb, 37, 38. His mosque at Jerusalem, 37. Sent forward by the Prophet to El Medinah, 64. Improves the Masjid at El Medinah, 73. Supplies the town of El Medinah with water, 90. Mosque of, at El Medinah, 104. His respect for the mosque of El Kuba, 117. His tomb defiled by all Persians who can do so, 143. His murderer Fayruz, 143.

Onions, leeks, and garlic, disliked by the Prophet, II. 67.

Ophthalmia in Egypt, I. 174. Rarity of, in Arabia, II. 99.

Orientals, their repugnance to, and contempt for, Europeans, I. 104. Discipline among, must be based on fear, 206.

Osman, the Caliph, his Cufic Koran, II. 77. His wish to be buried near the Prophet, 37, 38. The niche Mihrab Osman, 41. Assists in building the Prophet's mosque, 72. Builds the second mosque at El Medinah, 73. Enlarges the mosque of El Kuba, 118. Loses the Prophet's seal ring, 123. Visit to his tomb at El Baki'a, 179. His funeral, 180.

Osman, Bab, II. 72.

Oxymel. *See* Sikanjebin.

Palm-grove, the, of El Medinah, II. 70.

Palm-trees, venerable, of the hypæthral court of the Prophet's mosque, II. 49. Extensive plantations of, in the suburbs of El Medinah, 106. Loveliness of the palm-plantations of El Medinah, 108. Celebrity of its dates, 109. The time for masculation of the palms, 112. The Daum or Theban palm, 205, 215.

"Paradise, Mountains of," I. 217.

Pass, Arabic terms for a, II. 204.

Passports in Egypt (Tezkireh), inconveniences of, L 18. Adventures in search of one, 19. British carelessness in distributing, in the East, 47. Difficulty of obtaining one, in Egypt, 119 *et seq.*

Pathan (Afghan), the term, L 46, 21 L

Pebbles of the accepted, the, III. 59.

Pensioners, the orders of, at the Prophet's mosque, II. 84.

Perfumed pillar, the, in the mosque of the Prophet, II. 47.

Perjury, price of, at Jeddah, L 49.

Persia, tobacco and pipes of, L 172.

Persia, luxuriance of the plains of, L 244.

Persian Pilgrims, a disagreeable race, L 198. They decline a challenge of the orthodox pilgrims, 216. The Persians' defilement of the tombs of Abubekr and Omar, II. 35. Large number of, in the Damascus caravan, 142. Treatment of the "Ajemi" at El Medinah, 143.

Pharaoh, spot where he and his host were whelmed in the "hell of waters," L 191.

Pharaoh's Hot Baths (Hammam Far'aun), L 189.

Phœnician colony on the Red Sea, L 194.

Physicians, the Arabs as, not so skilful as they were, II. 98.

Pickpockets in Egypt, L 25.

Pigeons, the, sacred at Meccah, III. 53. Enter almost everywhere into the history of religion, 54.

Pilgrimage, ordinances of the, II. 280. Offerings for atonements in cases of infractions of, 280. Reckless pilgrimages of poor Indians, III. 64. Pilgrims, distribution of, at Alexandria, into three great roads, L 161. Steady decrease of the number of pilgrims who pass annually through Suez, 169, 170. Reasons

assigned for this, 170.
Takrouri pilgrims, 170.
The Hamail, or pocket
Koran of, 233. How they
live on the march, 206.
The change from Ihram to
Ihlal, III. 84. The little pil-
grimage, *see* Umrah.
Pilgrim's tree, the, L 147.
Pistols, the, of the Bedawin,
II. 247.
Plague. *See* Ta'un.
Poetry. Poetical exclama-
tions of the pilgrims on
obtaining the first view of
El Medinah, L 272, 273.
Tenderness and pathos of
the old Arab poems, II.
235. The suspended poem
of Lebid, 236. The poetic
feeling of the Bedawin,
241, 242. The Arabic
language suited to poetry,
242, 243.
Poison, the Teriyak of El
Irak, the great counter-
poison, II. 250.
Police of Egypt, curiosity of
the, L 2. Scenes before
police magistrates in Cairo,
111. The "Pasha of the
Night," 114.

Politeness of the Orientals,
L 203. Unpoliteness of
some "Overlands," 204.
Polygamy and monogamy,
comparison between, II.
233—235.
Pomegranates, the, of El
Medinah, II. 115. The
Shami, Turki, and Misri
kinds, 115.
Pompey's pillar, L 9, 29.
Prayer, the Abrar, or call to,
L 85. The Isha, or vespers,
228. Prayer to prevent
storms (Hizb el Bahr), 205.
This prayer recited, 205.
Prayers on first viewing
the city of El Medinah,
272. The prayer at the
Prophet's mosque, II. 25.
The places of prayer at,
24, 25. The Sujdah, or
single bow prayer, 26.
The position of the hands
during, 33. Prayer at the
Shubak el Nabi, 30. An-
cient practice of reciting
this prayer, 30. n. The
benedictions on Abubekr
and Omar, 34, 35. The
prayer at the Malaykah, or
place of the angels, 38.

INDEX.

That said opposite to the grave of the Lady Fatimah, 39. That recited in honour of Hamzah and the martyrs of Mount Ohod, 40. Prayers for the souls of the blessed who rest in El Baki'a, 40. That said at the Prophet's window, 41. El Kuba the first place of public prayer in El Islam, 117. The Niyat, or intention, 118. The Prophet's place of prayer at El Kuba, 118. The prayers at the mosque of El Kuba, 118, 119. The prayers at Hamzah's tomb, 135. The Talbiyat, or exclaiming, 279. The prayers on sighting Meccah, 290, 291. The four Makams, or stations for prayer, III. 15. The prayers at the Ka'abah, 43 *et seq.*, 90.

Preacher, the, at Meccah, his style of dress, III. 107.

Presents of dates from El Medinah, II. 109.

Pressgangs in Cairo, I. 110.

Price, Major, referred to, II. 93. n.

Pride of the Arabs, I. 241.

Procrastination of Orientals, II. 165.

Proverbs, Arab, I. 142.

Ptolemy, the geographer, I. 220.

Pulpit, the Prophet's, at El Medinah, II. 25.

Pyramids, the, I. 30. Their covering of yellow silk or satin, III. 93.

Rabelais, on the discipline of armies, I. 261.

Races of Arabs. *See* Arabs; Bedawin.

Radhwah, Jebel (one of the "Mountains of Paradise"), I. 217, 236.

Rafik, the (or collector of black-mail), II. 256.

Rahah, meaning of the term, III. 138.

Rahmah, Bab el (Gate of Mercy), II. 24, 72. Jebel el (Mount of Mercy). *See* Arafat, Mount.

Rahmat el Kabirah, the attack of cholera so called, II. 93.

INDEX. 251

Rain, want of, at all times in Egypt, L 173. The rainy season expected with pleasure at El Medinah, II. 91, 92. Rain welcomed on the march, 278.

Raisiyah minaret of El Medinah, the, II. 82.

Rajm (lapidation), practice of, in Arabia, III. 60.

Rakb, or dromedary caravan, the, II. 193.

Rakham (vulture), the, II. 205.

Ramazan, the, L 73. Effects of, 73. Ceremonies of, 74, 75. The "Fast-breaking," 77. Ways of spending a Ramazan evening, 78. The Greek quarter at Cairo, 79. The Moslem quarter, 79, 80. Beyond the walls, 82.

Ramlah (or sanded place of the Prophet's mosque, II. 23.

Ramy or Lapidation, ceremony of, III. 84—87.

Rasid, Bir (well of Rashid), the, II. 203.

Rauzah, El, or the Prophet's garden, at El Medinah, II. 24. Description of it, 27. Farewell visits to, 199.

Rayah (the Banner), the Masjid el, near El Medinah, II. 191.

Rayyan, the hill near Meccah, II. 288. n.

Raziki grapes, of El Medinah, II. 114.

Red Sea, view of the, on entering Suez, L 150. Injury done to the trade of the, by the farzah or system of rotation at Suez, 164, 171. Shipbuilding on the, 170, 180. Kinds of ships used on the, 171. Imports and exports at Suez, 171--173. Description of a ship of the, 179, 180. Course of vessels on the, 187. Observations on the route taken by the Israelites in crossing, 188. Scenery from the, 188. Bright blue of the waters of the, 188. Phœnician colony on the, 194. Christian colony on the, 194. Morning of the, 200. Fierce heat of the mid-day sun on the, 201. Harmony and majesty of

sunset on the, 201, 202. Night on the, 202. Marsa Damghah, 207. Wijh harbour, 208. The town of Wijh, 208. Coral reefs of the Red Sea, 212, 213. The shores of the, when first peopled, according to Moslem accounts, II. 56.
Religious frenzy (Malbus), case of, at Meccah, III. 54. Susceptibility of Africans to, 55.
Revalenta Arabica, II. 94. n.
Rhamnus Nabeca (Nebek or Jujube), the, of El Medinah, II. 114. n.
Rhazya stricta, used as a medicine by the Arabs, II. 278.
Rhyme of the Arabs, II. 243.
Ri'a, the (or steep descents), I. 243.
Rida, El (portion of the pilgrim dress), II. 279.
Rifkah, El, the black-mail among the Bedawin so called, II. 256.
Rih el Asfar (cholera morbus), the, in El Hejaz, II. 93.

Medical treatment amongst the Arabs in cases of, 93. The Rahmat el Kabirah, 93.
Ring, seal, the, of the Prophet, II. 123.
Riwaks, or porches, surrounding the hypæthral court of the mosque at El Medinah, II. 46, 118.
"Riyal Hajar," a stone dollar so called by the Bedawin, II. 79. n.
Riza Bey, son of the Sherif of Meccah, II. 290.
Robbers in the Desert, mode of proceeding of the, I. 242. Sa'ad, the robber-chief of El Hejaz, 249. Shaykh Fahd, 249. Indian pilgrims protected by their poverty, 258.
Rock inscriptions near Meccah, II. 288.
Ruasa, the (or chief of the Muezzins), residence of, II. 46, 83.
Ruba el Khali (the empty abode), its horrid depths and half-starving population, I. 3.
"Rubb Rummam," or pome-

INDEX.   253

granate syrup, of Taif and El Medinah, II. 115.

Rukham (white marble) of Meccah, III. 2. n.

Rukn el Yemani, the, of the Ka'abah, III. 10.

Rumat, Jebel el (Shooters' Hill), near El Medinah, II. 191.

Russia, opinions of the Medinites of the war with, II. 7, 8. The present feeling in Egypt respecting, 104, 109, 110.

Rutab (or wet dates), II. 111.

Sa'ad el Jinni (or Sa'ad the Demon), description of his personal appearance, I. 155, 156. His character, 155, 156. Equipped as an able seaman on board the pilgrim-ship, 181. His part in the fray on board, 185. Effects of a thirty-six hours' sail on him, 203. His quarrel with the coffee-house keeper at Wijh, 210. His sulkiness, 217, 218. Leaves Yambu', 236. His apprehensions in the Desert near Yambu', 237. Purchases cheap wheat at El Hamra, 247. His fear of the Bedawin, 254. Takes his place in the caravan, 265. Forced to repay a debt to the pilgrim, 269. Arrives at El Medinah, 274. His intimacy with the pilgrim, II. 15. Accompanies the pilgrim to Ohod, 128.

Sa'ad bin Ma'az, converted to El Islam, II. 63. Condemns the Kurayzah to death, 188, 189.

Sa'ad, the robber-chief of El Hejaz, I. 249. Particulars respecting him, 249. His opponent Shaykh Fayd, 249. His bloodfeud with the sherif of Meccah, 252. Description of Sa'ad, 253. His habits and manners, 253. His character, 253. He sometimes does a cheap good deed, 258. Conversation respecting him, 262. Description of his haunt, 262, 263.

Saba, the land of, II. 58.

Sabæans, their claim to the

Ka'abah as a sacred place, III. 9. a.
Sabil (or public fountain), of El Medinah, II. 99.
Sabkhah (or tutaceous gypsum), of the Desert, II. 274.
Sacrifices in cases of infractions of the ordinances of the pilgrimage, II. 280. At Munah, III. 97, 98.
Sadi, the Bayt el, the makers of the Kiswah of the Ka'abah, III. 95.
Safa, a hill in Meccah, II. 74. Ceremonies at, III. 125.
Sahal, sells ground to Mohammed, II. 68.
Sahn, El (or central area of a mosque), II. 23. 44.
Saidi tribe of Arabs, L. 138.
Saints, their burial-place at El Baki'a, II. 176.
Saj, or Indian teak, II. 74.
Sakka, the (or water-carrier of the Prophet's mosque), II. 43. 82.
Salabah bin Amr, II. 59.
Salam, not returning a, meaning of, L. 226.
Salam, or Blessings on the Prophet, I. 75.

Salam, the Bab el, at Medinah, II. 24. 28.
Salatah, the dish so called, L. 128.
Salih Shakkar, description of him, L. 158. Effects of a thirty-six hours' sail on him, 203. Leaves Yambu', 236. Arrives at El Medinah, 274.
Salihi tribe of Arabs, L. 138.
Salkh, the kind of, circumcision among the Bedawin so called, II. 252.
Salman, el Farsi, the Masjid, II. 190.
Salmanhudi, El (popularly El Samhoudi), his testimony respecting the tomb of the Prophet, II. 36. His account of the graves of the Prophet and the first two caliphs, 52. His visit to the tombs of the Hujrah, 78. n.
Salutation of "peace" in the East, 136. 144.
Sambuk, the, L. 171. Description of a, 179.
Samman, Mohammed el, the saint, II. 134. His

INDEX. 255

Zawiyah, or oratory, near Ohod, 134.
Sand, pillars of, in Arabia, II. 212. Arab superstition respecting them, 212.
Sandal, the Oriental, L 231.
Sanding instead of washing, when water cannot be obtained, L 254. n.
Sandstone, yellow (Hajar Shumaysi), of Meccah, III. 2.
Saniyat Kuda'a, near Meccah, II. 291.
Saracen, Gibbon's derivation of the name, II. 220. n.
Saracenic style of architecture, L 88, 89.
Sarf, El (or inflexion), study of, in schools, L 100.
Sariyah (or night march), disagreeableness of a, II. 210.
Sarraf, or money-changer, III. 116.
Sa'ud, the Wahhabi, L 235. Besieges the city of El Medinah, II. 78.
Saur, Jebel, Its distance from El Medinah, II. 87.
Sawadi, or black grapes, II. 114.

Sayh, El, the torrent at El Medinah, II. 104, 108, 129.
Sayhani, El, the date so called, II. 110.
Sayl, or torrents, in the suburbs of El Medinah, II. 89.
Sayyalah, the Wady, The cemetery of the people of, L 267.
Sayyid Ali, vice-intendant of the mosque of Meccah, III. 28.
Sayyidna Isa, future tomb of, II. 38.
Sayyids, great numbers of, at El Medinah, II. 148. Their origin, 148. n. The Sayyid Alawiyah, 149.
Schools in Egypt, L 99, 100. Course of study, in El Azhar, 100 et seq. Intonation of the Koran taught in, 101.
Scorpions near Meccah, III. 59.
"Sea of Sedge," the, L 188.
Seasons, the, divided into three, by the Arabs, II. 92.
Sehrij (or water tank), on Mount Ohod, II. 138.

Selim, Sultan, of Egypt, I. 138.
Senna plant, abundance of the, in Arabia, II. 215. Its growth in the desert, 215.
Sepulchre, the Holy, imitations of, in Christian churches, I. 93.
Sermons, Moslem, III. 22. The Khutbat el Wakfah (Sermon of the Standing [upon Arafat]), 76. That preached at the Haram, 106, 107. Impression made by it on the hearers, 107.
Sesostris, ships of, I. 180.
Shajar Kanadil, or brass chandelier, of the hypæthral court of the Prophet's mosque, II. 50.
Shame, a passion with Eastern nations, I. 37, 38.
Shami, Bab el (or Syrian gate), of El Medinah, II. 98. 102.
Shami pomegranates, of El Medinah, II. 115.
Shamiyah, or Syrian, ward of Meccah, II. 291. Quarrels of the, with the Sulaymaniya quarter, 292.

Shammas bin Usman, his tomb at Ohod, II. 138.
Sharai and Bi-Sharai, the two orders of Dervishes, I. 115.
Shararif (or trefoiled crenelles in the walls of El Medinah), II. 100.
Sharbat Kajari, the poison of the Persians, II. 229.
Shark, El, I. 259.
Sharki, the Dara el, II. 87.
Sharzawan, El, or base of the Ka'abah, III. 6, n.
Shaving in the East, II. 158.
Shaw, Dr., I. I.
Shawarib, Abu, the father of mustachios, II. 196.
Shaybah, Ibn, his account of the burial-place of Aaron, II. 57.
Shaybah, Bab Beni, the true blue blood of El Hejaz, III. 88.
Shaykh, explanation of the term, I. 10. Description of an Arab Shaykh, fully equipped for travelling, 230.
Shaykhayn, the "two shaykhs," Abubekr and Osman, II. 147.

INDEX.

Shaytan el Kabir (the Great Devil), ceremony of throwing stones at, III. 84-87.
Sheep, the true breeds of, in El Hejaz, II. 161. The milk of the ewe, 161.
Shems el Din Yusuf, El Muzaffar, chief of Yemen, his contribution to the fifth mosque of the Prophet, II. 77.
Sherifs, great numbers of, at El Medinah, II. 148. Their origin, 148. n. Their bravery, 284.
Sherifi, El, the grape so called, II. 114.
Shibr Katt, L 30.
Shibriyah, or cot, for travelling, II. 208.
Shipbuilding on the Red Sea, L 170.
Shisha (or Egyptian waterpipe), the, L 78; II. 264.
Shopping in Alexandria, L 10.
Shuab el Hajj (the "pilgrim's pass"), scene in the, L 265.
Shugduf, Dangers to, in "acacia-barrens," II. 212.
Shuhada (the Martyrs), L *Mecca and Medina. III.*

267. Remarks on the place, 267. Visit to the graves of the, at Mount Ohod, II. 132.
Shumays, Bir, yellow sandstone of, III. 2. n.
Shurum, the, L 138.
Shushah, the, or tuft of hair on the poll, L 156.
Sicard, Father, L 188.
Sidr or Lote tree of the Prophet's mosque, II. 49.
Sie-fa of the Bokte, in Tartary, L 60.
Siesta. The Kaylulah, or noon siesta, II. 15.
Sikander el Rumi, tomb of, L 11.
Sikanjebin (oxymel), used as a remedy in fevers in Arabia, II. 94.
Silk-tree, of Arabia. *See* Asclepias gigantea.
Simum, the, L 142. Its effects on the skin, II. 213. And on the traveller's temper, 267. The, on the road between El Medinah and Meccah, 269.
Sinai, Mount, L 194, 195.
Sinaitic tribes of Arabs, modern, observations on,

17

L. 137 et seq. Chief clans of, 138. Impurity of the race, 139. Their ferocity, 140. How manageable, 141.

Sind, dry storms of, L. 239, 258.

Singapore, pilgrims from, to Meccah, L. 172.

Silat el Rasul, referred to, II. 93. n.

Sittna Zaynab (our Lady Zaynab), mosque of, at Cairo, L. 96.

Sketching, dangerous among the Bedawin, L. 233.

Slaves, trade in, at Jeddah and in Egypt, L. 48. Abyssinian slaves style of courting, 61, 62. Condition of slaves in the East, 62, 63. The black slave-girls of El Medinah, II. 156. Value of slave-boys and eunuchs, 156. And of the Galla girls, 156. Price of a Jariyah Bayza, or white slave-girl, 156. Female slaves at Meccah, III. 115. The slave-market of Meccah, 133.

Small-pox in Arabia. *See* Judari.

Smoking the weed "hashish," L. 45.

Soap, tafl (or bole earth) used by the Arabs as, II. 124.

Sobh Bedawin, their plundering propensities, II. 202.

Sola, plain of, near Meccah, II. 289.

Soldiers in Egypt, L. 110.

Solomon, king, L. 205. Mosque of, at Jerusalem, connected with, II. 21.

Songs of the Bedawi Arabs, L. 137. Of Maysunah, the, III. 70. Specimen of one, 104.

Sonnini, his testimony to the virtues of the harem, II. 234.

Spears (Kanat), the, of the Bedawin, II. 247.

Stanhope, Lady Hester, her faith in magic mirrors, II. 95. n.

Statuary and pictures forbidden in mosques, L. 93.

INDEX. 259

Stoa, or Academia, of El Medinah, II. 50.
Stone, the, obtained near Meccah, III. 2. n. That of Panopolis, 3.
Stone-worship, III. 8. n.
Storm, description of one at Munah, III. 99. Dry storms of Arabia, I. 249.
Streets, the, of El Medinah, II. 100.
Students, Moslem, I. 99, 100. Wretched prospects of, 102.
Sudan, I. 170.
Suez (Suways), a place of obstacle to pilgrims, I. 120. Safety of the Desert road to, 149. The farzah, or system of rotation, in the port of, 164, 171. The George Inn at (*see* George Inn), 166 *et seq.* Decrease in the number of pilgrims passing through, to Meccah, 169, 170. The ship-builders of, 170. Kind and number of ships used at, 171. Imports and exports of, 171, 172. Average annual temperature of the year at, 173. Population of, 173. State of the walls, gates, and defences of, 174. Food of the inhabitants of, 174. Their fondness for quarrels, 174, 175. A "pronunciamento" at 176. Scene on the beach on a July morning at, 178.
Sufayna, El, the village of, II. 268. Halt of the Baghdad caravan at, 268. Description of the place, 270.
Sufat (or half-caste Turk), a, the present ruling race at El Medinah, II. 150.
Suffah (or Sofa), Companions of the, II. 73.
Sufiyan, Abu, his battle with Mohammed at Mount Ohod, II. 131, 134.
Sufrah, the, I. 75.
Suhayl, sells ground at El Medinah to Mohammed, II. 68.
Suk el Khuzayriyah (or greengrocers' market), of El Medinah, II. 99. The Suk el Habbabah (or grain market) of El Medinah, 99.

Sula, or Sawab, Jebel, near El Medinah, II. 191.
Sulaymani, the poison so called, II. 229.
Sulaymaniyah, or Afghan quarter of Meccah, II. 45, 291. Quarrels of the, with the Shamiyah ward, 291, 292.
Sumaydah, a sub-family of the Beni-Harb, L 249.
Sun, his fierce heat on the Red Sea, L 200, 201. Effects of, on the mind and body, 201. Majesty of the sunset hour, 202. Heat of the, in the Deserts of Arabia, 244. Hour at which it is most dangerous, 268. Adoration of the, by kissing the hand, III. 44.
Sunnat el Tawaf, or practice of circumambulation, III. 49.
Superstitions of the Arabs, II. 136. The superstitions of Meccans and Christians compared, 118, 119.
Supplication, efficacy of the, at the Masjid el Ahzab, II. 190.

Surat, tobacco of, L 172.
Surgery among the Bedawin, II. 250.
Surrah, the (or financier of the caravan), II. 84.
Suwan (granite), the, of Meccah, III. 2, n.
Suwaykah, celebrated in the history of the Arabs, L 268.
Suwayrkiyah, head-quarters of the Beni Husayn, II. 148. Confines of, 216. The town of, 263. The inhabitants of, 263.
Swords of the Arabs, L 241; II. 248. Their sword-play, 248, 249.
Syria, expedition of Tobba el Asghar against, II. 60.

Tabrani, El, his account of the building of the Prophet's mosque, II. 72.
Tafarruj, or lionizing, II. 24.
Tafi (or bole earth) used as soap, II. 124.
Taharah, the kind of circumcision among the Bedawin so called, II. 252.

INDEX.

Taif, population of, II. 102.
The "Rub Rumman" of, 115. The blue peaks of, II. 289.

Takat el Kashf (niche of disclosure), of the mosque of El Kuba, II. 119.

Takiyeh, or dervishes' dwelling-place, in Cairo, I. 83. The Takiyah erected at El Medinah by Mohammed Ali, II. 2.

Takruri pilgrims, II. 205. Their wretched poverty, 205.

Takhtrawan, or gorgeous litter, II. 127. Expenses of one, from Damascus and back, II. n.

Talbiyat (or exclaiming), the, when approaching Meccah, II. 279. Derivation of the term, 279. n. 280. n.

Talhah, friend of Mohammed, sent forward to El Medinah, II. 64.

Tamarisk tree, the, II. 113.

Tanzimat, the, folly of, I. 251.

Tarawih prayers, I. 78.

Tarbush, the, II. 59.

Tarik el Ghabir, the road from El Medinah to Meccah, II. 202.

Tarikh Tabari, the, referred to, II. 58.

Tarikah bin Himyariah, wife of Amru bin Amin, II. 59.

Tarshish, I. 180.

Tashrih, the Madani children's bodies marked with, II. 157.

Ta'un (the plague), never in el Hejaz, II. 91.

Tawaf (or Circumambulation) of the House of Allah at Meccah, II. 21. Ceremonies of, at the Ka'abah, III. 44. The Sunnat el Tawaf (or practice of circumambulation), 49.

Tawarah tribes of Arabs. See Arabs; Sinaitic tribes.

Taxation; no taxes paid by the Madani, II. 151.

Tayammum, the sand-bath, I. 254.

Tayfur Agha, chief of the college of eunuchs at El Medinah, II. 80.

Tayr Ababil, the, II. 93. n.

Tayyarah, or "flying caravan," the, II. 193.
Thamud tribe, the, of tradition, I. 216.
Theology, Moslem, observations on, I. 101 et seq. Poverty of an Alim, or theologian, 124.
Thieves in the Desert, I. 242.
Thirst, difficulty with which it is borne by the Bedawin, II. 213.
Tehamat El Hejaz, or the sea coast of El Hejaz, II. 87.
Teriyak (Theriack) of El Irak, the counter-poison so called, II. 250.
Tezkireh. *See* Passports.
Timbak. *See* Tobacco.
Tobacco (Timbak). The Shishah, or Egyptian waterpipe, I. 78. The tobacco of Persia and Surat, 172. The Shishah (hookah) of Arabia, II. 12. Its soothing influence, 206. Waterpipes, 206. Smoking among the Bedawin, 260, 261. Instances of the Wahhabi hatred of, 268, 282.

Tobba el Asghar, his expedition to El Medinah, II. 60. And to Syria and El Irak, 60. Abolishes idolatry, 61.
Tombs; that of El-nabi Daniyal (Daniel the Prophet), I. 11. Of Sikander El-Rumi, 11. Of Mahommed El-Busiri, 11. Of Abu Abbas El-Andalusi, 11. Of Kaid Bey, and the other Mameluke Kings, 95. The tomb of Abu Zulaymah, 191. Of Shaykh Hasan el Marabit, on the Red Sea, 212. Distant view of the Prophet's tomb at El Medinah, II. 2. Account of a visit to it, 20—53. The Lady Fatimah's at El Medinah, II. 38, 39. Exact place of the Prophet's tomb, 35. The tombs of Abubekr and Omar, 37. The future tomb of Sayyidna Isa, 38. Tomb of Mohammed, 69. 73. Attempted robbery of the tombs of Mohammed and his two companions, 76. The tombs

in the Hujrah visited by El Samanhudi, 78. n. The tomb of Aaron on Mount Ohod, 131. Hamzah's tomb, 133, 134. That of Abdullah bin Jaysh at Ohod, 137. Visit to the tombs of the saints of El Baki'a, 175 et seq. Tombs of Hagar and Ishmael at Meccah, III. 12, 13. Tombs of celebrity at the cemetery of Meccah, 130 et seq. Eve's tomb near Jeddah, 156.

Trade and commerce, condition of, at El Medinah, II. 153.

Trafalgar, Cape, L 7.

Travellers, idiosyncrasy of, L 16.

"Trees of El Medinah," the celebrated, II. 3.

Tripoli, L 182.

Tumar character, the, of Arabic, III. 95.

Tur, the old Phœnician colony on the Red Sea, L 194. Terrible stories about the Bedawin of, 194. The modern town and inhabitants of, 194. The delicious dates of, 197.

Tur, Jebel (Mount Sinai), L 195.

Turki pomegranates of El Medinah, II. 115.

Turks on the pilgrimage, L 183. Turkish Irregular Cavalry in the Deserts of Arabia, 241. Imbecility of their rule in Arabia, 251. Probable end of its authority in El Hejaz, 251. Douceurs given by them to the Arab shaykhs of El Hejaz, 258. Their pride in ignoring all points of Arab prejudices, II. 20. Their difficulties in Arabia, 70. One killed on the march, 267. Their dangerous position in El Hejaz, 244. The author's acquaintance with Turkish pilgrims at Meccah, III. 50.

Tussun Bey, defeated by the Bedawin, L 256. Concludes a peace with Abdullah the Wahhabi, II. 79.

Tutty (Tutiya), used in El Hejaz for the cure of ulcers, II. 98.

Ukab, the bird so called, II. 205.
Ula el Din, Shaykh, of El Medinah, II.
Ulcers, common in El Hejaz, II. 97. Antiquity of the disease in Arabia, 97. Death of Amr el Kays, the warrior and poet, 97. Mandate of Mohammed Abu Si Mohammed, 97. Popular treatment of, 98.
Umar bin Abd el Aziz, governor of El Medinah, II. 74.
Umar Effendi, his personal appearance, I. 154. His character, 154. His part in the fray on board the pilgrim-ship, 185. Effects of a thirty-six hours' sail on him, 203. His brothers at Yambu', 225, 234. His alarm at the Hazimi tribe, 227. Takes leave of Yambu', 235. His rank in the camel file, 236. His arrival at El Medinah, 274. His house in El Barr, II. 13. His intimacy with the pilgrim, 15. His account of the various offices of the mosque of the Prophet, 80, 81. His share of the pensions of the mosque, 85. Accompanies the pilgrim to Ohod, 129. Bids him adieu, 197. Runs away from his father at Jeddah, 153. Caught and taken back, 154.
Umbrella, the, a sign of royalty, III. 75.
Umrah (The Little Pilgrimage), III. 122. The Ceremonies of, 122 *et seq*.
Unayn, the Masjid, near El Medinah, II. 91.
Usbu, the (or seven courses round the Ka'abah), III. 46.
Usman Effendi, the Scotchman, II. 95. n.
Usman, the Pasha, the present principal officer of the mosque at El Medinah, II. 80.
Usman bin Mazun, his burial-place, II. 176, 177.
Ustuwanat el Mukhallak, or the perfumed pillar, II. 47.
Ustuwanat el Hannanah, or weeping pillar, at the Prophet's mosque, 47. Us-

tuwanat el Ayisha, or pillar of Ayisha, 47. Ustuwanat el Kurah, or pillar of Lots, 47. Ustuwanat el Muhajirin, or pillar of Fugitives, 48. Ustuwanat el Abu Lubabah, or pillar of Lubabah or of repentance, 48. Ustuwanat Sarir, or pillar of the Cot, 48. Ustuwanat Ali, or column of Ali the fourth caliph, 48. Ustuwanat el Wufud, 49. Ustuwanat el Tahajjud, where the Prophet passed the night in prayer, 49.

Utaybah Bedawin, ferocity of the, II. 276. Charged with drinking their enemies' blood, 276. Their stoppage of the Damascus caravan, 283, 284. Dispersed by Sherif Zayd, 284.

Utbah bin Abi Wakkas, the infidel, II. 139.

Utum (or square, flat roofed stone castles, in Arabia), II. 58.

Vegetables, the, of the plain of El Medinah, II. 113, 114.

Vena, common at Yambu', II. 96. Treatment of, 96.

Venus, worship of, by the Hukama, III. 41.

Verdigris, used in Arabia for the cure of ulcers, II. 98.

Victims, ceremonies of the day of, III. 83 *et seq.*

Vincent, on the Moors of Africa, I. n.

Vine, cultivation of the, in El Medinah, II. 114.

Visits of ceremony after the Ramazan, I. 109. After a journey, II. 7.

Volcanoes, traces of extinct, near El Medinah, II. 204.

Wady, the, el Ward (the Vale of Flowers), I. 143.

Wady el Kura, town of, founded by the Jews, II. 58. The route from El Medinah to Meccah so called, 202.

Wady el Subu, town of, founded by the Jews, II. 58.

Wady, the Masjid El, I.

Wahhabis, aversion of the,

to tobacco, II. 268, 283.
Their defeat of Tussun Bey
and 8000 Turks, I. 256.
Tenets of the II. 22. Their
rejection of Turkish rule
in El Hejaz, 70. Besiege
El Medinah, 78. Description of their march on the
pilgrimage, 281. Their
bravery, 284. Their appearance at the ceremonies
of the day of Arafat, III. 73.
Their unsuccessful attack
on Jeddah, 148.
Wahshi, the slave, slays
Hamzah, II. 142.
Wahshi, El, the date so called,
II. 110.
Waiz, the, in the mosque, I.
98.
Wakaleh, the, or inn of
Egypt, description of the,
I. 42. The Wakaleh Khan
Khalil of Cairo, 43. The
Wakaleh Jemaliyah, 43.
Those of El Medinah, II.
100. The Wakalat Bab
Salam, 100. The Wakalat
Jabarti, 100. The, of Jeddah, III. 149.
Wakf (bequeathed), established by the Sultan
Kaid Bey, II. 78. *See*
Aukaf.
Wakil (or substitute), in pilgrimage, III. 134.
Walid, El, the Caliph, his
magnificent buildings at El
Medinah, II. 74. Visits
the mosque in state, 76.
Mosques built by him at
El Medinah, 191.
Walis, the (holy men), of
Alexandria, I. 11.
Wallin, Dr. George, his admiration of Bedawi life,
II. 241.
Walls, the, of El Medinah, II.
100.
War Dance (Arzah), the, of
the Arabs, II. 128.
Wardan and the Wardanenses, I. 30.
Wasitah, El. *See* Hamra,
El.
Water bags in the East, I.
24, 118. Value of water in
the Desert, 142. Watercourses (Misyal) of Arabia,
243, 247. The water found
in the Deserts of Arabia,
247. "Light" water, II. 50.
Manner of providing, at
El Medinah, 90. Music of

the water-wheels, 109. Quantity of, in the palm-gardens of El Medinah, 112. Purity of the water throughout El Hejaz, III. 74.

Water-spout (Myzab), the, of the Ka'abah, III. 12. n.

Weapons, the, of the Bedawin, II. 247, 248.

Weeping pillar in Mohammed's mosque, II. 47.

Weights, the, of El Medinah, II. 111. n.

Wells, Moses', at Sinai, I. 197. The Bir el Aris at Kuba, II. 122. The Pilgrim's "Kayf" on the brink of the Bir el Aris, 122. Present number of wells at El Kuba, 123. The Saba Abar, or seven wells, 123. The three wells of the Caliph Harun at El Ghadir, 274.

West, Mr., sub-vice-consul at Suez, his kindness to the pilgrim, I. 163.

Wijh Harbour, on the Red Sea, I. 208. The town, 208.

Wind, the Simum, I. 142. The eastern wintry winds of El Medinah, II. 91.

Wishah, the style of dress so called, II. 279.

Wives of the Prophet, tombs of the, II. 182.

Wolf's tail (Dum i Gurg), the grey dawn, I. 147.

Women, flirtation and love-making at festivals, I. 108. The public amusements allowed to Oriental women, 110. The death wail, 110. An Armenian marriage, 116. Dress of the women of Yambu', 224. The face-veil, 224. Retired habits of the women at El Medinah, II. 13, 14. Soft and delicate voices of the Somáli women, 14. The Gynæconitis of Arab women, 14. A Persian lady's contempt for boys, 18, 19. The Bab el Nisa, or women's gate at El Medinah, 24. The women of the farmer race of Arabs, 116, 117. Women devotees at the Haram, 142. Dress and customs of the Indian women settled at El Medinah, 150.

Value of black slave-girls, 156. Price of a Jariyah Bayza (or white slave-girl), 156. Dress of the women of El Medinah, 159, 160. Their mourning dress, 160. Decency of the women of El Medinah, 163. Their pleasures, 163. Their bad language, 164. Arab marriages, 165 *et seq.* Uncomeliness of the women of El Hejaz, 228. Softening influence of the social position of the women among the Bedawin, 232. Polygamy and monogamy compared, 233 *et seq.* Heroism of women, 237. The Arab oath, "by the honour of my women," 237. Marriage ceremonies of the Bedawin, 252, 253. Frequency of divorces among them, 253. Dress of the Bedawi women of El Hejaz, 259. Strange dress of pilgrim women, 281. Wahhabi women on the pilgrimage, 281. Place for the female pilgrims in the Ka'abah, III. 17. Shrill cries of joy with which Arab women receive their husbands after returning from a journey, 38. The Kabirah (or mistress of a house), 38. Superstitious rite on behalf of women at Arafat, 69. Manner of addressing respectable Moslem women, 69. n. An adventure with a fair Meccan, 77—79. The slave market of Meccah, 133 Appearance of the slaves, 134.

Wounds, Bedawi method of treating, II. 98.

Writing and drawing generally disliked by Arabs, I. 233. Writing on noted spots, the practice both classical and Oriental, II. 140.

Wuzu (or the lesser ablution), I. 6, 75, 225.

"Ya hu," the exclamation, I. 72.

Y. S., the chapter of the Koran, II. 138.

Yambu', tribes inhabiting the deserts about, I. 138. Yambu' el Bahr (or Yambu' of the Sea), 220. The Jambia of Ptolemy, 220. Description of the town, 221. Varieties of the population at, 223. An evening party at, 227. Strength of the walls and turrets of, 235. Attacked by Sa'ud de Wahhabi, 235. Diseases of, II. 96, 97.

Yarab bin Kahtan bin Shalik bin Arfakhshad bin Sam bin Nuh, descendants of, II. 58.

Yasir bin Akhtah, plots against Mohammed, II. 69.

Yasrib (now El Medinah), settled by fugitive Jews, II. 58.

Yemen, tamarinds from, I. 172. The birth-place of the Aus and Kharaj, II. 58. Sufferings of the people of, from ulcers, 97. Mandate of the conqueror Mohammed Abu Si Mohammed, 97.

Yezid, son of the Caliph Muawiyah and his Bedawi wife Maysunah, III. 70. n. His contempt for his father, 70. n.

Yorke, Colonel P., I. 1.

Za'abat, the, I. 17.

Zabit, or Egyptian police magistrate, I. 19. Scenes before, 111, 112. The "Pasha of the night," 113.

Zafar, the Masjid Benú, also called Masjid el Baghlah, II. 187.

Zaghritah (or cry of welcome), III. 38.

Zananire, Antun, visit to his hareem, I. 115.

Zarb el Mandal, the magical science so called in Egypt, II. 95. n.

Zaribah, El, description of the plain of, II. 278.

Zat Nakhl (or "place of palm trees"), at El Medinah, II. 57.

Zawiyah, or oratory, the, of Mohammed el Samman, II. 134.

Zawwar, or visitors to the tomb of the Prophet, II. 41.

Zayd, Sherif, his bravery, II.

284. Disperses the Utaybah robbers, 284.

Zaydi sect, the, III. 15. n.

Zem Zem, the well of the mosque of the Prophet, I. 6, 70; II. 43. Its supposed subterranean connection with the great Zem Zem at Meccah, 50. Rows of jars of the water at the mosque of Meccah, III. 4. Description of the building enclosing the well, 17, 18. The Daurak, or earthen jars, for cooling the water, 18. n. Doubtful origin of the word, 40, 41. Esteem in which the water is held, 42. Its qualities, 42. How transmitted to distant regions, 42. Superstitions respecting it, 42, 49.

Zem Zemi, or dispensers of the water of the holy well at Meccah, II. 264. Ali bin Ya Sin, the Zem Zemi, 264.

Zemzemiyah, or goat-skin water-bag, I. 24.

Zikrs, or dervish forms of worship, in Egypt, I. 83.

Ziyafah, Bab el (or Gate of Hospitality), of El Medinah, II. 99.

Ziyarat, or visitation, of the Prophet's mosque, II. 21, 33. Distinction between Ziyarat and the Hajj pilgrimage, 21. Ziyarat el Wida'a, or "Farewell Visitation," 198.

"Ziyaratak Mubarak" (or "blessed be thy visitation"), the benediction, II. 42.

Zubaydah Kahtun, wife of Harun el Rashid, II. 202.

Zu'l Halifah, the Mosque, II. 74. Its distance from El Medinah, 87.

Zuyud schismatics, the, II. 151.

THE END.

www.ingramcontent.com/pod-product-compliance
Lightning Source LLC
Chambersburg PA
CBHW031952230426
43672CB00010B/2141